This Book Belongs to
barley Jaggart

A PASSION FOR
Ponies

A PASSION FOR
Ponies

JOHN & FRANCESCA BULLOCK

DAVID & CHARLES
Newton Abbot · London

Frontispiece:
A Welsh mare with her foal

Also available in this series

A PASSION FOR CATS
The Cats Protection League
Forewords by Desmond Morris
and Beryl Reid

A PASSION FOR BIRDS
Tony Soper

A PASSION FOR DONKEYS
Elisabeth D. Svendsen MBE
Foreword by Virginia McKenna

British Library Cataloguing in Publication Data
Bullock, John
  A passion for ponies.
  1. Livestock: Ponies: Care
  I. Title II. Bullock, Francesca
  636.1'6

  ISBN 0 – 7153 – 9371 – 5

Typeset and designed by John Youé
using a Macintosh system
and printed in Portugal
by Resopal
for David & Charles Publishers plc
Brunel House Newton Abbot Devon

Contents

Author's Note   6

Foreword by Joan Lee-Smith   7

Ponies and People   8

A Wide Variety of Choice   12

The Right Pony   26

Small Ponies   38

Ponycare   52

Ponies for Fun and the Family   72

Saddlery and Equipment   84

Working Ponies   93

The Pony Club   109

Competition Ponies   120

Show Ponies   132

Preparing for Competitions   145

Driving Ponies   156

The Pony's Health   174

Glossary   183

Useful Addresses   186

Acknowledgements   188

Index   189

To Blue Boy and all the other ponies
who gave us so much fun

Author's note

The term 'ponies' can be rather misleading. Horses and ponies are officially measured in 'hands', a 'hand' still being regarded as 4in (10cm) despite the advent of decimalisation, and ponies are usually considered to be horses which do not exceed 14.2 hands high when they are fully grown. However, the name is always used to describe the horses used for playing polo, and although a number of Arab horses are only pony size there is officially no such thing as an Arab pony.

The Norwegian Fjord horses are usually between 13 and 14.2 hands high, which makes them ponies in terms of size, and so are the Caspian horses, which are even smaller and average only about 11.3 hands.

The ponies of Iceland are also always referred to as horses, although the stallions are mainly no more than 13 – 13.2 hands high, with the mares rather smaller.

They are called horses, according to their breeders, because they ride like horses, and are often ridden by adults. As they are the only horses allowed into Iceland because of the strict import regulations there, it is fortunate for the Icelandic people that their ponies are so robust, and can be ridden by people of all ages.

Fallabellas, which are the legendary miniature horses of the Argentine, stand well under 34in in height, which makes them less than 9 hands high.

Whether a breed is usually referred to as a horse or a pony is consequently often a matter of preference, certainly as far as the breed societies are concerned, but for the purpose of this book we have decided to keep to the official height limit, and look upon all those horses who are 14.2 hands in height, or less, as being ponies in the true sense of the word.

Foreword

It gives me very great pleasure to have the opportunity of introducing John and Francesca Bullock's book.

I firmly believe it will become a classic of its kind – it is packed full of interest for all those who love a pony, whether they be breeders, exhibitors, or the average person who gets a thrill from merely being a spectator at a show. There is information on every breed of pony, as well as on the various equine Societies, including Ponies (UK), their history and background, which will give a great deal of pleaure to members who have no idea how the various Societies first began or what they stand for. The book will no doubt also be of controversial interest to a large number who cling to their own ideas, and regretfully cannot come to terms with present day progression.

Nevertheless, theoretical study can help many people who have only recently become pony owners, and the many and varied practical sections will help them to understand how to look after their pony, improve their riding, and take part in shows and other events. But there is plenty of fun, too, including first-hand accounts of (often amusing) experiences in the world of ponies, plus plenty of information on The Pony Club and all its activities.

I hope that everyone will find *A Passion for Ponies* as interesting, informative and enjoyable as I have.

Joan Lee-Smith
April 1989

Ponies and People

We all owe a great debt of gratitude to ponies, who have served man faithfully in peacetime and in war, and without whom civilisation would have taken much longer to arrive.

For centuries they were the only means of travelling long distances overland, enabling fresh territories to be discovered and commerce to be developed. They made men rich by carrying raw materials to the factories, and goods to the towns and ports; they worked down the mines, on the farms and in the cities; in times of war they carried their masters into battle and even provided them with food; in peacetime they carried produce to the market and then, when their work was done, became a means of enjoyment. They have hunted, and been hunted; been bred for work, pleasure, and food; learned how to survive under extreme conditions of hardship, and been asked to perform acts demanding courage and endurance – and all for the pleasure of their owners.

Only dogs have shown greater loyalty to their owners, and yet, as with dogs, loyalty has frequently been repaid by cruelty, sometimes intentional but far too often due to ignorance. There have, fortunately, been animal lovers in the past who felt strongly enough about the cruel way in which horses and ponies were being abused to ensure that they had some form of protection. The Irishman Richard Martin, a rich Galway landowner, even went to the lengths of building a stone prison on his estate, and servants who were cruel to any of his horses and ponies were imprisoned there until they promised never to ill-treat them again. He went much further, however, than ensuring that his own horses and ponies were not mistreated. As a Member of Parliament he managed to introduce a Bill in 1821 to protect horses and ponies generally throughout the British Isles, and enable anyone ill-treating them to be prosecuted. His Bill became law in 1822, after much controversy: and there were still many who insisted that 'man has a right to flog his own horse or pony' and that the Bill 'interfered with the liberty of a man to treat them as he wished'.

More than a hundred years later it was a woman, Glenda Spooner, who carried on the good work, and dedicated much of her life to promoting the well-being of ponies everywhere. Apart from forming the Ponies of Britain to promote the welfare of ponies and protect the nine native British breeds, she played a major part in the introduction of the 'Ponies Bill' in 1970.

Since the turn of the century and the development of motor

transport a new form of cruelty has developed. Horses and ponies are transported long distances, often without proper food and water, and with stallions, mares and foals being crammed in together in vehicles which are unsuitable for the purpose. The majority of them are destined for slaughter, often abroad for human consumption, and when they arrive at their destination their suffering is still not over. Fortunes have been made, and still are, by people connected with this vile trade, but the 'Ponies Bill' did prevent ponies from being exported which were below a certain value, and also established individual inspections and other safeguards to help protect ponies being exported.

Glenda Spooner died in 1981, but the welfare work of the Glenda Spooner Trust still continues. There is much more to be done, however, and the cruelty shown to horses and ponies at many sales needs further Government action. One of the problems is that ponies at sales are not even entitled to the same legal protection against cruelty and abuse provided by the regulations governing the sale of cattle and sheep. There are also far too few inspectors, and the journey from sale ring to slaughter house can sometimes cause as much cruelty and suffering as Richard Martin hoped to prevent with his Bill. Perhaps someone will come forward who has the same determination and dedication to ensure that a new Bill is passed

Wherever ponies are gathered for sale there should always be adequate fencing, with the railings spaced at distances sufficiently wide apart to prevent ponies from being trapped

Opposite:
*Taking a spread fence in good
style at a Junior Jumping
Competition at Hickstead*

which will take into account these new forms of cruelty, and there will be sufficient numbers of horse and pony lovers with the necessary compassion to do something about the situation.

Cruelty caused by ignorance is unlikely to be prevented by any Government action. When ponies were an essential part of everyday life they were owned and looked after by people who had been brought up with them, and who understood how to look after them. Many people today are owning ponies for the first time, and they don't always have the necessary experience to look after them properly.

Keeping any pony needs knowledge, time and money. In their wild state, when there were large areas of land over which they could roam and find sufficient food to enable them to survive, they were able to fend for themselves. In the confines of a field, or in a stable, they need frequent attention if they are to be happy and healthy, and be able to perform the tasks expected of them.

The Pony Club is doing a great deal to encourage children and their parents to understand more about pony welfare. Membership is growing, and more young people are now being taught not only how to ride, but also how to care for their ponies properly, and they will, in turn, be able to pass this knowledge on to their children.

A Passion for Ponies is intended as a tribute to the thousands of ponies, in Britain and in other countries, who give so much pleasure to their owners, and to be of help to those people who like to know more about their history, ability, breeding, and welfare. There is advice on choosing the right pony, how to go about buying him, where he should be kept and how he should be fed. When he is injured, or becomes ill, there is information on what to do to hasten his recovery, as well as making sure that the chances of him becoming ill again are reduced.

It is difficult to lay down hard and fast rules, because there are many aspects of horsemanship upon which even the most knowledgeable are still not able to agree – that is why it took some years for a panel of experts to produce the Manual of Horsemanship for the British Horse Society and the Pony Club. Experienced horse and pony owners, and instructors, all have their own methods, but they are based on expert knowledge and many years' experience.

There are, however, basic principles which must be followed in the selection, care and training of all horses and ponies. These we have included in *A Passion for Ponies,* along with the views of a number of people whose knowledge and experience create additional interest and further food for thought. In such a wide and passionate subject as ponies there will always be those who disagree with some of the advice and some of the views, but that would be true of any book which deals with so many aspects of pony ownership and welfare.

So many people have provided advice and information, particularly on the various breeds, that it would be difficult to mention them all by name. The authors would, however, like to express their thanks to everyone who has co-operated so enthusiastically in helping to make this book a tribute to the many thousands of long-suffering, and all too frequently abused, ponies throughout the world, but which remain a constant source of help, pleasure and inspiration to people of all ages.

A Wide Variety of Choice

The pony's ancestors

The five-toed mammal which was the ancestor of the pony emerged in the Eocene Age, millions of years ago. Only about the size of a fox, it had five toes like the fingers and thumb of a man's hand, and ran along on four of them. Scientists called it Eohippus.

After 10 million years it had grown to be the size of a sheep, and was running on three toes. It was then known as Mesohippus. After a further 10 million years it had grown to the size of a donkey, and although it possessed three toes it ran on only one of them, and was known as Merychippus.

By the end of the Pleistocene Age, 25 million years ago, the first hoofed ponies started to roam the earth. They were covered with long hair, and looked rather like the ponies which are still found in Siberia. Their toes had turned into hoofs, and the second and fourth toes had developed into splint bones, probably because they were no longer being used, and nature has a way of taking away things which are not needed any more. Although the origins of the different breeds of horses and ponies are sometimes rather obscure, it is known that Arab horses existed thousands of years before the birth of Christ, and there are drawings of them in China and ancient Egypt which were done years before the great flood. Hagar's son, Ishmael, raised a famous stud of Arab horses, which were also much prized in later years by King Solomon who, it is said, kept forty thousand stalls for his chariot horses.

Ponies can be found in all shapes and sizes, from children's fun ponies which are probably of rather obscure breeding but which still give their young riders an immense amount of pleasure, to the show ponies, dressage ponies, show jumping ponies, mounted games ponies, and driving ponies, which are usually bred for the task they are expected to perform.

Britain is fortunate in having the widest variety of ponies to be found anywhere in the world, and is unique in that within a comparatively small area there are nine separate breeds of native pony, each with its own characteristics. These have evolved over the centuries as a result of the different types of terrain and circumstances under which they had to exist, and have developed according to the uses to which they were put as living conditions changed.

PONIES IN HISTORY

It is unlikely that there were any ponies in the British Isles before 1500BC. The first ponies either migrated or were driven across the English Channel, which was then a marshy stretch, by the nomadic hunters of the continent. As these wild ponies settled in different parts of the country, they adapted to the various climatic and geographical conditions and developed their own characteristics. In due course, instances of cross-breeding, occasionally with foreign breeds, created differences in colour and size.

The Roman invasion in about 55BC resulted in the black Friesian horses being brought to Britain, and these had a considerable influence on breeds in the North. They came from Friesland, a province now divided between Holland and Germany, and are one of the oldest breeds in Europe. Their popularity then was largely due to their willing and docile temperament which enabled unskilled men to handle them, and their strength and ability to survive under difficult conditions. About 600 men and their horses were brought from Friesland to work on Hadrian's wall, which was being built from the Solway to the mouth of the Tyne.

Many of these Friesian horses were left behind when their owners returned home after their work on the wall had been completed, and the Romans also left many hundreds more in the north of England, mostly stallions, when they eventually departed from Britain. Because of this the Friesian horse undoubtedly had an important effect on the native breeds of the North.

NATIVE BREEDS

These famous native breeds, which have made Britain's ponies so well known and sought after throughout the world, have helped to create a wider range of pony so that the needs of every type of pony owner can now be satisfied. Although these native ponies are sometimes crossed with other breeds – and small Thoroughbreds and Arab horses in particular – to increase their size or performance, each native breed now has to maintain a standard laid down by its relevant breed society, which is responsible for keeping a register of all pure bred animals.

A FIRST PONY

Ponies are usually bred for their height, appearance, temperament, action and performance. When a child is learning to ride, however, size and temperament are more important than performance, looks or age. A real confidence-giver is what every parent should look for, and the right animal can be worth its weight in gold.

The pony should also not be too high, so that a rider who does fall off – and this will inevitably happen at some time or other – can get

The clean and streamlined looks of a show pony can sometimes be misleading, and they are very often much tougher than they appear. The characteristics of hardiness, honesty and strength are important

---

What does the word 'breed' mean?

A breed is a particular strain of horse or pony which continues to reproduce its own distinct characteristics with a certain degree of consistency. All native breeds as we know them today, however, originated from the wild European pony.

A narrow pony is better

The ideal pony for a child to learn to ride on should be narrow enough for the saddle to fit well, and to give its young rider a feeling of confidence – which he won't get if his legs are stuck out sideways because the pony is too wide.

back on without assistance. A pony which gallops off, squealing and bucking, can be very off-putting for a young rider sitting on the ground. One which will stand quietly and patiently to be caught will be more likely to instil confidence, and encourage the rider back into the saddle.

A SECOND PONY

When these beginners' ponies have become outgrown, or are perhaps no longer up to the ambitions of their riders once the rudiments of riding have been mastered, the choice of a second pony will need careful consideration. Parents often have a vision of their child astride a pretty little pony, cantering round the show ring, and winning rosettes and cups. If the child has the necessary dedication and ability, and the parents have sufficient money, these hopes can sometimes be realised, but there is more to riding ponies than winning prizes in show classes and much will depend on the temperament and ambitions of the rider.

Show ponies are usually expensive, and have been bred mainly for their action and looks. They are not always the best type of animal for a child to have fun with on their own, and anyway, thousands of

The Dales is a good example of a versatile pony which will carry an adult and jump well across country

A champion driving pony

children who enjoy riding have no ambition to compete other than to occasionally enter one of the classes at a local show. Others want a pony that is a good all-rounder, one they can use to go out riding with their friends, jump, hunt, take part in gymkhanas, and have fun with at local shows. Looks will again be of less importance than all-round ability, but because these ponies rarely shine at any particular activity, they will need to be replaced if their young riders decide to compete more seriously.

The choice of pony will then depend upon whether the requirement is for a show pony, a showjumping pony, a mounted games pony, a pony for dressage where action and paces will be important, or even one for driving.

Many young people have taken up driving as a sport, particularly since it has had such a rapid increase in popularity, and ride and drive ponies are becoming more commonplace. Ponies which have become outgrown are also being broken to harness for their owners or other members of the family to drive, instead of having to be sold.

Showing classes and show-jumping classes are usually based on the height of the pony, and so size can be very important when choosing a pony for these activities.

PONIES FOR ADULTS

Although the majority of ponies are owned and ridden by children, there is a growing passion for ponies among adults, partly due to an increase in the number of people who are now able to own their own horse or pony, but also because many ponies have been bred to be strong enough to be ridden by small adults.

Because ponies can be kept out at grass all year round – except for those used for the more arduous competitive activities – the cost of keeping them is considerably lower than for keeping horses, and this again has encouraged pony-ownership among those who want to ride or drive.

> **First ponies: never redundant**
>
> A beginner's pony will always find a ready home whatever its age, and can lead a useful life as long as it is sound enough to be ridden safely and without being caused any discomfort.

> **A wide choice**
>
> The choice is now probably higher than it has ever been and, apart from the wide range of British native ponies being exported, there are now many more overseas breeds which are being imported and bred in Britain.

MARKINGS

BLAZE

WHITE FACE

STRIPE

STAR

SNIP

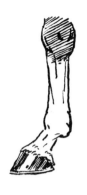

STOCKING SOCK

The names given to the different markings on a pony's legs:

Stocking
A white leg which reaches up as far as the knee or hock.

Sock
Involves the fetlock and part of the region near to the cannon.

White fetlock, white coronet or white pastern
Describes a particular part of a leg.

FETLOCK

PASTERN CORONET

The names given to the different markings on a pony's face:

Blaze
A broad white mark down the face. This usually spreads over the bones of the nose.

Snip
A white mark between the nostrils.

Star
A white mark on the forehead.

Stripe
A narrow white mark down the face.

White face
Where the colour includes the eyes, nose, part of the muzzle and the forehead.

Breed improvement

At the time when Exmoor ceased to be a royal forest, an industrialist, Mr John Knight, also became an important landowner in the area when he purchased 15,000 acres (606ha) and a number of ponies. He set about trying to improve the breed, however, by using Katerfelto, an Arab type stallion, but although the offspring sold well, they didn't have the hardy characteristics of the true Exmoor pony, and were not able to survive the winters in the open. They were consequently more expensive to keep, and the project ended when Mr Knight sold the estate in 1850.

THE EXMOOR   *An ancient breed*

The Exmoor pony's survival on the moors over many hundreds of years has been due to his quick-witted independent attitude to life, and his ability to think and act quickly in all circumstances. As the oldest of the British native breeds, the Exmoor is believed to be the closest descendant of the ponies which inhabited Britain 100,000 years ago, long before the arrival of man.

History

Where the Exmoor originally came from is uncertain, although fossil remains indicate that it is likely to be North America. The fossils show that ponies closely resembling the Exmoor in many ways, including colour and grazing habits, were prevalent a million years ago in many areas of the world. Those who survived the ice age, mainly by moving further south, were often victims of cross-breeding with some of the more exotic types of imported horses, which made them less suitable for coping with climatic conditions. Because Exmoor was an isolated area with harsh climatic conditions and populated by people who were more inclined to resist change, the ponies on the moor were left largely unchanged over the years.

It has been suggested that in about 1000BC the Exmoor pony was used as a chariot pony, and although there weren't any collars at that time which might have produced a heavy shouldered animal, this did result in a heavy-necked pony with well developed muscle due to the strain put on the neck by the draught pole and yoke. Although this feature was very noticeable in ancient drawings of chariot horses, it has been mainly bred out of the modern Exmoor pony. When chariots went out of use the Exmoor became less popular because of its small size, since larger animals were needed for riding and as war horses.

Written records of Exmoor ponies and other livestock kept on the moor appeared in the Domesday Book. Although the moor was not of any great value for agriculture or forestry purposes, it was good hunting country with a plentiful supply of deer, and by the time of William II's reign it had been designated as a royal forest. To ensure that there were enough deer for hunting, their breeding grounds were preserved, which meant that the ponies were also left to roam safely.

When Exmoor ceased to be a royal forest in 1818, large areas were enclosed and the last warden, Sir Thomas Acland, was given more than 3,000 acres (1,214ha) as compensation for the loss of office. He took some twenty of the best ponies to Winsford Hill and had them branded with an anchor, which was thought originally to be a mark denoting royal property. The Aclands were an important landowning family in the area and maintained a great interest in the ponies; however, the private stud books which they kept were unfortunately lost during World War II.

In an effort to improve the stock without cross-breeding, the next Sir Thomas Acland used to take some of the foals and graze them in the parkland which surrounded his Killerton estate, near Exeter, for their first two winters, before returning them to the moor. His son Richard later sold a part-share in the Acland herd to Mr Frank Green of Dulverton, who eventually became the sole owner of the herd. When he died, he left it to his great-niece, Mrs Ronnie Wallace, the wife of the joint-master of the Exmoor Foxhounds.

Exmoors abroad

Exmoor ponies have been exported in relatively small numbers to many parts of the world, including Denmark, Holland, Germany, the Falklands, America and Canada.

Those ponies not owned by Sir Thomas Acland and Mr John Knight were sold at auction in 1818, and fortunately many of them were bought by local farmers and other local people who had formerly enjoyed grazing rights when Exmoor was a royal forest. Many of today's Exmoor pony breeders are their descendants.

The Exmoor Division of the National Pony Society was founded in 1899, but the Exmoor Pony Society was formed in 1921 with Earl Fortescue as the first president. One of the aims of the society was to encourage the breeding of Exmoor ponies of moorland type, and a well-known horseman, Colonel Munkton, who was secretary from 1949 to 1969, produced the first stud book.

Registration

In order to protect the breed, stringent rules are applied in Britain and, unlike other breeds, registration is never automatic even if a pony comes from registered parents. Each autumn the herds on the moor are driven down to the farms and each foal is examined by two inspectors appointed by the Exmoor Pony Society. A foal may be failed because the inspectors feel that it is not true to type, or because it has poor dental structure. Colour is also important, and white markings on the body or feet are looked upon as denoting foreign blood. Borderline cases are usually deferred until the following year.

Foals that are considered eligible for registration are branded with

As driving ponies

Because of their staying power and strength, Exmoor ponies are becoming increasingly popular for all driving activities, and are ideal when driven in pairs or as a team as there is never any difficulty in finding well matching ponies.

An excellent example of the true Exmoor pony

THE PROBLEMS OF BORROWING OR LEASING

Owning a pony can be expensive, but the purchasing cost can sometimes be avoided by borrowing or leasing. The concept of leasing as opposed to buying seems very attractive: provided that there is somewhere to keep the pony, there will only be the cost of a saddle, bridle and headcollar and the 'running expenses' to be considered.

Sometimes owners don't wish to sell their ponies when they become outgrown, and look for someone to exercise them and share expenses. Others may be going away to school and need somebody to look after their ponies while they are away.

The British Horse Society strongly recommends that whenever a pony is leased, a written agreement should be drawn up for both parties to sign; the Society emphasises that leasing is preferable to borrowing.

Circumstances can vary, but the following points should be covered in the course of the discussions, and the main ones included in the written agreement:

* There should always be a Declaration of Intent as to what will happen when the lease comes to an end, also as to whether the person leasing will have first refusal in the event of the owner deciding to sell the pony.
* The duration of the lease and the review date should be clearly stated along with notice required for cancelling the agreement.
* Both parties should have adequate third party cover; in the case of the pony, the owner should take out a policy but the person leasing may be asked to reimburse the premium.
* If tack is included with the pony, it should be insured and there should be a clause confirming that it will be returned in a good state of repair.
* It should be made clear whether the pony may be ridden by only one named rider or whether it may be ridden by other people.
* The owner may wish to specify which veterinary surgeon should treat the pony, and may also wish to be informed in advance of any major surgery or if for any reason the pony has to be put down.
* There should be general agreement as to where the pony is to be kept and whether it should be kept regularly shod.
* The person leasing should be made aware of any vices or allergies or any special medicines required.
* The rights of the owner to visit the pony and the frequency of any such visits should be clarified.

Many of these points may be taken for granted, particularly if the pony is being leased by a friend, but circumstances can change and it is only sensible to be businesslike and have a signed agreement to which both parties can refer.

a star on the near shoulder and the number of the herd beneath the star; the foal's own number within the herd is branded on the near hindquarter. All the details are then recorded in the stud book and a registration certificate issued to the owner. Even if the registration papers are lost, each pony can always be recognised by the brand. Arrangements are made for foals bred in other areas to be inspected in the same way, and although this means a considerable amount of travelling for the inspectors, it does ensure that a strict check is kept on the breed. Some ponies are freeze-marked by their owners because of the number of thefts of horses and ponies, but this is not an alternative to the society's own branding system.

Ownership

Visitors to Exmoor may gain the impression that the ponies on the moor are wild, and do not belong to anyone. This is not the case: all the ponies have an owner and a particular area in which to roam. Not all the ponies running on the moor are Exmoors and there are now quite a number of cross-bred mares, but only those with a brand are pure-bred ponies.

The foals are born in the spring and early summer, and spend the rest of the summer running with their mothers and learning about life on the moor. The stallion in charge will protect and guard his mares, and make sure that they are in foal for the following year. In the autumn, farmers mounted on horseback drive the mares and foals down to the farms; the foals are now old enough to be weaned and branded and the colts are usually sold, along with some of the fillies, while others go back to the herd to breed foals in due course.

The herd is then returned to the moor with either the same stallion, or perhaps a different stallion exchanged or leased from another owner. This practice of exchanging stallions helps to ensure the continuity of the breed. In the old days this would have been a natural process when a young male would come along and fight off an ageing stallion and take over the herd.

Showing

The stallion parade is traditionally held at Exford in early May. Both local stallions and those from other parts of the country go to Exford to parade and compete for valuable premiums. It is something of a get-together for breeders and enthusiasts, and for new members to become acquainted with the breed. Yearling and two-year-old colts also compete for premiums and the colts are later considered for their potential as stallions. The society holds an annual show at Exford every year on the second Wednesday in August. It is always a very popular event and there are classes for all categories of Exmoor pony, including in-hand, under saddle and in harness.

Special climatic adaptations

In order to withstand the winter conditions the Exmoor has developed a rather special type of two-layered coat – the longer, greasy outer hair repels the rain which runs off, helped by strategically placed whorls that direct the water away from the sensitive parts of the body; and the undercoat of short, wool-type hair. Research has shown that ponies without this type of special coat structure do not survive as well in the open. Even in the heaviest snow, which can lie on a pony's back for days, the two-layered coat retains the body heat so well that the pony remains warm and dry and the snow stays frozen.

THE IDEAL PONY

Choosing a pony can be a difficult task, and it is often a good idea to ask for an expert's opinion. Colonel Alec Stuart gives his own inimitable and light-hearted view of the ideal requirements, which perhaps shouldn't be taken too seriously.

The height of the animal is immaterial. The shorter the legs, the less there is to be damaged, the easier the pony is to mount, and the less the distance for the rider to fall. Whilst selecting a pony for her child, this latter point must have a great influence on a mother's heart, but she must also bear in mind that the rider's inside foot should not actually touch the ground when moving round a corner.

The pony's head should be carried low to help the perception of any obstacles that might make the convenient placing of the hooves difficult in any way. Indeed, the kind owner will provide a small two-wheeled trolley on which the animal may rest its chin and so save it from the fatigue of supporting its head.

Very long ears are a distinct advantage. All experts are emphatic that the rider ought to look between his pony's ears. Under conditions of poor visibility, such as at dawn or dusk, short ears are difficult to see, and so the rider is unable to look in the correct direction, and may thus become lost.

The legs should, in principle, be of a length and be so shaped and placed that, when motionless, the hooves are underneath an appropriate part of the animal. For the comfort of the rider, a gliding motion is of the greatest value, and so the less the forelegs are raised, the better. Such an action will also clear from his path those stones over which he might stumble, and should his toes turn out, the stones will be kicked to one side and so he will not suffer the necessity of kicking them twice.

If purchasing a pony, remember that a certificate proffered by a veterinary surgeon is quite superfluous. If the animal has splints, spavins, or any of the other ills to which horseflesh is prone, rejoice. As all ponies get them, you are consequently at an advantage by gaining possession of a beast that already has them. Moreover, they give you a ceaselessly interesting topic of conversation.

A famous Exmoor cross

Although the Exmoor has in the past been an important means of transport, its main use now is in the growing range of leisure activities. It is also being crossed with small Thoroughbred horses and other breeds to produce competition horses and show ponies which are often of a very high standard, particularly where stamina and performance are required. Piglet II, ridden so successfully by the well-known three-day-event rider Rachel Hunt, is a typical example of Exmoor pony blood being used to produce a brilliant event horse.

Distinctive colours

The Exmoor pony's colour is very distinctive and patches of white or white markings are not permitted. The colours range from a special kind of dun which is unique to Exmoors, to bay or brown with black points. The light buff, mealy colouring round the eyes, on the nose, inside the flanks and under the belly is also unique, and the large dark eyes are surrounded by a rim of light hair, which makes them seem to stand out – this is known as a 'toad eye' appearance. A heavy ridge of bone above the eye gives added protection.

Most of the major shows in Britain have classes for Exmoor ponies and many of the smaller ones have mixed mountain and moorland classes – the ridden mountain and moorland championship is held in London at Olympia in December. The breed society presents special rosettes at a number of the major shows to members exhibiting the highest placed Exmoor pony in ridden or in-hand classes. The society also runs its own performance competitions each year where ponies and riders can gain points for successes in the show ring and for taking part in other activities. Records are kept throughout the season and presentations made to those with the highest scores in the junior and senior sections.

Apart from the specialist showing classes, Exmoor ponies are especially suitable for the popular family pony classes as well as junior jumping and working hunter pony events. When properly schooled they are excellent mounts for Pony Club activities, and being up to weight they will last a child longer than most breeds of a similar height.

It is in the show ring, however, that there is the greatest concern that the Exmoor pony should retain all its important characteristics and temperament, and with the popularity of showing increasing, more judges are needed. The Exmoor Pony Society has its own panel of judges who carry a great responsibility for the future success of the breed. New judges have to be proposed and seconded and if accepted as being potentially suitable, they must then attend three shows a year for three years, in the company of a senior judge, before being considered for acceptance on the panel. All the shows receiving support from the society must select their judges from those listed on the official Exmoor judges panel.

The judges look for all the important features which have made Exmoor ponies so popular over the years. Large ponies would find it difficult to survive the cold wind and rain on the moor during winter, when food becomes scarce and where sufficient good shelter is not available, so the height for an Exmoor has become established as being up to 12.2 hands for mares and 12.3 hands for stallions and geldings. Very small ponies, however, are not encouraged.

Conformation

The Exmoor must always be a sturdy pony, with good bone and up to a lot of weight in relation to its size. Even so, due to its well proportioned frame and good shoulder, its action is that of a lighter type of animal, with a long, low and smooth stride which gives a balanced, comfortable ride. Exmoors are also extremely sure-footed.

Although many native breeds of pony have small heads, the Exmoor has a large, well shaped head with plenty of space for the essential functions of thinking, breathing and eating in order to survive. The nostrils are wide to enable them to inhale a good supply of air, which is warmed as it passes over a large area of mucous membrane on its way to the lungs.

The teeth are also important, and the Exmoor has a long, deep jaw to accommodate the long, strong molar teeth which are set at an angle to enable it to survive on poor grazing; the front upper and lower teeth meet exactly so as to cut off the grass cleanly without damaging the roots. Pure-bred ponies with faulty teeth are not accepted for registration.

Exmoor ponies are well adapted to living in their natural environment, and can live outside all the year round on large acreages like the moors where they can range freely to look for food and shelter; however, they may need extra food and shelter when they are kept in smaller fields. When they are not being used a supply of good hay is sufficient, but 'hard feed' in the form of pony cubes or bran, barley, and sugar beet needs to be fed to ponies being worked, according to the work done. Oats are best avoided unless the ponies are being ridden by an adult, or worked very hard.

Although they appreciate being stabled on occasions, perhaps to keep them away from the flies in summer, Exmoor ponies hate being shut up and it is unwise and unkind to keep them stabled for long, unless they are in regular work. There is also the danger of giving too much food, particularly if they are turned out in rich pastures in the grass-growing months of May, June and July. Too much rich food can lead to laminitis (fever of the feet) and other problems.

The Exmoor's feet are hard and well shaped, and in their wild state they don't usually need any attention because they are kept sufficiently worn down by moving over the hard terrain. Away from their natural habitat, however, their feet do need regular attention – as do all other ponies' – and they can sometimes be ridden unshod, provided that they do not have to do fast work over hard or stony ground.

An Exmoor pony and her foal

23

YOU CAN'T KEEP A PONY IN THE GARAGE

On a hot August afternoon, while I was on holiday with the George family, Frances wandered over to see me and asked if I would give her some advice. 'Of course,' I said, 'Pull up a chair. What do you want to chat about?'

'Well' she said, by this time she was beginning to wriggle and appear excited, 'Daddy has at last said that I can have a pony.'

I smiled at Frances and she grinned back, the grin getting bigger and bigger and bigger. Frances is nearly eleven, small and slight, and pony-mad, and has been longing for a pony for years. Her father, however, had sensibly waited to see whether this mad passion would be a passing phase, as dancing and learning the piano had been.

But month after month Frances had doggedly repeated that she wanted a pony and spent many hours, regardless of the weather, sitting on a gate across the lane watching a neighbour's pony. She had also been for a lesson each week at the local riding school and, until we had come away on holiday, had been spending the mornings of her holidays mucking out and helping to catch the ponies needed for lessons, in exchange for the occasional free ride.

'What super news,' I said. 'What do you want to know?'

'Well,' she said, again squirming excitedly, but with a very earnest expression on her face. 'Please could you tell me how to be kind to my pony!' I immediately liked Frances even more, as she had obviously realised that wanting to be kind is not enough. You have to know how to be kind, which often means doing something, rather than thinking about it.

We embarked on a lengthy discussion on the practicalities of buying and keeping a pony, and the whys and wherefores of the kindest pony keepers. Frances wanted to buy a pony straightaway, as soon as we returned home, so that she could ride it for the ten days before she went back to school because, as she pointed out, it was perfect riding weather.

This idea, however, gave cause for concern. She was right, the weather was beautiful, but a couple of weeks after returning home Frances was starting at her new school. The hours would be longer, and she would have further to travel and much more homework to do than she had ever had before. Her family owned one field, which she thought was just over an acre of not very good ground, and so I didn't think that her pony would be able to live out for the winter without

quite a lot of attention.

Frances assured me she wouldn't mind all the extra work, but when we talked about the field and the care involved she became more thoughtful. No less enthusiastic, but a little more practical towards the idea of actually owning a pony, and doing what was best for it, rather than perhaps just what was best for her, as the two things did not necessarily quite go hand in hand.

I first asked her father exactly how big the field was, and he said it was an acre and a quarter, which is quite a marginal size for keeping a pony. An acre is the barest minimum, but the pony would then need a lot of supplementary care. I asked Frances what the grass was like.

'Oh, there's masses and masses,' she replied cheerfully, but on closer reflection she admitted that there were definitely stinging nettles, especially down by the stream, and she knew there were also docks, as she had used them on a nettle sting only the week before.

She hadn't realised that horses and ponies do not like really long grass. It gets very tough to eat, and they would rather starve than eat the really rank stuff. Unlike cattle, they won't eat nettles and most weeds, and some of the brighter-coloured field flowers, which Frances loved to see, are actually poisonous to ponies.

We decided that the field really needed grazing by a group of quite grown-up cows, who would not mind eating rough stuff, and we could then see how much suitable grass there really would be for a pony. Frances's father did not think that finding the cows would be too much of a problem, as they were on good terms with the local farmer and bought their potatoes and logs from him.

We then thought that if we were going to graze anything in this field we ought to consider the fencing. The very best fencing is obviously post and rails, which is stock-proof and nice to look at, but sadly rather expensive. Frances explained that the top of the field was fenced with barbed wire, and consequently unsuitable for ponies, as the barbs could cause a nasty cut. Two of the other sides were fenced by walls around gardens, which at 4ft 6in should be high enough, although we would have to check that the pony couldn't reach over and eat anything precious, or worse, something poisonous in the gardens. The remaining side, which faced on to the road, was a type of wooden lattice fencing, which was quite new and so reasonably strong and safe, although it would perhaps not last as long as some other forms of fencing.

Her father agreed they would need to replace the top fence and we thought that strong, plain wire fencing with three strands would be the answer. The top strand should be 4ft (1.2m) high with a rail along it, and posts every 2yds (1.8m). The bottom strand would be 18in (45cm) from the ground. This would be safe and strong providing that the wire was reasonably thick and kept very taut. Then, if Frances persisted with her pony craze, the fencing could be replaced with post and rails, which is obviously the safest fencing for ponies, as there is no possibility of the animals becoming entangled in it. Without a doubt it is also the most pleasing to the eye.

I asked about watering the pony, and Frances replied there was a stream. We agreed that at 18in it seemed to be a good depth; if a stream is too deep, ponies will be frightened to use it, and if too shallow, they could drink mud and sand and get colic. It was pollution-free, as it came from a spring only two fields away, and it never dried up in the summer. In the end, however, we decided that it would not, after all, be suitable as it got very boggy around the approach in the winter, which would make a pony reluctant to drink as often as it should.

We considered buckets, but they would be difficult to keep full with Frances at school all day, especially when it was very hot or in freezing weather. There was an old tank in the garden shed, but that was rejected as it had sharp edges which could cut the pony. Eventually, we decided that they would have to invest in a new water tank especially designed for animals; there was no mains water in the field, but it could be filled with a hosepipe from the garden every couple of days.

Frances then enquired if she would need a shelter, as the family across the road had one for their pony. I thought that as their ground was limited, they might have to shut the pony in sometimes and perhaps a shed, which would double as a stable, ought really to be considered a necessity. If they had had slightly more ground, sheltered either by a thick clump of trees, a big hedge or a good wall, the pony could, perhaps, have got sufficient shelter from the flies in the summer and the worst of the weather in winter. However, if she wanted to stop her field from getting too cut up, it was best to be able to shut her pony in for the night during the winter.

The shelter would have to be about 10ft by 12ft (3x3.6m) with an open front, and should be sited on a dry part of the field, facing away from the prevailing winds, preferably towards the gate. It should not be built of corrugated iron, as this is noisy, ugly, and rusts easily, and furthermore a pony could cut itself badly if it kicked through the side of the shelter.

Asbestos isn't a lot better, although it doesn't rust. The shelter would be best if it was built from something which would blend in well with the natural surroundings.

Frances and her father thought they would buy a purpose-built wooden one, which would be a nice compromise between the cheap iron and expensive brick or stone. It should wear quite well, and would be assembled by the firm from which it was bought.

Frances then asked why the ground should not be allowed to get cut up, or poached – muddy to those not familiar with the horsy terms. It is because in the spring the first thing to become established on the bare earth is weeds, long before the grass has time to get going, and weeds obviously aren't such a good keep for ponies. By the following winter they would also disappear into mud much faster than grass, and so they would be there in even greater proportion by the following winter. 'Is mud a problem then?' she enquired, and I assured her it was a tremendous problem, particularly with limited grazing.

I told Frances that if it was my field I would first graze it with cows to eat up all the old and rank grass, and then clear out the stream to allow the field to drain better and discourage the marshy plants which a pony won't eat. I might also perhaps consider draining it, if the field was very wet.

Then I would pull up and burn all poisonous plants and large weeds, and hand broadcast with seed any patchy bare earth. Finally, I would fertilise it and rest the field until next spring.

'You mean you wouldn't buy a pony now?' she asked sadly. 'No,' I replied, 'I think it would be kinder and more sensible to wait another few months and buy your pony in the spring when your field is ready. By then your father will have arranged to have it fenced properly, sorted out the grass, erected a shelter and bought a water tank.

'It would also be a horrid time of year to start looking after a pony, in the dark after school. Much better to give the field the best chance of staying mud-free by not keeping a pony through the worst months of the winter.

'It would also give you a chance to get to know him in the warmth of the spring, and let him get to know you when you can give him more time. After all, it isn't kind to buy a pony only to leave him to stand alone in a strange field all winter.'

Poor Frances, she was disappointed, but being very sensible and kind agreed not to think of looking for a pony until about March of next year, and I said that I would then help choose just the right pony for her.

Vicki Macdonald

The Right Pony

The decision to buy a pony is not one which should be taken lightly because, even when ponies are living out all the year round, they do need frequent attention. They must have sufficient good grazing which is well fenced and free of dangerous trees and plants, plenty of fresh water, and shelter from the flies in summer and the wind and rain in winter. Pony owners must also have sufficient knowledge, or experienced help, to ensure that their pony is well looked after, whether at grass or stabled. But it is also most important to choose the type of pony which will fulfil all, or at least most, of its prospective owner's requirements. And the choice can be difficult with so many different types and sizes of pony from which to choose.

THE RIGHT TYPE

The first consideration should be the purpose for which the pony is required. Is it going to be a first pony, for a child that wants a safe and reliable mount, which will give confidence? Or is it for someone who is becoming more ambitious, and wants to compete? Is it to be used for riding, or driving, or perhaps both? Maybe there are other plans for the new pony.

The rider's knowledge, experience, and level of competence must also be considered, in addition to the facilities which are available for keeping the pony, and the money required for its purchase and keep. The eventual choice will probably have to be influenced by a combination of all these factors, rather than by any one requirement.

The type of pony to look for will obviously depend on the rider's ability, age and ambitions. Parents are unfortunately sometimes too ambitious for their child, and buy too good a pony before the child is ready to compete at top level; there are many young riders who would be far better off being left simply to enjoy their ponies and gain confidence, before being asked to perform on their own in front of other people, on a pony that is probably unsuitable for their ability and experience. Some children are put off ponies altogether because they dread having to compete, but they have to do so because their parents have bought them an expensive pony and have visions of them becoming a Ginny Leng or a Marie Edgar of the future.

There are, of course, many young riders who are keen to compete, and cannot wait to show how good they and their ponies are. They are to be encouraged, of course – but parents should always spare a thought for the child who just loves ponies, and wants one simply as

Opposite:
A nice type of pony for a child

a friend and for a great deal of fun. They will still have the satisfaction of learning to look after an animal, and this will give them confidence and a sense of responsibility which will stand them in good stead in later years.

RELIABILITY

There will always be a demand for reliable ponies which will take their riders hacking through the countryside and along the roads with a good degree of safety and comfort, but which also have enough ability to perform well out hunting, and in Pony Club competitions. Few ponies, however, do everything well, and it is usually a matter of finding a pony which will fulfil most requirements satisfactorily. When someone is learning to ride, the age of a pony is only important in that it should not be too young, and looks shouldn't matter at all. A pretty young pony may in fact be flashy and unreliable and could prove a disastrous choice for an inexperienced young rider, who might be put off ponies altogether. Far better to find a sensible old pony who is well schooled and sensible, who is not a slug, but has enough sense to look after himself and his young rider.

PRICE

A pony which is too quiet, however, may be almost as unsuitable, except in the case of very small children. One which is reluctant to go out of a walk, no matter how hard its rider tries, can quickly become a source of considerable frustration for an ambitious child and will do nothing to improve riding ability. The price of a really good first pony will therefore usually depend more on reliability and temperament than ability and looks; although very often owners are more concerned to let these ponies go to a really good home when they have become outgrown, than they are about the price. Such ponies are usually looked upon with great affection by parents, as well as their young riders, and their future wellbeing and happiness is of major importance. Anyone lucky enough to know when one of these ponies becomes available would be wise to purchase it without delay, because there will always be knowledgeable parents looking for that type.

A few scars and bumps are not important because the pony will not be aimed at the show ring; it should be viewed more as a safe and

Patience is a virtue in a beginner's pony

*A useful type of all-round pony
that will give its owner a
great deal of enjoyment*

reliable pet, who will behave well inside and outside the stable. Although it should be sound and not be suffering from any problems which could affect its usefulness, or make it expensive to keep, there is no need for it to match up to the requirements for a good competition pony.

SUITABILITY

Some people have the mistaken idea that buying a young pony for a young rider will enable them to grow up together. Others look for a pony that is too large because they hope that their child will 'grow into it'. Young ponies and young riders never go well together, because neither the pony nor the rider has the necessary knowledge or experience to be of help to the other. Buying a pony that is too large is also a mistake and will mean an unhappy time for the child until it reaches the age when it can handle and ride the pony properly. Ponies are always quick to realise that they are in the hands of someone who has little or no control over them, and will probably decide to take full advantage of the situation. By the time the young rider is sufficiently experienced and old enough to cope, the pony may well have become unmanageable.

Beware!

Never consider buying a pony with anything but a friendly and obliging nature. Bad-tempered ponies are a menace, particularly in the hands of a child, and are to be avoided at all costs. So are ponies which are unsound, unless the unsoundness is obviously only temporary. It costs far more to keep an unsound pony, whatever its past record of successes, than it does a sound one.

PROFESSIONAL ADVICE

Anyone buying a pony for the first time would be well advised to seek professional advice, or at least get help from someone who is really knowledgeable, and discuss their particular requirements. Write down exactly what type of pony is required, with all the essentials on one side of the page such as size, ability, whether it will have to live outside all the year round and the maximum price to be paid; and those which may not be so important like, perhaps, its age, colour and looks, on the other. Except for insurance purposes, the age of a pony is not usually such an important consideration unless it is too young, because ponies can go on performing well much longer than horses, and many are still going strong when they are well past twenty.

ADVERTISING

Although good ponies are often purchased at sales, a well worded 'Wanted' advertisement in a suitable newspaper or magazine can be a perfectly satisfactory way of finding the right animal. Select the most suitable local replies – there is little to be gained by travelling hundreds of miles to look at ponies if there is a suitable animal nearby. The 'Ponies for Sale' columns can sometimes produce a suitable pony, but remember that owners very often view the ponies they have for sale through rather rose-coloured glasses, and it will be up to the purchaser to decide how much of the information is correct. When going to see a pony, look for one which will suit the ability and temperament of the rider as well.

CONFORMATION

The conformation, or the way in which the pony is put together, is very important although few are perfect in this area. However, those with poor conformation are usually more susceptible to injury and illness, and a riding pony is more comfortable if it has a reasonable length of neck, sloping shoulders, and good withers (although saddle fitting can be difficult if the withers are particularly high). Strong quarters and thighs help a horse to jump, and a pony which has a frame that is well-sprung, or rounded, will be easier to keep in good condition.

Ask the owner to stand the pony out in the open so that it can be examined from all angles – and first impressions often prove to be correct. By standing back a little it is possible to get a good overall impression of the pony from both sides, and from the front and rear. Imagine a square drawn from the front of the withers along the back to the top of the hindquarters, from the top of the buttock to the floor, and from the front of the chest down to the floor. A well proportioned pony should fit nicely into that square.

It was once thought that the chest could not be too broad, probably because ponies that are too narrow at the front are likely to have forelegs so close together that they will not only brush against each other and cause injury to the joints and lower limbs, but may also cross their legs and stumble. Too wide a chest, however, will produce a rather rolling action, particularly at the canter and gallop, so it is better to ensure that the chest is not too wide, simply that there is enough room between the front legs. To test for this and for straightness, stand in front of the pony and imagine a line being drawn from the point of the shoulder to the ground at right angles –

if the pony's conformation is correct, the line will pass through the centre of the knee, fetlock and foot.

A pony with a deep girth will have plenty of room for the lungs to expand, which is important; the depth of girth has nothing to do with the amount of heart room, however, as some people believe. The back needs to be strong and well muscled on either side of the spine, but strength should not be confused with width. A pony with a back too broad in relation to its size should be avoided, as it will cause saddle fitting problems and will also be uncomfortable for the rider.

LIMBS AND FEET

Good, strong limbs are obviously important, particularly with ponies that are going to have to gallop and jump. The joints should look hard, and not have a tendency to roundness and puffiness. Knees need to be flat and well defined, the cannon bones should be short, and the tendons must be clean, cool and strong, and not puffy or bowed. The fetlocks need to be clean and hard and the pasterns fairly short and sloping, not long or straight. The feet should be well shaped and open, with frogs that are well developed and not shrivelled, soft, or smelly. A pony with small 'boxy' feet is to be avoided, and so is one with feet that don't match or which has one foot smaller than the others – the toes should never turn out. Hooves should be free from cracks and ridges which may indicate that a pony is prone to laminitis. However, even a perfectly proportioned, sound pony is of little use if it has not got a good temperament, and a large, kind eye is always most important.

> **'Cold-backed'**
>
> If a pony is described as being 'cold-backed' and lowers its back when the saddle is put on, this is more likely to be the result of some former injury, or perhaps an arthritic condition, and is nothing to do with the back being cold.

Out for a country ride

PONY SALES

*This Code of Practice by the British Horse Society is endorsed by the Livestock Auctioneers'
Market Committee for England and Wales and the Institute of Auctioneers and Appraisers
in Scotland, and should be strictly followed by those of its member firms
which conduct the sale of horses, ponies and donkeys.*

*   The number of animals presented at a market, sale or fair should not exceed the capacity of the accommodation available.

*   There should be adequate fencing around the market or saleyard to prevent breakaway.

*   Saleyards must be of suitable design and construction. They must be adequately maintained so as to prevent injury to animals. It is essential that pen railings should be spaced at distances sufficiently wide apart to prevent ponies from becoming trapped. If possible, right-angled passageways should be avoided, or treated with extreme care.

*   The inward-facing sides of pens and access ways should be smooth and without dangerous projections.

*   Concrete or other solid floor areas should be bedded or rendered slip-proof.

*   Holding pens should be available for stock before and after the sale; they should provide a suitable form of shelter for animals kept overnight. When also bedding must be provided.

*   There should be enough pens or suitable tying space to allow the proper segregation of one category of horse or pony from another; ponies should be kept separate from horses.

*   Mares with foal at foot, and stallions, including rigs, should also be penned separately from other horses.

*   There should be separate entrances and exits which must be kept clear for the passage of animals to and from the sales ring. Where scales form part of the entrance or exit, these should be wedged to immobilise the scales. A head room of 6ft 6in (1.9m) minimum is a requirement.

*   There should be an isolation pen away from the main sales pens.

*   Every animal within the saleyard must be provided with an adequate supply of suitable clean drinking water as often as is necessary to prevent it suffering from thirst.

*   Whilst ideally all animals should be removed on

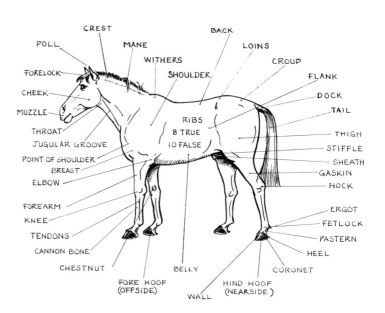

THE POINTS OF THE PONY

the day of the sale, animals kept overnight in the saleyard should be offered suitable food at appropriate intervals. Hay should be offered in racks and feeding stuff in troughs or buckets; the animals should not be fed on the floor.

* Ideally a veterinary surgeon should be in attendance at all horse sales. If a Ministry veterinary officer is not present then the auctioneer should either ensure that a veterinary surgeon be employed or is on call. It should be the responsibility of the auctioneer, on the advice of the veterinary surgeon where appropriate, that ailing or injured animals should not be presented for sale.

* Foals should not be offered for sale at under four months of age, except when 'at foot' and with their dams. A foal of any age which is considered weakly or immature should be refused entry to the sale, together with its dam.

* Broken horses should be led by a suitable method; horses not broken to halter should *not* be led.

* The local authority should ensure that any conveyance used for the transport of horses complies with the Transit of Animals (Road and Rail) Orders 1975 and 1979, or current government regulations in force, (Statutory Instrument Number 1024 – 1975) (1013 – 1979).

* Saleyards should be so planned as to allow easy loading and unloading, with sufficient loading bays for the number of horses sold, to achieve quicker clearance from the saleyards.

* Auctioneers should ensure that there are enough experienced stock handlers to deal with the number of horses and ponies presented for sale, particularly at the end of the sale when there is most need for them to assist with loading.

* Drovers should be clearly identified and be responsible to the auctioneers. Electric goads and the use of whips and sticks etc are prohibited, and where possible horses should be led.

* Only one person other than the vendor should be allowed in the sale ring at any one time, and that person should be one of the official drovers or a steward.

* Artificial lighting should be available to deal with sale activities after dark.

* Payments on unwarranted horses should be withheld for seven days for security purposes.

* Any person who considers that transgressions of this Code are taking place, should report these to the Animal Health and Welfare Officer at the market office immediately.

ACTION

A pony's action can be checked by having it walked and then trotted up on some hard and level ground. Apart from checking the way in which the pony moves, this is also a good time to see whether he trots up willingly, or whether he is inclined to be rather tardy and unco-operative. If, by this time, you are a little doubtful about the pony, it is nonetheless good manners to ask to see it ridden, preferably by someone connected with the owner. If the pony is going to misbehave and you are a parent, you will no doubt prefer that someone other than your own child should be riding it at the time!

UNDER SADDLE

If the pony is being jumped, ask to change round some of the fences. It is important to know whether the pony is inclined to hot up when jumping, and rush his fences, and if he is clever at sorting himself out before a fence. When you are satisfied that the pony will be all right for your rider to try, it is important to make sure that the two look right together. The object is to obtain a suitable pony. Young ponies need capable, experienced riders, while novice riders need older ponies which have learnt their business. Over-ambitious parents should restrain their ambitions until their children are ready for the challenge. Show jumping ponies in particular need selecting with knowledge and care – those of the tearaway variety, festooned with all sorts of gadgets, are not for the novice rider, no matter how many prizes they may have won.

Be careful

Riding the pony in an indoor school will not be an adequate test. Insist on seeing the pony ridden out in the open, and take a note of the tack he is wearing. A pony that is all trussed up with a double bridle and martingale rather than a plain snaffle will have to be rather suspect, particularly if it is being purchased for an inexperienced child to ride.

Find out about your pony

When buying a pony it is always wise to try and find out as much about it as possible. Quite apart from its temperament, manners and ability and whether it is easy to catch and box, it is also helpful to know whether it has any stable vices which, apart from anything else, may well affect its value.

HEIGHT

Height can be important in the case of show jumping ponies and those required for the show ring, and even if they have a life certificate for their height, it is always wise to have them measured again, preferably by a veterinary surgeon. Far better to be wise before buying the pony than to find it will have to compete in a larger class because it is a fraction over-size for the class intended.

REGISTERED PONIES

Ponies which have been jumping in British Show Jumping Association affiliated competitions, or have been shown in British Show Pony or the National Pony Society classes will also be registered, and details of their competition successes as well as their age and height will be known. Breed societies can also be very helpful in supplying information for people wishing to purchase native ponies.

Members of Pony Club branches frequently buy outgrown ponies from one another, and this is particularly the case with mounted games ponies who are often passed on from one team member to another, rather than let them get into the hands of a rival branch.

Remember, expert and helpful advice is never wasted, and even though the urge to buy a pony as quickly as possible may be great, it is always wiser to wait until the right pony can be found, which will then become a joy to own and fun to ride.

An ideal child's pony

Their versatility as a pony with quality and substance, moorland toughness, and superb temperament makes Dartmoors particularly attractive as childrens' ponies; and with full and flowing mane and tail and low, straight, free-flowing action, the Dartmoor is a very good-looking riding pony.

THE PONIES OF DARTMOOR

The Dartmoor pony is similar in a number of ways to the Exmoor, but the two breeds should not be confused and they each have their own enthusiastic supporters. The earliest reference to the Dartmoor pony appeared in the year 1012 in the will of Aelfwold of Crediton, a Saxon Bishop; however, there must have been ponies on the rugged wastes of Dartmoor, in the extreme south-west of England, many years before then.

In 1898 the Polo Pony Society set up a local committee to produce descriptions of all the native breeds, and their description of the Dartmoor was almost identical to the present-day pony, except for the height. The height limits then were 14 hands for stallions and 13.2 hands for mares, but few ponies reached that size. Only two of the 72 mares registered in the first stud book reached the maximum height, and of the five stallions, Brentor Confidence was the largest at 13.1 hands.

The two mares were registered by the director of convict prisons based at Dartmoor, and were probably two of the ponies ridden by warders as they escorted prisoners out on the moors to and from their work; the warders at Dartmoor Prison continued to use ponies to escort convicts until the early 1960s.

World War I had a very detrimental effect on the Dartmoor, like so many other breeds. However, at about the same time the Duchy Stud, which was owned by the Prince of Wales, began buying Dartmoor ponies to use in a breeding programme aimed at producing an all-round saddle horse. One of the stallions they used was a desert-bred Arab called Dwarka, a bay with a real pony-type head, and two outstanding ponies were produced as a result of this breeding policy, The Leat and Heatherbelle VI.

Opposite:
The lovely head of
White Willows Darwin,
a champion Dartmoor pony
stallion

Miss Calmady-Hamlyn

A great supporter of the Dartmoor pony for more than fifty years, Miss Calmady-Hamlyn had an important influence on the breed during the early 1900s. She bought her first Dartmoor in 1910 and showed her ponies with considerable success in London and at all the local shows in Devonshire. To begin with, many of her mares which she showed in Dartmoor classes were not pure bred, but were used by her to produce polo ponies – polo was another of her great interests. She won the Lord Arthur Cecil Cup for the champion mountain and moorland brood mare at the Polo and Riding Pony Society's Show for the first two years that it was awarded with her best Dartmoor mares, Junket and Diana II, in 1914 and 1915 – a remarkable performance, particularly as she stood reserve for the cup as well.

The Breed Society

The 1920s were an important period for Dartmoors. The Breed Society was formed in 1924, the height limit was finally fixed at 12.2 hands, and some of the most influential bloodlines of today relate back to the 1920s and 1930s, as do many of the breeders who are also now well known. Although the Breed Society failed for a while, it was re-formed by Miss Calmady-Hamlyn and her friend, Miss Norah Dawson. It was mainly thanks to the lengthy period that Miss Calmady-Hamlyn was the society's secretary, and to her tremendous enthusiasm for the breed, that the Dartmoor became such a successful pony.

Registration

Many of the ponies that she bred became champions and had a considerable influence on the breed during the 1930s. There were, however, very few registered ponies left after World War II – registration by inspection was introduced to try and build up the herds, and the winners at various selected shows automatically became eligible for registration.

Membership and registrations increased during the 1950s, so much so that after 1957 no further registrations made solely on wins or by inspection were permitted, and only those ponies whose parents were already registered were eligible for the stud book. The breed was also beginning to become popular in other parts of Britain, including the south-east, the Midlands and the north-east; there were also some breeders in Scotland, and a number of ponies had been exported to America.

Changes

Doctor Roberts took over as secretary in the 1960s and considerable changes took place during the twelve years that he was in office. A new constitution was introduced and a supplementary register was opened for up-grading ponies, as many members felt that the stud book had been closed too early in 1957.

Competition today

Dartmoors are now taking part successfull in many different kinds of competition, from carriage driving to the Mountain and Moorland Ridden Championships at Olympia, as well as in working hunter,

*Debbie Ogle and her attractive
pair of Dartmoor ponies,
Skerraton Peanuts and Foxglove*

Acceptable colours

Dartmoors are bay, brown, black, grey, chestnut or roan in colour, and any white markings on the head or legs should be fairly small. Piebald or skewbald colouring is not allowed.

jumping, gymkhana and ridden show and in-hand classes.

Conformation

A true Dartmoor should have a strong but not heavy neck of medium length and a small, well set-on head, with large and expanding nostrils. The eyes should be bright, mild, intelligent and prominent; ears need to be small, well formed, alert and neatly set, and the throat and jaws should be fine and not show any signs of throatiness or coarseness.

Medium in length, the body should be strong, well ribbed up, and have a good depth of girth with plenty of heart-room. Good shoulders are most important, and they should be well laid back and sloping, but not too fine at the withers. With strong loins, well covered with muscle, the hindquarters need to be of medium length, neither level nor steeply sloping, and with a tail set well up.

Dartmoors should never be 'sickle' or 'cow-hocked', but have hocks that are well let down and with plenty of length from the hip, clean cut and with plenty of bone below the joint. Their forelegs must never be tied in at the elbows and the forearm should be muscular, with the knee fairly large and flat on the front. The cannon bone should be short from knee to fetlock and have an ample amount of good, flinty, flat bone. The pasterns must be sloping but not too long, and the feet should be sound, tough and well shaped.

The ponies that roam the moors in a practically wild state have for many years been in serious jeopardy. In the early 20th century, Shetland stallions were indiscriminately introduced onto the moors in order to meet the need for very small pit ponies; the result was an indifferent type of Shetland cross, which continued to increase in numbers at the cost of the true Dartmoor.

The Dartmoor Society has managed to reinstate the true Dartmoor breed, but nowadays the ponies on the moor are in danger from the thousands of motorists who visit the moor each year. These tourists are being advised to leave the ponies in peace, and not to encourage them to come to the cars looking for food. With so much interest in the Dartmoor pony, however, it seems very likely that there will be Dartmoor ponies on the moors for many more generations of children to enjoy.

Dartmoor cross-breds

The Dartmoor pony has also proved of great value as foundation stock for cross breeding, the aim being to produce quality riding ponies. In 1965 a Part-Bred Dartmoor Register was opened and stud owners were encouraged to cross Dartmoors, or registered part-bred Dartmoors, with Thoroughbred, Arab, Anglo-Arab, or registered riding ponies. The cross-bred ponies almost always inherit the kind and generous temperament of the Dartmoor, and many have proved to be brilliant performers in a number of different activities. They have been consistent winners in the show ring, for example such ponies as Devon Minettie, Oakley Benjamin, Redwoods Concerto and Vean Ringlet, and have also proved to be tough and reliable in endurance riding events – that great little horse Dubonnet on which the European and World Three-Day-Event Champion, Virginia Leng, won the Junior European Three-Day-Event Championship as a teenager, was a combination of Dartmoor and Thoroughbred blood.

Small Ponies

Measuring the Shetland

Because of their small size, Shetlands are usually measured in inches.

Shetland Grand National!

THE SHETLAND PONY

The smallest breed of British native pony is the Shetland, which has maintained its small size in its native Shetland Islands for more than 2,000 years. Along with the Exmoor, it is also probably one of the purest of all the native breeds. When there has been any alteration in type, it has usually been due to a change in the work the ponies have been expected to do. Shetlands must not exceed a height of 40in (1.01m) by the time they are three, or 42in (1.07m) by the time they are four years of age or over.

Registration

The Shetland Pony Stud Book Society was formed in 1890 and the registering of pure-bred ponies has been kept up ever since. Volume One of the Stud Book states: 'The horse is accredited as the noblest of the lower animals, and the Shetland pony stands at the head of this noblest race, as the most intelligent and faithful of them all'.

It was, however, the formation of the Londonderry Stud in Bressay, Shetland, in about 1870, with a selected number of stallions and mares that was mainly responsible for fixing the type and character of the pure Shetland pony, and led to the foundation of many other high-class studs. When the Londonderry Stud was dispersed in 1898, many of the animals from there were exhibited at leading shows, which helped to popularise the breed.

The Shetland has a double coat in winter and a smooth one in summer

Small but versatile
The inhabitants of the Shetland Isles came to rely on the ponies not only as a means of transport, but also for haulage because, despite their lack of height, they are remarkably strong and capable of carrying heavy loads. When there was a demand for ponies to work in the mines, the Shetland was found to be ideally suited to the task, and large numbers were taken to the north-east of England for that purpose. It was probably because so many of them were used for hauling coal underground that Shetland ponies became predominantly black in colour – the mine owners only wanted dark-coloured ponies and so the breeders producing for them set out to breed black Shetlands, the other colours being used for different purposes.

Although registered Shetland ponies must not exceed 42in (1.07m) in height, they are tremendously strong and sturdy and as well as being popular as children's riding ponies, they also make excellent

The hardy Shetland

The extreme hardiness of the Shetland pony enables it to thrive under very adverse weather and grazing conditions, but they can do well in most climates, and since 1890 nearly 7,000 Shetland ponies have been exported from Britain to thirty-eight different countries, including India and Russia.

SMALL IS BEAUTIFUL

*Debbie Sly met 13-year-old Shetland stud
owner Oliver Joyce in the spring of 1989.*

Many children are born with ambition. 'When I grow up I want to be . . .' For some, their hopes remain a pipe-dream, for others, those hopes are a goal which they may spend much of their life working towards. Oliver Joyce became what he wanted to be before he had time to do much growing up, for he has been running his own Shetland pony stud since he was eight years old.

Quimper Stud and its tally of eighteen ponies and numerous show successes to date, is the result of five years of hard work put in by a young boy and his family.

Oliver had always wanted Shetland ponies. He had been riding since he was very young, but since he was four had voiced a preference for Shetlands. When he was seven, he had a bad fall and hurt his back; he announced that he was not going to ride again, but was going to breed Shetlands. Oliver's mother was not overkeen on these shaggy little creatures, and when Oliver turned up with an unrideable Shetland which he had bought for £25, his mother thought she had a safe bet when she said if he could break it, he could buy the brood mare he had always wanted.

Within three weeks he had succeeded, and with £300 from the sale of his first riding pony, he secured his mare. Oliver picked Canella out of a field of identical ponies, or so they would seem to those less familiar with these little ponies. She belonged to Mrs O'Brien who runs the Anwood Stud in Sussex, and who has given Oliver much help and advice since he bought Canella. This little mare proved she was something special by winning at the first show she was entered in.

She gave Oliver his first home-bred foal by producing Caramella in 1985. Oliver also bought a foal from Mrs O'Brien who, at four years old, is now his best mare – Francesca is obviously the apple of his eye and he describes her simply as 'the best'. Her impressive show record is proof of his faith in her and he hopes she will be the one to fulfil another of his ambitions to show his ponies at Olympia.

Oliver finds it hard to define exactly what he looks for when choosing a Shetland. Temperament is his number one criterion; all the ponies encountered at Quimper are incredibly sweet-natured – even the stallion (leased from Mrs O'Brien) allowed himself to be dragged by his forelock into position for his picture to be taken. Oliver prefers the sturdier, more traditional type of Shetland, so plenty of bone is essential, as is a pretty head and kind eye. Long backs and long legs are definitely out.

By 1987, Oliver's hobby had grown into a rather expensive one, as he had four ponies and a great many more things he wanted to do besides. He therefore wrote off to about twelve local companies to see if he could get any financial backing. The Gresham

Shetland pony sales

Pony sales are still held annually in Britain, in association with the Shetland Pony Stud Book Society, where only Shetland ponies are sold, and the great majority of these are pedigree animals. The sales are held in mid-October at Lerwick and Baltasound in the Shetlands; at Kirkwall, in the Orkneys; and at Aberdeen. A further sale is also held in late October or early November at Reading, in Berkshire.

driving ponies, particularly in scurry competitions when their courage and agility make them extremely popular with the spectators.

Colour and coat

Native Shetlands can be of any colour including skewbald, piebald, dun and palomino, but must not be spotted. In winter they have thick woolly coats through which grows the long straight hair that sheds the rain and keeps their skin dry in the worst weather. In the summer, however, their coats are short and carry a beautiful, silky sheen.

Conformation

Despite their stocky appearance, the well bred ponies have small heads with a wide forehead and small, well placed ears. They should have large, prominent eyes; their faces must not be dished or roman nosed, but they should have a broad muzzle, and a correct jaw with good teeth. Shetlands do have rather thick necks, but they should still have a good head carriage and it is important that the neck is properly set onto a sloping shoulder and ends in a well defined wither.

Their power comes from a strong body, with plenty of heart room,

Assurance Group offered him £1,000 towards his expenses, and subsequently he was so successful that in 1988 his new sponsors agreed to increase that amount to £3,000 per year for three years.

Actors may be warned never to go on stage with children or animals, but Mike Bourne, the public relations and sponsorship manager for Gresham Assurance, was very taken with the combination of this young boy and his ponies.

Their involvement had started when Oliver was just over 11 years old, and even at that age he was full of plans and ambitions.

'In fact, he's probably got more plans than we have got money' said Mike Bourne, 'but we are happy to help where we can, and though the commercial aspect did not come into it at first, and is still not paramount as regards his success, we are, of course, getting good publicity.' Mr Bourne explained that they did not want to go overboard on the commercial aspect, and that the sponsorship must remain in Oliver's best interests. But, of course, when the ponies get to Olympia, they will certainly be carrying Gresham's colours.

Oliver is not one to rush into things. When the sponsorship was offered, he politely said he would like to discuss things with his grandfather and would let them know his decision. For many youngsters it would have been a temptation to become a little complacent with £3,000 in their pockets, but Oliver's first thought was to go around all the banks and see who would offer him the best deal. 'After all, there's a lot of interest due on £3,000.'

Oliver's original breeding policy was to produce

Quimper Stud is very much a family affair, and some of the ponies are ridden by Oliver's sister Victoria

the black, sturdy type of pony similar to his foundation mares and the stallion he was using. However, in 1989 he bought his own stallion; while it still has good bone, he is hoping the new sire will add a little more refinement to the mares' offspring, being a rather elegant chap himself. The stallion is from the Transy Stud, which is one of the oldest in the country. His progeny will probably be more suited to riding than

continued overleaf

well sprung ribs, and strong, muscular loins. The quarters should be broad and long, with a well set tail. Manes and tails are an important characteristic with the hair long, straight and profuse, and the feathering on the fetlocks should be straight and silky.

Although their legs are short, the forelegs should be well placed, with well muscled forearms, strong flat knees, flat joints and plenty of bone. When looked at from behind, the hind legs should not be set too wide apart; the hocks must not be turned in, but be well shaped and strong, neither 'hooky' nor too straight, and the thighs strong and muscular. Finally, their feet should be round, open, and very hard, and their action should be free and straight, making full use of the shoulders, knees, and hocks.

Shetlands thrive best on a large run of rough grazing, but they can also do well in small fields and paddocks, providing that they have constant fresh water and plenty of hay in winter when there is not enough nourishment in the grass. If protection from hedges, trees or walls is insufficient, they will also need an open-fronted shelter to protect them from wind and rain in winter, and from heat and flies in summer.

Famous Shetland ponies

The Shetland Pony Stud Book has two sections, one for ponies of only two recorded generations, and the other for those with three or more. The ancestry of many fully pedigreed ponies, however, can be traced back for ten or more generations, and many of the most successful show animals can still be traced back to those famous sires of the Londonderry Stud, with such romantic names as Laird of Noss, Lord of the Isles, Multum in Parvo, Odin, Oman, and Prince of Thule.

continued

their more stolid mothers.

Black ponies were always Oliver's favourites, but he was tempted by a little dun and a very pretty bay, both of which he bought as foals. The new stallion is also bay and Oliver has already managed to breed his first bay foal.

One of his most successful mares is Sylvia, whom he rescued. She had been through eight homes and no-one had got round to even removing her headcollar; Oliver bought her for £50. He backed her three weeks before taking her to the Hampshire show, and she was placed fourth.

Gingham, his second pony, was another great success and he has two foals by her. Sadly, he only had one foal from his original mare, Canella – her second foal was born dead and the vet advised that the outlook for the mare was not good and that if she lived she would never be able to walk again: it would therefore be kinder to have her put down. However, Oliver spent two weeks sleeping in the stable with her, having as a last resort called in a spiritual healer, then treating her with herbs. She is fully recovered now, and lives happily on the stud, presiding over her successors. It appears that spiritual healing has also put another pony, suffering with navicular, on the road to recovery.

The stud is very much a family affair. It is part of Mrs Joyce's 50-acre farm, and Oliver relies on his mother for much of the help with the ponies, and of course their transport. In the winter, she does the ponies for him in the morning, but Oliver fits in as little school as possible, and rushes home to his ponies in the evening. All the ponies live out, so they do not need too much attention in the winter months – although this is when the early preparation for the show season starts.

In summer, Oliver spends all the daylight hours he can find with the ponies. The shows keep everyone busy, and all the ponies need to be ridden and schooled. Younger sister, Victoria, and even younger brother, James, are also called in to help. Victoria is very keen and has her own little grey Shetland, called Liza. It was Oliver's suggestion that she learn to ride side-saddle as a way to show the ponies off better, and maybe this bit of showmanship will help get them to Olympia.

Little James is not so keen unless he is winning prizes, but he has his own donkey which he shows. This was so that he would have something to occupy him during the long showing season, and even the donkey has won prizes.

Sponsorship has enabled Oliver to do many of the things he had hoped to do – before this financial assistance came along, he would get money for his birthday and Christmas presents so as to pay for a stud fee. However, he could not afford to keep a mare and foal, and pay another stud fee in one year, so he could only afford a foal every other year.

Oliver keeps all the filly foals to see how they develop, and so as to learn by experience the best time to show and sell them. Some of the mares produce adorable foals, but by the time they are two they are going through a really ugly stage – they grow out of this by the time they are about four. Oliver was nearly caught out by this the first time, and even put one up for sale as he could not stand the sight of her. But he gradually appreciated that she was developing into a more beautiful young lady – like the ugly duckling – and so she stayed.

The colt foals are gelded, except for those that may be good enough to be future stud stallions; Oliver breaks the geldings in and sells them on.

Oliver was originally concerned that the Shetland pony in its traditional standard form would die out, as so many breeders were showing a preference for the miniature Shetland. His foundation mares will ensure that the traditional pony remains a familiar sight in Sussex at least, but for one so young, Oliver is painfully aware that the stud has to make money to survive. In 1988 he stood his leased stallion at stud and had five visiting mares – the stud fees he collected covered the cost of the lease and the stallion's keep. He bought his own stallion because its purchase price was not much more than the lease payments he had been making, and was therefore a true investment. He also hoped it would help produce the type of pony he knows will sell.

The £3,000 has not gone to Oliver's head, either. He knows a side saddle will cost him £600, and on top of that he will have to finance Victoria's blue tweed habit. There are feed and veterinary bills to be met, entry fees to be paid, and the horsebox has to be kept on the road.

Oliver keeps his own set of books in which every transaction is faithfully recorded. There are sections in his business book for finance, plans, breeding records of all the mares, a record of all the stallions and geldings sold, a foal list, a show record, and one for transfers and animals bought and sold. The back section is modestly called 'My hobby'; it includes a history of the Shetland breed, and the story of how Oliver started the stud, and its progress to date.

Oliver's ambitions have not stopped with the formation of the Quimper Stud – he likes all the native breeds and would like to produce all of them! He also wants to produce and show other people's ponies, and to this end is going to spend two years with Len Bigley in Herefordshire; Len used to have the Lanarth Stud but now he produces and shows ponies. Here, Oliver will learn to deal with somewhat more flighty and delicate creatures than his own trusty Shetlands.

On top of this he wants to have a team of black, home-bred Shetlands to rival Prince Philip's team of Fells. He spent two weeks with Frank Skillet where he learnt as much as he could about driving, and will probably return there when the new stallion arrives, since it is broken to harness; he has also bought a driving mare. Scurry driving appeals to him equally, and to help pay the bills, he plans to hire out a Shetland and carriage and transport the bride at weddings!

With so much planned, it is obvious that he means it when he says: 'When I leave school at eighteen, there won't be enough time left in my life to do all the things I want. If I start now, I might just manage it!'

Oliver's new-found success makes further demands on his valuable time. He has appeared on television twice and has been interviewed for countless newspapers and magazines. He also took part in a documentary called 'Low Down', about children who are doing something a little bit different – this required eight days' filming and Oliver was surprised at all the fuss. But far from this fame going to his head,

Oliver is still only happiest talking to people who are genuinely interested in his ponies.

Oliver does not have the grand facilities often associated with studs. The family does have planning permission to build four stallion boxes and two barns, one for hay and straw, the other to contain twelve loose-boxes – but this will cost about £20,000, and they have to buy the farm first, if they can, which is another £40,000. That represents a lot of stud fees and prize money, and may be one of the things that will just have to wait.

Oliver appears to be just an ordinary little boy trying to do something with his ponies on 50 acres of cold, windswept pasture on the seaward side of the downs: but hopefully he won't have to worry too much about what he wants to do when he grows up.

Oliver and his younger brother James riding Francesca, who was the Points Champion at the Shetland Breed Show

THE TINY HORSES FROM ARGENTINA

A pony that will wander about the house and even go upstairs like a dog may seem a little far-fetched: but not, of course, if it is a Falabella miniature horse. It is not to be confused with the Shetland pony which, despite its small size, has been known to carry a 12 stone (76kg) man for 40 miles (64km) in one day – the Falabella stands well under 34in (86cm) and cannot be ridden.

They are, however, perfect miniature horses in every way, with very finely boned legs in perfect proportion to their bodies, and very small feet – they have been described as being rather like a hunter when looked at through the wrong end of a telescope.

History

The history of the Falabellas is surrounded by mystery and there are many stories as to how they came to be so small, all of which add to the romantic nature of the breed.

Lady Fisher keeps a herd of Falabellas at Kilverstone, not far from Newmarket; when she visited Argentina she was told that the chief of the Cayak Indians had passed the secret of breeding these miniature horses to the Falabella family. However, this seems unlikely in view of the warlike nature of the Indians who inhabited the area in the past, and their need for war ponies rather than miniature horses.

Some maintain that a herd of horses was trapped in a canyon in Argentina hundreds of years ago, and that the only food they had to eat were cactus plants. Over several generations the horses got smaller and smaller until they were found by the Falabella family, who winched them from the canyon and took them to their ranch.

Others claim that the horses had been found hidden in a valley in the Andes, a sort of Shangri-la where everything, including all the

Opposite:
A whole new meaning to the term 'hunter trial'?

Lord and Lady Fisher with some of their Falabellas at their miniature horse stud at Kilverstone Wildlife Park in Norfolk

The true Falabella breed

The Falabella breed has within it the blood of many other breeds, and all the colour markings, but the rarest of all are the spotted ones. The height remains small because the Falabella carries a dominant gene which has the effect of shrinking down in size the offspring of any larger horse that it is crossed with. Although the Falabella family have been breeding miniature horses for more than 130 years, the Falabellas are still a breed in the making; first of all they are crossed with the larger breeds of horse, and it then takes many generations of breeding and selecting to get them down to the mini size of less than 34in (86cm). It is , however, because they are crossed with other breeds that the Falabellas are perfectly proportioned replicas of larger horses.

The prize spotted stallion Menelek shows his jumping ability

plants, were small and different!

There is also the suggestion that the grandfather of the present Señor Falabella had sent some Thoroughbred horses to a very barren and windswept part of Patagonia, and then forgotten about them. Some years later his grandchildren remembered the story of the horses and set off to look for them. When they did eventually come across them, they found that only the smallest had survived since the only shelter and grazing was the low-growing scrub.

The most unlikely story is that the Falabella family at one time employed a number of Japanese on their ranch who somehow managed to reduce the size of the horses. However, the true story of their origin is even more fascinating. This was told to Lady Fisher by Señor Julio Cesar Falabella, whose grandfather founded the breed.

Last century there were in parts of Chile and Argentina a number of tribes of nomadic Indians that even the Spaniards had failed to subdue. They hated the white man, and waged a constant war on the settlers. Periodically, they would descend on the ranches, burning, looting and killing, and taking away with them prisoners and cattle which they would later sell. Their captives were treated in a most hideous way, and few if any survived. One of the early settlers was Señor Falabella's maternal grandfather, an Irishman called Newton who, like so many of the Irish, had a deep knowledge and understanding of horses.

He had built a water mill on the banks of the river which passed through his land, and every night stones were placed inside the mill wheel, and the rumbling noise could be heard for miles. The Indians, who were very superstitious, thought that he must be some kind of

MINI
HICKSTEAD.

magician, and kept well clear of Señor Newton's ranch.

There was a ford below the house and, as it was the only watering-place for some distance, horses and other animals often went there to drink. Some of them would still have their saddles and bridles on, or would still be harnessed to a cart or wagon whose blood-stained seats indicated that their owners had been attacked and probably murdered by Indians.

One day there appeared at the ford a small horse that was quite different to anything that Señor Newton had ever seen. It was a perfectly proportioned horse in miniature, and Señor Newton was so fascinated by the little stallion that he decided to keep it and breed miniature horses for his daughter, who was Señor Falabella's mother.

It was the offspring of that little stallion that laid the foundation of the Falabella miniature breed. No-one ever found out where the stallion came from, to whom he belonged, or how he came to be that size, and it remains one of the great unsolved mysteries of the horse and pony world.

Although Señor Falabella now keeps some 400 horses of many different sizes on his ranch, only a few are the true small miniature, and it may take several generations to breed down to the very smallest sizes of all.

The Lady Fisher with Pandora, who is almost hidden by the wildflowers in the garden at Kilverstone Hall

---

Falabella celebrities!

Visitors to Kilverstone can see the miniature horses putting on a remarkable free jumping display; the little Falabellas also make charity appearances, and have appeared on television in Britain and abroad. They have been exported to Australia, New Zealand, America, Italy, Spain, East and West Germany, the Middle East, Sweden, Holland and Japan.

Kilverstone: the first European stud farm

When Lady Fisher met Senor Falabella on his ranch, he agreed to sell her Menelek, his prize spotted stallion who was running with some of the 15-hand Appaloosan mares he was using to breed down from. There were also three other herds, one containing a number of little mares and a tiny stallion, another with normal size Falabellas, and the third consisting of very small ones. Lady Fisher was allowed to select three other stallions and a number of mares, and these were all shipped to England to form the basis of the herd at Kilverstone Wildlife Park at Thetford in Norfolk, which became the first Falabella stud in Europe.

Coming from the dry climate of Argentina, the Falabellas took a little time to become accustomed to the cooler, moister climate of Britain, and particular attention had to be paid to the temperature and humidity of their indoor accommodation. They all have their own night rugs in the stable, and weatherproof day rugs when they are turned out during the colder months.

They are fed like other ponies except in smaller quantities, and an acre of grazing is sufficient for two Falabellas – if they are kept in a small space they can be taken for a walk like a dog. However, as long as they have enough room to run around and kick their heels up they can get all the exercise they need.

At Kilverstone they have already crossed the Falabella stallions with mares of larger breeds to produce miniatures. When a 15-hand Arab mare was crossed with Chico, a Falabella stallion who is only 29in (53.6cm) high , the foal was born the same height as his father, and could only just reach his mother's milk by standing on tip-toe.

The gestation period for Falabella mares can be up to 13 months, instead of the normal 11 months taken by other horses and ponies, and Pepita, the first of the mares to foal at Kilverstone, carried her foal Evita for 12½ months. This longer period could be the result of the different climatic conditions in Argentina, because since then all the other mares have taken the usual 11 months. Other ponies usually grow until they are five or six years old, but Falabellas make 90% of their growth in the first year, and are fully grown by the time they are three. They have two ribs and two vertebrae fewer than other horses and ponies, but although they are too small and delicate of bone to carry a rider, they can be harnessed to a lightweight cart and will pull an adult or several children.

THE MINIATURE HORSES OF IRAN

Although only the height of a small pony, the Caspian is thought to be related to the ancient miniature horses of Mesopotamia, and it has the temperament and gaits of a horse. Even so it is an ideal ride for a child, and is one of the most attractive breeds now being used for riding and driving. It is highly intelligent, alert, kind and willing, with the fine, silky summer coat and the mane and tail of a Thoroughbred – but in winter it has the coat of a mountain pony.

History

More than 3,000 years ago there were Caspians around the southern shores of the Caspian Sea, and they were used by such famous rulers as King Darius the Great for ceremonial purposes and as carriage horses. Their breeding grounds were between the forested northern slopes of the Elburz mountains and the Persian shores of the Caspian Sea in northern Iran, and they were probably taken there from Media by tribesmen from Kermanshah when they moved to that area of Iran.

Little is known of them, except that they were either running wild or, until the 1960s, being used as working ponies by the peasant community in the area. The breed was discovered again in northern Iran in 1965, when the American wife of an Iranian found a stallion called Ostad, only about 11 hands high, harnessed to a crude and heavy cart. He was a slim, bay horse, with a bright, glossy coat, slim legs and tiny hooves, and had the body and carriage of a well bred oriental horse.

He was bought and taken to the green pastures of Norouzabad, near Tehran, and gradually he was joined by more ponies found pulling heavy loads and rescued from thoughtless native owners. Most of the Caspian ponies were thin and sick and covered in sores, and two years passed before a small breeding herd could be established.

The rice paddies and cotton fields of Mazanderan were searched for more examples of the breed, but famine, disease and lack of care had taken their toll, and by the end of the 1960s only about thirty Caspians had been found. However, a stud was established at the royal stables outside Tehran and interest in the breed began to develop. Less than twenty years after being rediscovered, however, the little Caspian horses were facing danger again as a result of the revolution in Iran. Luckily, Caspian mares and stallions had been exported to Britain between 1971 and 1978, and some of those bred in the United Kingdom were sent to Australia, New Zealand and Canada; Caspian studs and societies were then established there.

This has fortunately meant that despite the political upheaval in Iran, the breed has been saved. Since 1975, the maintenance of a register of pure and part-bred Caspians bred in Britain has been undertaken by the British Caspian Society and Trust, which is a registered charity. A regular stud book is published, and the society is helping to promote the breed through show classes and driving events. An annual breed show is held, with in-hand, ridden and driven classes, and the society also promotes classes for Caspians at other shows throughout the year. There is also a points performance scheme in operation, to encourage the use of Caspians in as many equestrian activities as possible.

Ability and performance

There is no doubt that the Caspian's natural floating action – it has a long, low, swinging trot, a smooth rocking canter, and a rapid flat gallop – and a strength belied by its appearance, has made the breed increasingly popular for riding and driving. It is an ideal leading rein or first ridden pony, and gives a small child the sort of comfort and control which adult riders have with a well schooled horse. Its calm, willing temperament gives a child confidence, and its elegant appearance and well-balanced action have been attracting favourable attention in the show ring.

Being a natural jumper, the Caspian has considerable potential as a child's hunter, showjumper or eventer, particularly if it has been properly trained and is in the hands of an enthusiastic young rider. It is well-proportioned and compact, and has the speed and turning

Ancient ancestors

Evidence of a small, pony size horse from about the end of the seventh century AD is present in ancient seals, statuettes, and writings. The most famous is the trilingual seal of Darius the Great, about 500 BC, now in the British Museum. It shows a pair of tiny ponies with very fine legs, small ears, and vaulted foreheads, pulling the royal chariot on a lion hunt.

The Caspian Stud Book

The International Caspian Stud Book is the parent body to which the national societies in Britain, Australia, New Zealand, and North America are affiliated, as well as horses in Iran.
It approves the stallion licensing procedures of the affiliated societies. Stallion licensing can be applied for when Caspian colts are more than two years of age.

A child's pony

The Caspian can be a good first pony for a child, and it can keep up with a normal sized horse without any difficulty, except at a flat gallop.
Stallions are regularly ridden together by small children, and can be turned out together in the same field.

These two ponies from the Dark Horse Caspian Stud, Winstay Shah Jehan (left) and Darkhorse Avval, are typical examples of the Caspian breed, which is thought to be related to the ancient miniature horse of Mesopotamia

ability required of a mounted games and gymkhana pony, and even young and newly broken Caspians have been successful in gymkhana competitions.

They make graceful and energetic harness ponies, and more of them are now competing successfully as single, pair and tandem turnouts in driving trials. Their acceleration and manoevrability have also been bringing them success in scurry competitions.

Conformation and colour

As with most native ponies, there are rules regarding the appearance and temperament of the Caspian. They are normally between 10 and 12.2 hands in height – averaging 11.2 hands – and are usually bay, grey or chestnut in colour. Some Caspians are black and cream, however, and they can have some white on their face and legs.

They should have a wide, vaulted forehead and deep cheekbones in a short, fine head that tapers to a small muzzle; large, almond-shaped and often prominent dark eyes, and large nostrils set low. The ears should be wide apart, alert and finely drawn, and often turn in at the tips.

Caspians are characterised by their slim body, with a graceful neck, long sloping shoulders, and a deep girth; slender limbs, with strong, dense, flat bone, and little or no feathering on the fetlocks; neat, oval hooves which are immensely strong all round, often with a small frog and which seldom require shoeing.

As with native breeds, they are very hardy, and can winter out in most climates providing that they are in a field which has shelter from the wind and rain, and sufficient food in winter. They should not, however, be allowed too much rich spring and summer grass.

THE TRUE COST OF A FOAL

There is often a great temptation to breed a foal from an outgrown pony mare, but in many cases the results are far from happy. Thousands of foals are bred each year by people who don't realise the problems involved, and they end up unwanted and doomed to the knackers' yard.

It is estimated that more than 10,000 ponies every year end up as food on European dinner tables, bought by the growing body of meat men who have contracts to fulfil for slaughterhouses and are regular buyers at pony sales throughout Britain.

These ponies, who are looked upon as being surplus to requirements, are to a large extent the result of thoughtless breeding. The increase in the cost of feeding stuffs, veterinary expenses, farriers' charges, transport, stallion fees and insurance, all make the cost of getting a mare in foal higher than many owners would expect, and if they had worked out the true cost beforehand they would probably have decided against trying to breed a foal.

The facilities needed should also be taken into account, for instance there must be somewhere to keep a foal after it has been weaned. So often people don't look as far ahead as weaning, and they have no idea of the amount of time and care involved.

Foals have to be kept for at least three years before they can be ridden, and during that time owners have to cope with all their requirements: daily attention, paying veterinary fees, arranging 'flu and anti-tetanus injections, worming regularly and coping with farrier charges – all this, even when the foal is healthy.

Then there will be the cost of breaking the pony in, and expenses are rarely recovered, even when he has been broken; and keeping him until he is much older involves yet further expense.

So, unless an owner is prepared to accept the problems and the costs, and to plan ahead for a period of some three to four years, the answer must always be: 'When in doubt, don't breed'.

It's difficult to resist – but do bear in mind the true cost before breeding a foal

Ponycare

Good strong post and rail fencing is by far the best

KEEPING A PONY AT GRASS

Ponies are natural foragers and being kept at grass suits them well as this is closer to their natural condition. However, they should not be left to fend for themselves entirely, and accidents and illness can often be avoided with a little foresight. A pony needs an acre, and preferably more, of well drained and well fenced pasture if he is kept out all year round. Plenty of fresh water is essential, and so is some form of shelter to provide protection from the wind and rain in winter and the flies in summer. Ideally the grazing area should be divided into two or more sections, so that one section can be rested while the others are being grazed.

Fencing

Ponies are inquisitive and would explore far beyond the confines of their paddock if they could, so fencing must be secure and safe. Post and rail fencing about 1.5m (5ft) high is ideal – it is expensive, but does last a long time. Post and wire is a cheaper alternative, but the posts must be strong and the wire needs to be kept taut and in good repair; barbed wire does not make good fencing for ponies as it can cause injury. Hedges and walls form natural fencing in some parts of the country, and can provide shelter from the wind. Again, they must be kept in good repair as ponies will quickly push through any gaps in a hedge.

Gates

Gates must open wide so that a pony does not injure himself when he is led through, and they need to have a secure fastening which the pony cannot undo. Ponies need shelter and this can either be a shed of some kind or a thick hedge and shady trees, though trees provide little shelter when they lose their leaves. A field shelter must be high and wide enough for the pony, with a wide doorway to prevent injury – if ponies share a shelter then plenty of room is vital, otherwise a bullying pony may force his companion out, and they must be able to get through the doorway quickly. A felt-covered wooden roof is ideal; corrugated iron should be avoided as it will get very hot in the summer.

Pasture

Although grass grows naturally with very little help, it does not grow consistently all year round. In the winter the field will become bare and the pony will need hay and extra feed to keep him fit. However, in spring rather the opposite occurs – the grass grows fast and lush and ponies can quickly get overfat, and they will then be extremely susceptible to 'grass laminitis'. This is when there is a lot of heat in the hooves, and the pony *must* have his feed reduced and be treated by a veterinary surgeon.

Ponies will not eat grass that has grown old or long, nor will they eat the tufty grass anywhere near their droppings. To prevent the pasture becoming 'horse-sick', a few measures can be taken. Droppings should be picked up at frequent intervals and removed to a dung heap – if this is not possible then they should be scattered with a rake, or the field should be chain-harrowed. This will encourage a pony to be less selective and will also reduce the build-up of worms which are found in the pony's dung. Fields will benefit if they are topped occasionally, to get rid of the longest grass and thistles; similarly, a good way to keep grass in better condition is to let cattle graze it as well as ponies, because cattle are not such selective feeders and will eat the longer, older grass.

Poisonous plants

Unfortunately, poisonous plants also grow in fields amongst the grass a pony eats, and can make him very ill. These plants should be pulled up from any grazing areas and also from fields which are to be made into hay for the pony. Ragwort is a very common plant which can cause liver damage; it grows in the more open, sunny parts of the

Watch out

Poisoning should be suspected when a pony suddenly becomes ill after feeding, or shows signs of digestive problems, excitability or convulsions. Poisonous plants can be most dangerous when they are at the succulent stage in fields where good grass may be scarce. During a very dry summer, or in late autumn and winter when there is no growth of grass and supplementary food is not provided, ponies can often be tempted to eat plants which may be poisonous to them. Remember that spraying some poisonous plants with weed killer can even make them more palatable to ponies, and mouldy hay or silage may easily contain toxins. A veterinary surgeon must always be called immediately if a pony shows any signs of having been poisoned. Any delay could prove fatal.

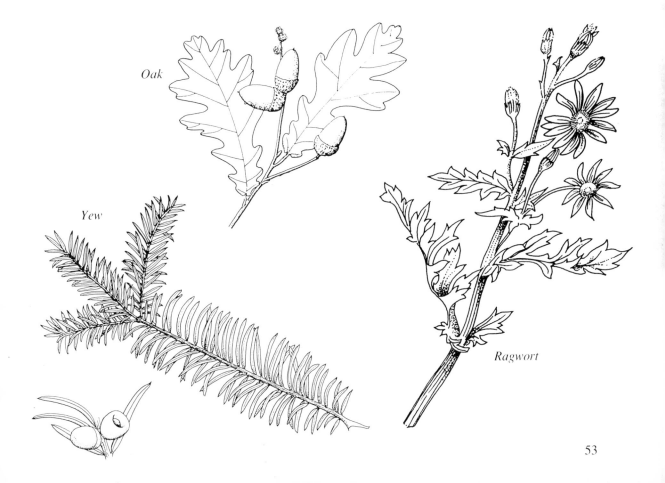

Oak

Yew

Ragwort

field and should be pulled up by the roots as soon as it appears. The plants should be burnt or carefully disposed of, as ragwort is even more dangerous when it is dead.

Deadly nightshade and other members of the hemlock family prefer damp ditches and hedgerows, and gloves should be worn when these are pulled up. Privet and yew are also poisonous and should be cut down or fenced off. Grass cuttings must on no account be fed to ponies as they can make them ill. Acorns, if eaten in large amounts, can also be fatal and if many fall they should be picked up. Fortunately, when there is plenty of grass a pony will not usually be tempted to nibble anything dangerous, but it is best not to take any chances.

Winter feeding

During the winter, ponies will need to be fed hay and probably a concentrate feed, according to the breed of pony and the work he is doing. If it is very mild and there is still plenty of grass, hay will not have to be fed until later in the year, but by about November it will usually be necessary, though once a day should be plenty up until Christmas. If the pony is being hunted or ridden regularly he will also need a concentrate feed, which can be made up of horse and pony nuts, oats, flaked maize or bran.

From Christmas until April, ponies will probably need two feeds of hay each day as well as a concentrate feed. Ideally, hay should be fed in nets, as less is wasted than if it is spread on the ground, but the haynets should always be tied high enough so that when they are empty they will not become entangled in the pony's feet.

When it is frosty or snowy, ponies will not be able to break the layers of ice in the water-trough by themselves, and it will be necessary for the ice to be broken at least three times a day. Ponies

The straps at the rear of a New Zealand rug should always be crossed over and undone first of all when the rug is being removed

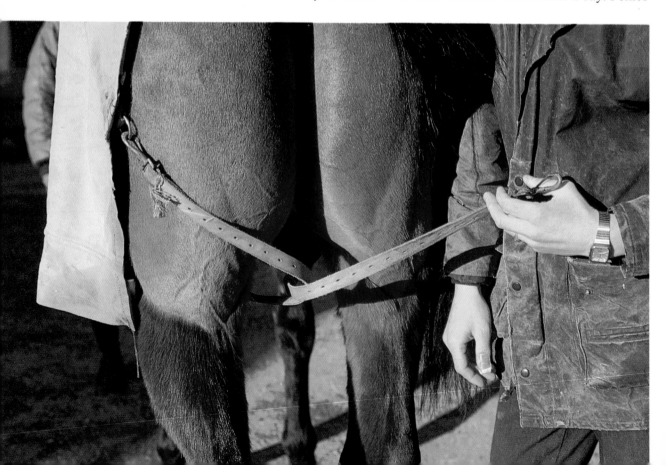

that are unshod can suffer bruising when the ground is very hard, and they may need front shoes.

Welsh ponies in the snow

Clipping

If a pony is ridden regularly in winter he may need to be clipped and the most popular for a pony turned out is the trace-clip; the pony may then need a New Zealand rug, a weatherproof rug with a warm lining, kept in place with leather straps. It must fit properly so that it does not rub the skin and should be taken off and put back on again at least once a day. Mud should be removed from the pony's coat before the rug is put on. A good feed of warming and energy-making food is also needed, as a rug alone does not make up for a lack of coat.

Catching

When a pony is being brought in from the field he should never be approached from the front. The best way is to go up to his nearside and stand with your back to his tail. With a tit-bit in your left hand, and talking to him all the time, put your right hand round the pony's neck; the rope can then be taken from the left hand and held round his neck, and the noose of the halter slipped over the pony's nose and up over his ears. The neck rope can then be released and the pony led away. Tit-bits should always be carried when catching a pony.

If a pony is difficult to catch, he should be let out with a short piece of rope attached to his headcollar – this will be more easily caught

---

Feeding in the field

If several ponies are fed together, hay may have to be fed on the ground – it should be left in a large circle, in heaps which are wide enough apart so the ponies cannot kick each other. Bowls of feed should also be placed well apart so that ponies will not be too close together while they eat. There should be one more heap or bowl than there is number of ponies, ie six ponies, seven heaps

The Peruvian

For centuries Lima was the headquarters of the Spanish occupation forces, and so more Andalusian and other Spanish breeds were imported into Peru than any other country in South America. The first were brought over by Pizarro and Almagro in 1531 and 1532, and pure Andalusians were bred in and around Lima for hundreds of years. Some inevitably escaped and went wild and their descendants are a Peruvian type of Criollo pony, sometimes called Saltenos; they are usually smaller than the Argentine Criollo, although some make 14 hands or more, and they are noted for their soundness and lively action. Another native type is the Serrano, a heavily built mountain pony, often used as a pack pony or for draught work on the highland plateaux. There is also the Morochuquo: more heavily built than most Criollos, although seldom exceeding 13.2 hands in height, the Morochuquo branch of the Criollo family make invaluable pack transport and saddle ponies in the cold and inhospitable Cordillera mountains.

Worm your pony regularly

Most cases of colic are due to red worm which needs to be treated regularly, preferably every 6 – 8 weeks by a wormer in paste form so that you are sure it has been swallowed. The type of wormer should be changed at regular intervals to prevent worms from becoming resistant to any one particular drug. Pony droppings should be collected once or twice a year and sent to a veterinary laboratory for testing to make sure that the wormers used are being effective.

hold of than the headcollar when he comes up to sniff at a tit-bit. If the pony is really bad to catch he should be turned out each day into a bare yard with a longer trailing rope fixed to the headcollar. With very little to eat he will soon become bored, and be pleased to see someone approach with a small feed or tit-bit. A real fuss should be made of him when he comes to call, but he should always be left wanting more. After a week or so in the bare yard he should be ready to be turned out into a larger field, but he should still have a short length of rope fixed to the headcollar until he is happy to allow people to go up to him without running away.

Illness and injury

A pony can become ill or injured while out at grass. Sometimes a little first-aid can put things right, but in more serious cases a veterinary surgeon must be called. 'Ordinary' cuts and wounds must be washed with clean cold water and dressed with cream or powder, but deep cuts and puncture wounds will need veterinary attention.

Sweet itch is an eczema which causes the mane and tail to become itchy, and the pony will often rub these areas and can make them bleed. Soothing lotions can be put on the sore areas and the pony should be kept inside during the day if possible. Lice may be seen in the hair of the mane and tail in the spring, but lice powder can be bought from a chemist to deal with these parasites.

It is not always possible to tell exactly what is wrong with a pony at a glance, but it is easy to see when he is ill. He will usually stand with his head down and ears back, his coat will be staring and he will look tucked up and miserable. The vet should be called and in the meantime the pony should be brought into the stable, if one is available, and then dried with straw if he is wet. His ears should be rubbed to warm them and he should be given a rug with a blanket underneath if it is very cold.

Even in a secure field with plenty of grass, it is important to check the pony each day. He may have escaped, or become ill or injured. Like most inquisitive animals, if there is something to investigate or get caught up in, ponies will probably manage to get into mischief.

A warning about worms

All ponies are infested with worms, and their beds if they are stabled, and paddocks if they are turned out, are also likely to be infected by worm eggs or young worms. Regular action, ie worming, is needed to prevent the worms from getting the upper hand; if they do, a pony will quickly lose condition and its performance will be affected. Worm infestation may cause indigestion, colic, or even death.

Ponies at grass are usually infected with the eggs of the bot fly during late summer, and these develop into larvae which live in the stomach of the pony during the winter months. It is therefore important to find a medicine which is effective against the bot fly larvae which you can use during the winter.

As mentioned earlier, whenever possible a ponies' field should be divided up into smaller paddocks so that each section can be rested for at least three months of each year. When there are a number of owners sharing a field it is important that they all treat their ponies for worms at the same time, and make sure that the droppings are collected regularly to reduce the areas of worm infestation.

THE DALES PONY
Toughness and versatility

Although bred originally as a pack pony, the Dales, a native of the eastern slopes of the Pennines, has become known as 'the great all-rounder' of the pony world. Although Dales ponies can be found from the High Peak in Derbyshire to the Cheviots near the Scottish border, their favoured breeding grounds have always been the upper dales of Tyne, Wear, Allen, Swale and Tees.

History

From Roman times until the mid-19th century there was a flourishing lead-mining industry in that area and the Dales pony was bred specifically for pack work; it carried ore, fuel and lead on its back, and became renowned for its great strength, iron constitution, endurance and the ability to get over rough country at speed.

There were two distinct types of pony in the Middle Ages: amblers for riding, and trotters for pack and army requirements, and the great abbeys of the time had large studs of them, although instead of the darker colours, they usually preferred greys.

In 1513, on a roll of tenants of Jervaulx Abbey, the ponies requisitioned for army purposes were classified by gait, and the majority of the 253 selected were described as being 'trottyng'. There were some greys, but most of them were black or bay, which is the principal colour of the Fells and Dales of today. The 'trottyng' ponies were listed as having mostly white markings, and the Dales pony carries more white than the Fell.

During the late 17th century, the Scottish Galloway was considered to be the best pony for fast pack-work, and replacements were bred near the lead mines. Suitable native mares ran with the breeding herds and farmers also liked to run a few Scottish mares with the native breeds on the fell. The largest, strongest, and most active ponies were chosen for pack work, and were always well fed to ensure fitness and speed. The black Galloways of the mixed herds eventually replaced the Scottish Galloways which were nonetheless famous for their 'peculiarly deep and clean legs, and their qualities

The Criollo

A cross between pure-bred horses and Arab and Barb strains, the Criollo ponies were brought to South America at the time of the conquest. For more than 300 years the breed survived the extreme hardships of living wild, and this has produced hardiness and the ability to endure great exposure. Usually between 13.3 and 14.3 hands in height, they stand on very short legs and are mostly khaki, dun or skewbald in colour which means they blend easily with the sandy wastes and burnt-up pastures of their native land. Aimé Felix Tschiffely, who was born in Switzerland but became a naturalised Argentinian, earned great fame by riding two Argentine Criollo ponies some 10,000 miles from Buenos Aires in South America, to Washington USA; when they set out on their remarkable journey in 1925, Gato was 15 and Mancha was 16 years of age, and rider and ponies endured great hardships, including hunger and extremes of heat and cold. The journey was intended to prove the stamina of the Criollo breed of ponies which Tschiffely believed was dying out.

Gato died at the age of 36 and Mancha at 40, and models of them in their own skins can be seen in the Colonial Museum in Buenos Aires.

Snowhope Purple Heather, who was foaled in 1929, proved to be a very influential Dales stallion

Opposite:
*After being a successful brood
mare, Sunglow Karalina had
considerable success in the
showring from the age of eleven,
including wins at the Ponies of
Britain Show at Peterborough
three years running*

of speed, stoutness and sure-footedness over a rugged mountainous
country'. It is obvious where the Dales gained many of these
remarkable qualities.

As the Scottish Galloway had always been the favourite mount of
both Border raiders and Scottish drovers, there was no shortage of
supply, but by 1831 the breed was considered to have become
extinct. Their reputation for excellence, however, had by that time
led to them being used to found new breeds or to improve existing
ones such as the Norfolk roadster, the Clydesdale and the Dales. The
Clydesdale and Dales were bred along different lines, but they do
have several features in common, including beautiful feet and legs
and very flexible joints which give both breeds a distinctive jaunty,
free action when walking.

In the days when the ponies were used as pack animals in the lead-
mining industry, the rakes of lead were all situated on the high moors;
the washing places were by streams; the smelting holes needed to be
on a hill; a good supply of wood for fuel had to be nearby, and the lead
then had to be transported to the ports of the north-east coast, and
when the local wood ran out, coal had to be brought back.

Versatility
The Dales pony also became recognised as a comfortable riding
animal, strong enough for draught work and able to thrive on the
bleak uplands of the Dales. These abilities were not lost on farmers

*Dales ponies are often good
jumpers and Sunglow Karalina is
seen here competing in a working
hunter pony class*

PONYCARE

The typical action of a Dales pony is shown here by the mare Brymor Mimi

who found them ideal for work on small farms throughout the year. They could pull a ton in a cart; were sturdy shepherds' ponies, capable of covering great distances across the fells; and could carry up to twelve stones (76kg) of hay, often with a rider as well, and sometimes in deep snow. A pair could pull a plough or a reaper/binder, had a fast trot and were able to take a farmer to market in style. Being willing and clever jumpers, they could also give him an occasional day's hunting.

Because of these qualities, when the railways superseded the pack

The same mare, Brymor Mimi, is accompanied by her foal Millstone Hotspur while gathering sheep

trains, the ponies found a niche on the farms of the Dales, and many of them were also taken for work in the lead and coal mines of the north-east. When better roads were constructed, there was a demand for faster horses for the mail and stage coaches, and the fastest and stoutest roadsters of the day were Norfolk cobs.

Trotting ponies

The best of the Norfolk breeds were imported by Yorkshiremen to improve the Yorkshire trotters, and the result was the marvellous Yorkshire roadsters of the mid-19th century. Stylish trotters became the rage, and as the Dalesmen enjoyed trotting races but found it uneconomical to keep an extra pony solely for that purpose, they used the best of the Norfolk and Yorkshire blood to breed the brilliant little mares which added an extra sparkle to the fast Dales trot. In this way they created the spectacular action of the good Dales ponies, but without spoiling them as farm workers and riding ponies.

> ### In the early days
>
> Bronze age horse tackle has been found in Weardale, and it is recorded that Barnard Baliol in 1131 included rights of pasture for 60 mares and foals above High Force, in Teesdale.

The Dales ponies Ackram Rose and May Queen IX are the winners of many tradesman and light commercial driving classes

The Galloway

Well-known as a riding pony in Galloway, in the south-west of Scotland, the Galloway stands about 14 hands and was a popular breed there more than 400 years ago. In 1706 Daniel Defoe, in his *Tour Through Scotland* wrote:

'Here in Galloway they have the best breed of strong low horse in Britain, if not Europe, which we call pads [pacing as distinct from trotting saddle horses] and from whence we call all truss [compact], strong, small, riding horses Galloways; these horses are remarkable for being good pacers, strong, easy-goers, hardy, gentle, well-broke, and above all, that they never tire; and are very much bought up in England on that account.'

The Dales Galloway

Although extinct as a breed for more than 150 years, the importance of the Scottish Galloway is still remembered, and the black Galloways of the mixed herds which superseded them and became known as the black-hill Galloways of the Dales, are still called Dales Galloways by many Dalesmen.

The Shales family

The most notable family of Norfolk cobs was the Shales, whose foundation sire was Shales the Original, foaled in 1755. His sire was Blaze, the son of the thoroughbred, Flying Childers, by the famous Darley Arabian. The same stallion was also the foundation sire of most of the world's finest trotting breeds, and at least one line back to him can be found in the pedigrees of most of today's registered Dales ponies.

Vanners

During the early part of this century there was a tremendous demand for smart vanners for town work, and gun horses for the army. Many fine Clydesdale stallions were being travelled so that they could be used on Dales mares to produce vanners which gave farmers a good return, but they did become a threat to the pure Dales breed of pony.

Registration

In 1916 the Dales Pony Improvement Society was formed, and the Dales Stud Book was opened in a section of the National Pony Society Stud Book. Many of the ponies were taken for the army during the 1914–18 war and the War Office gave premiums to Dales stallions; between 1923 and 1924 the army took 200 Dales ponies.

The registration of ponies was instituted just in time to prevent the real Dales ponies from being cross-bred out of existence – before 1916 there were no Dales stallions travelling, but there were many magnificent Clydesdales on the road. By the mid-twenties, there were hundreds of Dales ponies working in northern towns; however, the Fells were going through a bad time and the breed almost disappeared. Fortunately, the situation improved and royal patronage helped the Fell breed back to safety.

Decline...

Dales ponies were taken by the army again during World War II, as well as for work in the town when petrol became scarce. Even the young mares were taken, and many were used for breeding the vanners needed for the railway's express delivery service. After the war, horses and ponies no longer needed because of the return of petrol, disappeared into the slaughter houses of Europe in their thousands. It was nearly the end of the heavy ponies. Registrations lapsed, to the stage where only four ponies, all of them fillies, were registered in 1955, and only the dedication of a few Dalesmen saved the breed from dying out altogether.

... and recovery

The breed did pick up slowly, however, although there were few good stallions. In 1963 the Dales Pony Society was reorganised, and the word 'improvement' was dropped from the title. Lost ponies were sought and inspected for type, height and colour before being registered. Many of the ponies had lost their papers, or had never previously been registered, and a grading-up register was introduced for these inspected ponies.

It was a far-sighted plan which proved to be extremely successful, and since the grading-up register was closed in 1971, the number of registered Dales ponies has risen steadily, and so has the quality. Until 1969 there was a shortage of Dales stallions, and a number of those by Fell sires with Dales bloodlines were used. This does show how close the two breeds have been until quite recently, and even the influential Dales stallion, Stainton Prince, was by a good Dales stallion, Mountain Prince, out of a Fell mare.

Dales ponies were originally bred for a specific task in a harsh environment; and when they were no longer needed for that specific job, they were successfully adapted for other uses. All the qualities and abilities have been retained, however, and their combination of strength, agility, hardiness and courage, as well as their good conformation and calm, intelligent nature, makes the Dales an excellent riding and driving pony, and a true all-rounder.

The Dales pony can now be up to 14.2 hands in height, and black, brown, grey or bay in colour. White markings are only allowed to the fetlocks of the hind legs, or as a star or snip. It must have a neat and pony-like head, broad between the eyes which must be bright and alert, and ears which should curve slightly inwards; there should be a long forelock of straight hair down the face, and a long flowing mane. The neck should be strong and have sufficient length, and the stallions need to display a bold outlook with a well arched crest. Shoulders must be long and sloping with well developed muscles, but the withers should not be too fine.

A short-coupled body, deep through the chest, with well sprung ribs; deep hindquarters, which are lengthy and very muscular; a tail well set on, not too high but with plenty of long, straight hair reaching the ground; broad, flat and clean hocks, well let down with plenty of dense, flat bone below; short and very muscular forearms, with broad, well developed knees. All these are important features of the modern Dales pony.

It must also have the very best of feet and legs, with flexible joints, showing quality without coarseness. The cannons should display between 8 and 9½in (20-24cm) of flat, flinty bone, and well developed tendons. The pasterns should be nicely sloping and of good length; Dales ponies should have ample silky feather on the heels, and large, round feet open at the heels and with well developed frogs. They are great characters, living and working until their late twenties, and many are still going strong when they are well over thirty years of age. The title of great all-rounder is certainly well deserved.

KEEPING A PONY STABLED

Looking after a pony requires a lot of time and hard work at the best of times, but a stabled pony is even more demanding. A stable need not be expensive but it should be roomy, draughtproof, light, airy and well drained. The pony must be able to lie down without getting stuck against the walls, and the stable must be strong enough to stand up to a few kicks and knocks, and the weight of the pony leaning against the walls.

The stable

Stables should be built on well drained ground with their backs to the prevailing wind. Floors should slope gently towards the door and there should be a drainage gully outside.

The door must always open outwards and be in two parts so that the top half can be fixed back to let in plenty of air. Some ponies can escape over the bottom half of a door, and if this happens a grille may have to be fitted across the top to keep them in.

There should be nothing inside the stable on which the pony can hurt himself; light fittings and switches must have guards and be out of the pony's reach. A manger will not be necessary because ponies can be fed from bowls on the floor, but they will need plenty of fresh water. A container to hold a salt lick is also a good idea. The haynet should be tied to a strong ring fixed into the wall; this can also be used

---

Army Ponies

General Bates, the army buyer, would not consider any animal which showed any sign of cart-horse blood. He wanted ponies between 14 and 14.2 hands in height, over five years of age, with a girth of 68in (1.7m) weighing half a ton (508kg) and able to carry 21 stones (134kg) in mountainous country with the Mountain Artillery.

Impressive action

The action of the Dales pony is one of the most striking of the Mountain and Moorland breeds, being clean, straight and true, and going forward with tremendous energy. In addition the knees are lifted, and the hindlegs flexed well under the body for powerful drive.

The Konik

Although it stands only about 13 hands the Konik is considered more a horse than a pony, and the name means 'small horse'. It thrives on hard work and a meagre diet, making it popular with many small farmers in Poland and throughout Eastern Europe. These ponies have been bred in Poland for many centuries, and the breed is officially recognised by the Polish authorities because of its importance to small farmers and the demand for it in other countries. Noted for its quiet temperament, the Konik retains many of the characteristics of its wild Tarpan ancestors. Herds of them run untended in reserves, fending for themselves as they used to do centuries ago. They are easily broken to harness and soon settle down to work.

1

2

3

The four stages of mucking out

1 The soiled portions of the bedding should be separated from the clean with a pitchfork

2 Throw the dry bedding back to the sides of the stable to enable the floor to be brushed clean. The straw can then be replaced for the pony to stand on during the day

3 The soiled bedding should be taken away in a wheelbarrow and put straight onto the muck heap

4 A smart stable yard is usually a sign of good stable management, and after all the boxes have been mucked out the yard should be swept clean

4

for tying up the pony, though a piece of string should be used as a link between the headcollar rope and the ring – the string will break if the pony pulls back in panic and this will prevent the headcollar from breaking, which can become expensive.

Bedding

Straw, woodshavings or even shredded paper can be used as bedding and should be spread deep enough so the pony does not hurt himself on a hard floor. Dirty bedding and manure should be taken out every day and fresh bedding added as required, although a deep litter system can sometimes be used, in which fresh bedding is added on top of the old bedding after the droppings have been taken away. The box must be airy and have enough headroom as the bedding builds up. All the bedding, however, should be cleared out every two or three months.

A stable routine can be adapted to suit individual needs, but it is

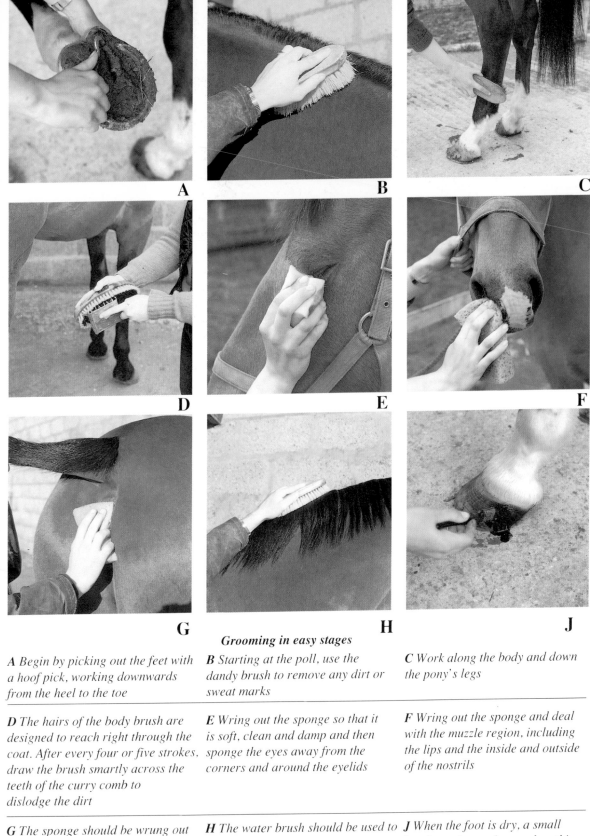

A

B

C

D

E

F

G

H

J

Grooming in easy stages

A Begin by picking out the feet with a hoof pick, working downwards from the heel to the toe

B Starting at the poll, use the dandy brush to remove any dirt or sweat marks

C Work along the body and down the pony's legs

D The hairs of the body brush are designed to reach right through the coat. After every four or five strokes, draw the brush smartly across the teeth of the curry comb to dislodge the dirt

E Wring out the sponge so that it is soft, clean and damp and then sponge the eyes away from the corners and around the eyelids

F Wring out the sponge and deal with the muzzle region, including the lips and the inside and outside of the nostrils

G The sponge should be wrung out again and used to clean out the dock area, lifting the tail as high as possible

H The water brush should be used to lay the mane by dipping the end hairs of the brush in water, shaking them out, and brushing the mane from the roots downwards.

J When the foot is dry, a small brush can be used to apply a thin coating of hoof oil to the whole hoof, including the bulbs of the heel as far as the coronet

continued

Some stable requirements

For a medium-size pony a stable should be at least 12ft (3.6m) square and with sufficient headroom, and the door must be high enough so the pony does not bang his head on the lintel. The roof should slope away from the stable door, and there needs to be a protective canopy in front of the stable.

The grooming kit

The grooming kit should be kept neat and tidy in a box or bag, and should include these essential items:

Body brush This has short, dense, soft bristles and is used to remove dust and scurf from the pony's coat, mane and tail.

Curry comb A metal curry comb is used to clean the body brush and a rubber one is used to remove caked mud from the pony's coat.

important that feeding, grooming and exercise form a regular routine. A stabled pony must be groomed every day and his feet picked out again after exercise; and time should be taken during grooming to check the pony over for any cuts or bumps.

Grooming

Grooming not only keeps a pony looking smart and tidy, it also benefits his health by keeping his skin in good condition. It is a methodical process which will take an experienced groom half to three-quarters of an hour – someone less practised may take longer, as good grooming takes quite a toll on unaccustomed muscles.

Before grooming can begin, the pony should be tied up securely and his rugs removed. If it is very cold the rug can be folded back over his loins while his front end is groomed, and over his shoulders while his quarters are done.

The feet should be picked out first and each hoof and shoe examined carefully; check the shoe is not loose. Grooming can then begin with the dandy brush, starting at the poll and working back to the hindquarters – it is used in short movements, backwards and forwards, to remove caked dirt and sweat, and should not be used on tender parts of the body. A clipped or thin-skinned pony may object to it, in which case the body brush can be used for the same purpose.

The body brush is used in short circular motions, working in the same direction as the coat grows. The short, dense bristles reach through the coat to the skin and draw out any scurf and dust. It can also be used on the mane and tail, brushing a few locks at a time.

The headcollar is then fastened around the pony's neck while his

DIFFERENT TYPES OF FEED

Oats are a great all-round feed for horses but are heating, and should be fed sparingly to ponies which may become difficult to ride if fed too many. Oats can be fed whole but are more easily digested if they are bruised, rolled or crushed. The grains should be hard and clean, and should be fed with bran and chaff.

Cubes are commercially sold mixtures of different ingredients and have had vitamins added to them so as to comprise a balanced diet. Feeding cubes means the pony always receives a consistent diet, and it saves several feeds having to be stored and mixed. They are less likely to cause a pony to 'hot up' than oats, but they are expensive and can become a bit mundane for the pony. Feeding the cubes with chaff or bran will encourage the pony to chew them properly before swallowing.

Barley can be fed instead of oats as it has a similar food value. It is less likely to cause the pony to hot up and should be fed rolled, crushed or preferably flaked.

Boiled Barley can be fed warm and mixed with bran to encourage a shy feeder. It is especially good for gaining weight or for feeding after a hard day's exercise such as hunting. The barley should be brought to the boil and simmered until the grains split – this can take four to six hours.

Flaked maize is suitable for a pony which needs fattening, but should be fed sparingly as it can cause the blood to overheat.

Wheat should only be fed to ponies as bran.

Bran encourages the pony to chew his feed. It helps his digestion, provides bulk in the diet, and is especially good for sick animals. It should not be fed in excess as this can affect health and growth.

Bran-mash is a very suitable warm feed which is useful after hard exercise. Bran is put in a bucket and boiling water is added until it is completely soaked. A few ounces of salt and a handful of oats or barley are stirred in, and then the bucket is covered and left till it is cool enough to eat. Linseed jelly can be added to make it tastier and it offers a convenient way to

head is gently brushed. After replacing the headcollar, the wisp can be used to tone the muscles and bring a shine to the coat by stimulating the oil glands. A wisp is made from a twisted piece of hay or straw, but leather-covered massage pads can be used to serve the same purpose. The wisp should be dampened and then brought down firmly on the muscular areas of the body, in the same direction as the coat growth – the loin area should not be wisped at all.

The pony's eyes, mouth and dock need to be wiped over with a damp sponge – it may be preferable to keep a separate sponge for the dock area. The mane can be set in position by damping it down with a water brush (similar to a dandy brush but dip it in water before use); this can also be used to wash any mud off the hooves which should then be oiled. The pony can then be given a final rub over with a dampened stable rubber, to smooth the coat and remove the last traces of dust.

This complete grooming procedure is known as strapping, and is most effective if carried out after the pony has been exercised, when the skin is warm, the pores have been opened up, and the scurf comes to the surface easily.

Quartering is carried out first thing in the morning and gets its name because a quarter of the animal is cleaned at a time. After the feet have been picked out, the rug is unbuckled and folded back so that the front end of the pony can be groomed first. The rug is then replaced and the back end folded over so that the hind quarters can be groomed. Any stains can be removed using a sponge or water brush, and then the rug can be re-buckled. In the evening, the pony may be given a quick brush-over before his rugs are changed.

continued

Dandy brush A brush with long, stiff bristles used for removing heavy dirt and dust, especially on grass-kept ponies.
Hoof-pick A metal instrument used to remove mud, bedding and stones from the feet.
Hoof-oil This is brushed onto the hooves to stop them becoming brittle.
Mane and tail comb These are metal or plastic, and used to remove tangles.
Stable sponge Sponges are used to clean the eyes, nose, nostrils, mouth and dock.
Stable rubber A piece of cloth used to give the pony a final polish over.
Wisp A pad of plaited hay or straw which is used to massage the body to promote circulation.

disguise medicines and wormers. A bran-mash acts as a laxative, which makes it suitable both as a once-a-week feed for ponies in work, and for invalid ponies.
Beans should be split or bruised before feeding to ponies, and are very heating. They should only be fed sparingly (a double handful twice a day in the feed) to ponies kept out in the winter, but not to stabled animals.
Linseed is usually only fed in the winter and has a high oil content which improves the condition and gloss of the coat. It is fed as a jelly or tea and ponies can have up to ½lb (226g) of the seed twice a week.
Linseed jelly is prepared by placing a handful of seed in a saucepan and covering with water. It should be soaked, with the lid on, until the next day. This soaking can be done over a cool or slightly warm oven. More water is added and the linseed is brought to the boil. Unboiled linseed is poisonous. Once the linseed has cooled it should set like a jelly and can then be added to the feed.
Linseed tea is prepared in the same way as linseed jelly except more water is used. It is then mixed with bran to make a linseed mash.

Oatmeal gruel is a very welcome pick-me-up for a tired pony, although some do not like the taste. A double handful of oatmeal is mixed in a bucket with boiling water. When it is cool enough, it is given to the pony to drink.
Molasses is a sugar by-product which makes a very tasty and nutritious treat for ponies. It comes in meal or liquid form and is added to the feed – a very good way to encourage a shy feeder.
Dried sugar beet pulp offers energy and roughage in the diet and helps maintain weight, and adds bulk to the diet of a pony not in fast work. Sugar beet pulp must always be soaked for twelve hours in cold water before feeding, otherwise it can cause choke or colic as it swells up in the stomach. No more than 1.4kg (3½lb) soaked weight should be fed in a day, and the pulp should be soaked in 2½ parts water to 1 part cubes. Once soaking is completed it should be fed immediately. If it is left too long, the fermentation process, which begins once the pulp is wet, can make the pony ill.
Salt is an essential part of the pony's diet and is best fed as a salt lick in the stable. Otherwise, table salt can be added to the feed.

TYPES OF HAY

Seed hay is cut from land that has been reseeded and is excellent for ponies as it contains good grasses such as rye, clover, timothy and meadow fescue. Seed hay should be greenish brown in colour and crisp and hard to touch, with a sweet smell. A musty smell, or a yellow or dark colour means the hay has deteriorated and should not be fed.

Meadow hay is cut from permanent pasture and has a less coarse stalk than seed hay, which means it is not so good for the digestion. Its nutritional value will vary depending on the grasses in the field, but it should be greener than seed hay, soft and sweet smelling. Hay less than six months old should not be fed to ponies, neither should mouldy hay, or hay containing docks, thistles or ragwort.

Chaff is hay, or a mixture of hay, straw and any other greenstuff, which has been chopped up short and is then added to the feed. It adds bulk, and prevents the pony bolting his feed.

Horsage or Haylage is suitable for feeding to ponies who are allergic to hay. It is a cross between hay and silage (fermented grass) and is not as dusty as hay. Care should be taken not to feed too much as it often contains more protein than ordinary hay.

THE PONY'S FRIEND

Over the years, ponies have been subjected to many forms of cruelty and abuse, largely due to man's greed and ignorance, and it is only comparatively recently that their welfare has been governed by laws and regulations. The introduction of the 'Ponies Bill' in 1970 helped to protect ponies being exported from Britain by bringing in minimum export values, individual inspections and other safeguards. A major part in this new legislation was played by Glenda Spooner, who worked tirelessly for much of her life for an improvement in the treatment of all horses and ponies.

Her concern for all animals was the predominant factor throughout her life, and led to the formation, nearly forty years ago, of the Ponies of Britain club which was launched to promote the well-being of ponies everywhere. Glenda Spooner's lifelong devotion to ponies began, however, as a child before World War I and was chiefly due to a little Arab stallion called Claremont.

The pony spent his early life in India and was bought as a four-year-old by Glenda's father, Sir Frederick Graham, from the Ali Ben Talib stables in Bombay. That same evening, he was put to a dog cart and driven to the local polo ground where he took part in two chukkas before being driven home again. Although he may well have been ridden before, he had certainly never been driven.

When the family returned home to Scotland, Claremont was shipped back to Britain and joined his owner's team of polo ponies which was based near London. In those days, a polo pony really was a pony and did not exceed 14.2 hands, and as Sir Frederick weighed almost 14 stones (88.8kg), it is hardly surprising that Claremont broke down in both forelegs.

Sir Frederick gave the pony to his children on condition that they got him sound, and young Glenda spent many hours at the family's estate in Scotland, sitting on a stool with a book in one hand and a hosepipe in the other, applying cold water to Claremont's legs. Eventually, the heat and swelling subsided and after a long rest, the legs became hard and the pony was sound again.

The attempts of Glenda's elder brothers to ride the pony ended with them on the floor and as a result they soon lost interest, leaving Claremont to a delighted Glenda. The sight of the 11-year-old girl riding the little Arab stallion in all weathers over miles of Scottish moors soon became a familiar one and caused little surprise, even though she often rode bareback and equipped only with a headcollar.

Several years later when Glenda went to work in London, Claremont was stabled at Marble Arch. After a while, however, he became bored with rides in the park and was sent to live with friends in the country. At the age of 27 he was taken cub hunting for the first time by Glenda, and followed his new pursuit with great enthusiasm. Not until Claremont was well over 30 did his physical condition begin to deteriorate, and he was put down before he began to suffer.

Glenda went on to become well known as an actress, journalist and author, but after the death of her husband Captain Hugh Spooner in a flying accident in 1937, she returned to a life of caring for ponies and horses.

In 1952, Major Crocker Bulteel proposed that she

Feeding

A stabled pony is not free to eat as and when he pleases and relies upon someone to bring him food. Ponies have small stomachs and need to be fed little and often; they all need roughage, and hay provides this in an ideal form. A concentrate feed may also be needed, but this will vary depending on the size and type of pony and how much work he is getting. This feed can be made up from straight grains such as oats, barley, maize and bran; or from horse and pony cubes, rootcrops and commercial mixes and supplements. Small ponies should only be given oats in very small quantities. Horse and pony cubes provide a ready-mixed diet and may be sufficient for a pony. Different brands do vary and ponies may get on better with one particular type.

A stabled pony will appreciate being able to graze for a few hours or so each day if this is possible. If not, he must have plenty of bulk feed such as hay. He should be fed at the same times each day and

ran a show at Ascot racecourse in aid of equine welfare charities. A club was subsequently formed, run by a committee of people who were concerned with the welfare of horses and ponies; it had as its patron HRH Princess Alice, Duchess of Athlone, who was followed by the Duke and then the Duchess of Norfolk. Glenda named the club Ponies of Britain and it had as its object not only the welfare and benefit of ponies everywhere, but also the protection and promotion of the nine native breeds.

The inaugural show proved to be a great success and after some initial difficulties, Ponies of Britain went from strength to strength. The shows helped to finance the welfare activities of the club, acted as a shop window for the breeders of native ponies, and helped to raise the general standard of ponies and their management.

Glenda Spooner continued to work tirelessly for the cause of all ponies. Following her death in 1981, the Glenda Spooner Memorial fund was set up as a tribute to her many achievements in the field of equine welfare and to ensure that her work for the improvement in their conditions and treatment should continue. Six years later, in January 1987, the Glenda Spooner Trust was founded and has taken over all the welfare work of the Ponies of Britain; the original club has since been dissolved. The aims and objects of the trust are to prevent ill-treatment and alleviate suffering; to increase public awareness of the widespread areas of cruelty and exploitation; to take every opportunity to educate, advise and inform in order to extend the range of good equine management. The work includes active support for all efforts to strengthen, improve and enforce protective legislation for ponies, particularly that which concerns conditions at sales and markets, the treatment of horses and ponies sold to the meat trade, and the investigation of reports of horses or ponies in distress.

The trust is also concerned with conditions on common land such as the New Forest and Dartmoor, and the plight of ponies in urban areas turned out or tethered on areas of waste land with little grazing and no shelter. It is prepared to undertake prosecution in cases of cruelty and neglect, and will also support other welfare organisations in their efforts to do the same. Conscious of the fact that so much cruelty is the result of ignorance, the trust produces leaflets on subjects ranging from buying at sales to caring for a pony in winter, and gives advice on how to report cases of ill-treatment.

The current patron is Her Grace, the Duchess of Devonshire, and Her Majesty the Queen has also made a recent donation. The director is Mrs Vivien McIrvine, and the trustees include the former international surgeon Trevor Armstrong who is a breeder, judge and exhibitor of riding ponies.

The trust deals with enquiries on all manner of subjects, including many from people who want to adopt or give a home to a rescued animal. Although it does not run its own rescue and rehabilitation establishment, it does have connections with other societies that do, and great care is always taken in ensuring that rescued animals are only loaned to suitable homes. Sadly, many rescued ponies have clearly passed the stage of rehabilitation, and these are humanely destroyed in order to end their suffering.

Through the Glenda Spooner Trust, the work of this remarkable woman is continuing and a number of people are now carrying on the campaign for the welfare of ponies. There is also a Junior Supporters Group which was formed to encourage young people to become involved in the cause. Members receive a badge, a certificate and regular newsletters, and have the satisfaction of knowing that they are helping to fight the battles which ponies are unable to fight for themselves.

FULL CLIP

HUNTER CLIP

BLANKET CLIP

TRACE HIGH CLIP

never exercised immediately after a meal. Water should be freely available. If it is restricted, he may drink straight after being fed and this will not be good for him.

Rugs

Although ponies can put up with the cold when they are turned out in a field, once they are standing in a stable they will become quite susceptible to cold and will need a stable rug, which is usually made of jute with a blanket lining, or of a polycotton/nylon mix with a lightweight synthetic filling. It is held in place by a surcingle or cross-straps and will keep the pony warm, and in very cold weather a blanket can be put on underneath.

A sweat rug looks very like a string vest and works on the same principle. It is used to help the pony dry out when he is wet or sweating. If he is turned out to grass at all in the winter, particularly if he has been clipped, he will also need a protective New Zealand rug.

Clipping

In the winter, a stabled pony should be clipped to prevent him getting too hot when he is exercised. A trace clip is the most popular clip for ponies, when only the hair on the lower part of the neck and body is removed – on the upper body and legs it is left long for warmth and protection. A blanket clip is when the hair on the head, neck, and belly is removed; a hunter clip involves removing the hair from everywhere except for the legs and usually the saddle area; and a full clip means removing the hair on the legs as well.

Grooming the grass-kept pony

A pony kept at grass will keep his skin in good condition quite naturally. He should only be groomed when he is to be ridden, and a dandy brush and rubber curry comb are good for this purpose. The body brush can be used on the mane and tail, but if used too much on the body it will remove the natural oils which help keep the pony warm and 'waterproofed'.

Vices

Ponies can become bored when they are stabled and left alone for long periods, particularly when there are no other ponies around. When this happens they can develop some very bad habits such as windsucking, weaving or crib-biting. Wind sucking is when a pony will stand with his head raised and his neck arched and suck in and swallow air. While he does this he makes a peculiar noise, and may curl his tongue over his lips.

Crib-biting is another vice often associated with windsucking in which the pony grabs hold of his manger or the top of the stable door before going through the same strange sucking process. The front of his incisor teeth become worn down and can eventually end up looking like the bevelling on a chisel. These vices may look harmless but they can cause digestive problems. A chronic crib-biter will lose condition and is hard to keep fit.

Weaving is an even stranger habit. A pony will stand in a doorway moving his head from side to side and simultaneously shifting his weight from one foot to the other like a pendulum – rather like someone being hypnotised.

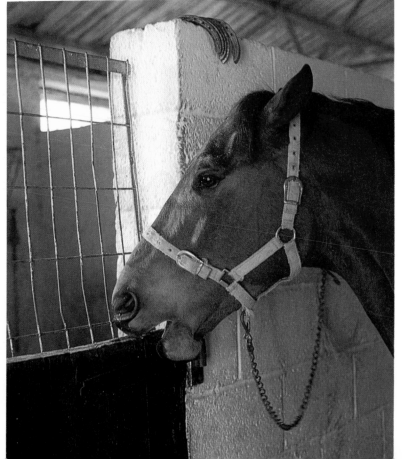

A horse or pony that crib bites will grab hold of the manger or the top of a stable door with its teeth, and make a strange sucking noise

Ponies for Fun and the Family

A PONY ON HOLIDAY

For people who don't own their own pony, a riding holiday is the chance to have one all to themselves to look after and ride during their holiday.

Holiday courses are also available for those who want to learn more about driving, and advice can be had on choosing the right sort of pony and driving vehicle, the choice of tack, harnessing up a pony correctly, as well as daily lessons in driving and stable management.

Indeed, a riding holiday will give pony lovers an insight into what keeping a pony really entails, whether it is for riding or for driving, and can help them decide whether they really do have the necessary dedication and time available to ensure that the pony is looked after properly.

Whatever the choice of holiday, whether in Britain or abroad, the one important thing in common will be the horses and ponies, and the opportunity to ride or drive them every day.

For many young pony lovers, the chance to have their very own pony for a week or more will be a dream come true. However, there are so many places now offering riding holidays that it is sometimes difficult to decide where best to go, and the standard of accommodation, instruction, food and entertainment, quite apart from the horses and ponies, can also vary very considerably.

Many of the good places do get booked up well in advance, particularly in the height of the season; if an establishment does have vacancies at late notice, it is always wise to try to find out why there should be plenty of accommodation available, when other riding establishments nearby are fully booked. It may be because they have only recently started to do riding holidays, so they have not had time to build up their list of return visits – young riders and families who enjoy being there so much that they book to go back year after year. However, there could be other reasons, and perhaps the standard of food and accommodation or the quality of their ponies leaves much to be desired.

Always ask for a brochure, and study exactly what is being offered, whether the prices being charged include any extras, and the amount of riding and instruction you will be getting each day. The majority of establishments do offer value for money, but there are some which are of a much lower standard. It is therefore important to make sure that you know what you will be getting, and that the

---

A use for the outgrown pony

A riding holiday can suit the whole family: the children can spend their time riding, the parents may like to learn to drive, and may thereby find a new use for the outgrown family pony.

Is it an approved riding establishment?

Check whether a riding establishment is one of those approved by the British Horse Society, the Association of British Riding Schools, the Ponies Association (formerly the Ponies of Britain), or the Pony Trekking and Riding Society of Wales, if you feel at all concerned about the facilities. There are, of course, some places offering very good riding holidays which do not necessarily have this kind of approval. However, if tuition is being offered it is important to make sure that the instructors are well qualified and that those in charge of rides are experienced riders, who would know what to do in an emergency.

Under instruction

establishment has the necessary facilities to provide you with the type of holiday you are looking for; also you should check that the surrounding countryside has not been spoilt. A look at a map, and a quick call to the nearest Pony Club branch secretary will probably provide the answer.

Decide first of all exactly what you are hoping to get from your holiday. Obviously you want to have plenty of riding, but are you more interested in daily rides without instruction, or are you hoping to improve your knowledge and riding ability while you are on holiday?

Do you want to be given a pony to ride and look after yourself? Maybe you have your own pony already, in which case do you want to take him with you?

What sort of riding do you want to do while you are there? Would you like to take part in competitions of some sort? How much money do you want to spend? Prices vary considerably according to the type of activity, the quality of the ponies available and the amount and standard of instruction required.

Trekking

Trekking holidays are extremely popular with riders of all ages, because they can enjoy plenty of fresh air and glorious scenery from the back of a sure-footed and safe pony, travelling at a leisurely pace.

Most trekking centres will cope with beginners and novice riders as well as the more experienced, and again, this can be an excellent holiday for all the family. Even parents who may not be particularly horsey can often be persuaded to take part, and enjoy exploring the countryside from horseback. If they do get tired or bored, they can always choose to do something different the next day.

The length and pace of the treks will vary from centre to centre, but there will usually be half-day or full-day rides, with picnic lunches provided. Sometimes additional refreshment is provided along the

---

Native ponies are ideal

Native ponies, particularly the Dales and Fells, are frequently used for trekking, and they provide safe and reliable mounts for almost every size of rider.

Trail riding

More experienced riders often prefer trail riding where the pace is usually faster, with overnight stops at farms, hostels or pubs. The ponies have to be fitter because of the additional speed and the great distances covered each day, and so do the riders. Trail riding is not a holiday for the very novice rider, but it can be tremendous fun, and a good way of getting really fit at the same time.

Nowadays there are even classes for trekking ponies at show

route, and there is entertainment in the evenings.

Some establishments provide a mixture of instruction, daily rides and well-organised competitions, which may take the form of mounted games, show jumping, hunter trials, dressage, or classes such as handy pony. There are usually picnic rides and barbeques, visits to local shows and places of interest, and talks on equestrian subjects, and centres situated near the coast sometimes include other activities like swimming and sailing.

Accommodation can vary from sharing a caravan or mobile home to log cabins, living as a member of the family in a farmhouse, or simply bed and breakfast at a local cottage or nearby hotel. Some places offer self-catering accommodation for the whole family, so the children can enjoy all the riding and the parents can use it as a centre for other holiday activities.

Instructional holidays

Those looking for instruction – with or without their own pony – also have a choice, depending on the level and type of training they require. Keen riders can now get first class instruction in dressage, show jumping, cross-country riding, polo or carriage driving, from people who have been successful competitors themselves and who know what is required to improve the individual performance of pony and rider. It is important to have reached a fairly advanced standard, however, in order to gain the most benefit from a week or more of such intensive instruction, but the results can be surprising and well worth the price.

The overall cost will depend more on the calibre and qualifications of the instructors than the type of accommodation available. Once again, there is very often a choice of accommodation, a room in a

local cottage or farmhouse or perhaps more luxurious quarters in a hotel. The main objective, however, is that the riders – and their ponies, in the case of those who take their own – return home better prepared to face their next competition, and with more chance of success.

THE FELL *A family pony*

It has been suggested that a Fell pony cannot be put to the wrong job, and although this may seem rather a sweeping statement, the Fell is probably the most versatile of all the native breeds. They are excellent riding and driving ponies and have been successful in a wide variety of equestrian activities; they also vary considerably in weight and size, so a Fell pony may be found to carry almost any rider.

The Fell owes much of its inherent qualities of stamina and hardiness to the tough, swift-footed wild ponies who had to glean their keep by covering great distances daily in the extremes of

The only way to travel. A Dales mare transporting her owners through the countryside in a traditional Bradford cart, which is a very popular vehicle in the north of England

The Galloway pony

The Galloway pony evolved like the Fell, from native pony mares and Friesian stallions, and was the Scottish equivalent of the Fell pony. They were used by the Scots to carry them and their goods over the border to the market towns and horse fairs of the Lake District. The Scots were also great horse dealers, and many of their Galloway ponies were sold in the north of England and eventually became crossed with the Fell ponies, so much so that in some parts of the Lake district they are still referred to as Fell Galloways. Trotting matches between the visiting Scots and local farmers became an integral part of the horse fairs, and led to some very exciting contests and considerable wagers.

The sad demise of the Galloway and its eventual extinction was due mainly to the introduction of Clydesdale blood to cater for the demands of industry and agriculture, and prevented Britain from having a tenth native breed. This change in demand did, however, lead to the development of the Dales pony which is now a heavier animal than the Fell, standing up to 14.2 hands, but still having the same equable temperament and similar dark colours.

climate to which the Lake District is prone. Only the fittest survived the winters, and they were also prey for the packs of wolves which then roamed the country, as well as the local inhabitants who were not averse to hunting the wild ponies for food. The result was a pony no more than 13 hands in height, and probably bay, brown or dun in colour, which formed the ideal basis for the Fell breed.

History

The Fell pony really owes its origins to the Friesian horses which were brought to Britain by the hundreds of workers from Europe, employed by the Roman Emperor Hadrian in about the year 120AD to help build the famous Hadrian's Wall which stretched across Britain in the north. When these workers and the Romans left, many Friesian horses were sold and local inhabitants crossed them with their own ponies. About a thousand Friesians, mainly stallions, were left in northern England and their influence led not only to the breeding of the Fell pony, but also to the Old English Black, which has since been merged into the Shire horse and the now extinct Galloway and Fen ponies.

Exactly when the Fell pony breed as such became established is still uncertain, but it was probably early in the 5th century, although the name Fell – which really means a tract of high moorland such as the Lake District – did not come into use until the 19th century. The Roman invasion certainly had an important influence on the breed, particularly as the Friesian horse, when used to improve other breeds, almost invariably passes on its black colour as well as its strength, thriftiness, and equable temperament.

The Anglo-Saxons also did much to improve the breed because of the way in which they kept their ponies. The majority of them were kept on the rough land outside their settlements which meant that only the toughest and strongest survived, although the ponies they used for packwork or pulling their sledges were kept in an enclosure in the centre of the settlement for the sake of convenience.

Wheeled vehicles were very rare because of the nature of the land and the lack of good roads, and so pack animals became essential. During the hard winter months the breeding stock were fed on 'browse', the dried leaves of deciduous trees, collected and stored in barns. Although this helped to ensure that all breeding stock remained hardy and strong, it did not guarantee any standards of quality, good conformation or size, and in-breeding was commonplace.

When the Normans invaded and attacked the settlements, shortage of time usually prevented them from rounding up the horses from the rough ground outside, with the result that when they had gone the good breeding stock was usually left untouched – only the poorer quality stallions used for work around the settlements were taken.

As well as relieving them of many of their surplus stallions, the Normans did those early horse breeders in the north of England a considerable service by introducing the practice of gelding. Until then, for reasons of prestige, only stallions had been used for riding. Now, however, the colts which were surplus to breeding requirements could be gelded and used for work on the land. Inevitably this led to less indiscriminate breeding and a better selection of stallions for stud purposes.

However, the development of the breed throughout the later

Middle Ages and Tudor times was a slow process, and there was little scope for variation in conformation, colour and size. The similarity to the Friesian horse has always been striking but the inhospitable hills of northern England, unlike the fertile, sandy lowlands of Friesland, prevented the Fell pony from developing to be as large as the Friesian.

The Lakeland farmers, however, were quick to appreciate that the Fell pony was able to trot for long distances at a steady speed and they saw in the Fell a lucrative source of income, by breeding and training 'rakkers' to sell to the wealthy gentry and townspeople. The ponies could carry their owners at a fast pace comfortably and safely over all types of terrain, and these qualities made them very popular. Although Henry VIII's laws regarding ponies being kept below a certain size had little effect in the north of England, he did in fact have an influence on the Fell breed: during his reign many of the monasteries and abbeys were dissolved – the monks had encouraged the breeding of white cattle and horses, and when their white stock was dispersed after the Reformation, the horses merged with the Fell stock. Although black remained the dominant colour, grey had been introduced and is now not uncommon in the Fell breed.

Use and performance

The industrial revolution led to the development of iron ore mines in the north of England, and both Fell and Dales ponies were used for transporting the ore long distances. The needs of industry reduced the number of Fell ponies working on the land, particularly as many were also used in the mines. Old pack-horse tracks exist all over Cumbria, and there are still several of the narrow stone bridges which were just wide enough to allow a pony to cross when the river was too deep to be forded.

The unique pack-horse bridges always had low stone walls on either side, but were high enough to prevent the animals from falling into the water if they stumbled. Some of them are still in use, but now they carry the thousands of riders who enjoy trekking across the beautiful countryside, instead of the iron ore, coal, wool and dairy produce the Fell ponies used to carry more than 150 years ago.

> ### Taking the easy way out...
>
> There are many humorous stories told of the men and ponies who transported goods from Kendal, Penrith and other Lake District towns, in the days when the pack pony was the most obvious method of transport in the north. The ponies travelled loose in droves, and the ones which worked the Kendal to Whitehaven route were led by a wise old black stallion who set the pace, the others following on in the usual manner. The man in charge was mounted on another old pony and like many overseers of the time, he was rather too fond of alcohol. He used to ride on ahead to the first inn, leaving the black stallion to lead the drove along the usual route, and stay there until the drove had passed. When he had had his fill at that inn he would ride on past the drove again until the wise old stallion arrived with the rest of the ponies. The process was repeated all the way to Whitehaven and back!

His Royal Highness the Duke of Edinburgh has been very successful in driving trials with the team of black Fell mares owned by Her Majesty the Queen

Turf ponies

Fell ponies were also used for another kind of racing, and were specially bred as turf ponies; before grandstands were built, instead of having to watch a race from a carriage on the course, many sporting owners and spectators were mounted on turf ponies, who took up their positions on the rails and then galloped alongside the runners for as long as possible. They obviously had to show considerable speed in order to be able to do so.

Typical characteristics

Although there is a height limit of 14 hands, the ideal Fell should be about 13.2 hands; it should be strong and active with great bone and show true pony characteristics, with the lively and alert appearance peculiar to all mountain ponies.
It should have a small head with large nostrils, big bright eyes and short ears, sloping shoulders, and a deep strong body with well muscled quarters. The legs must be strong with plenty of flat bone and fine silky feather, the feet round with the characteristic blue horn. It is also important that Fell ponies should have a long stride at all paces, with a good knee and hock action. The mane and tail should be long, and the feather must not be trimmed for showing.
The Fell is a breed where hereditary unsoundness is practically unknown; being so hardy they suit the rider of limited means and can be kept out all the year round providing that they get hay in the winter and hard feed if they are in regular work. They are ponies which come from hardy stock, and have been particularly adaptable to the requirements of their fortunate owners for many hundreds of years.

At one time it was estimated that three hundred Fell ponies left Kendal each day for other Lake District market towns, as well as Manchester and London. The arrival of the railways meant the end of many of the pony teams and the ostlers and others connected with them, but the Fell pony survived and reverted to being an all-purpose pony. It was also used a great deal for shepherding, being sure-footed and patient.

Trotters

Early in the 19th century the Dargue family of Bow Hall, Dufton, near Appleby in Westmorland, began to breed a strain of Fell ponies to be used particularly for trotting races. Over the years they took on particular characteristics, being lighter in bone than the normal Fell pony, and many of them were grey. In 1886 one of these ponies – five years of age and standing 13.2 hands high – was advertised as going well in harness, and being able to trot a mile in three minutes carrying twelve stones (76kg). The trend at that time was for ponies to be broken to both ride and drive so that they would be of the greatest practical value.

Another pony of the Dargue strain, a 13.2 grey mare called Strawberry Girl, won many trotting races, including the Borough Stakes at Blackpool on 17 July 1882 for a first prize of £60, which was an amazing amount in those days. She won under saddle and in harness, and many of the Dargue ponies showed considerable versatility, proving to be good jumpers and hunters.

The fame of the trotting Fell ponies became well known in other parts of Britain, and in the late 1850s Comet, a Welsh cob stallion, was sent from Wales to Westmorland to compete with the local trotting ponies. This 15-hand horse trotted ten miles (16km) in thirty-three minutes on the main Shap turnpike, carrying twelve stones (76kg) on one occasion; while he was at stud in the Orton area he was visited by many of the local mares with great success.

Gradually the trotting races which had begun as rather rough and ready affairs at the shepherds' meets held at the end of the summer, developed into much more sophisticated affairs, carrying large cash prizes; the stone markers used to indicate the various lengths of the races can still be seen in some places.

A 'working' foal

Although the industrial revolution led eventually to a considerable drop in the use of horse power, the Lakeland farmers were inclined to be cautious about mechanised farm implements and preferred to keep a mare who, in addition to doing all the routine work, was expected to produce a foal each year. The mares would work until the foal was due and be back at work again when the foal was only a few days old.

The foals were usually sold as 'suckers', but when they were old enough to be weaned they were then kept by somebody else until they were 'stags', or unbroken three-year-olds, when they would be sold again at one of the big horse sales.

In harness

When broken to harness Fells were very popular for pulling tradesmen's carts in the industrial cities, and a few were used as pack

Her Majesty the Queen's Balmoral Bramble, who was Champion Fell Pony at the Royal Windsor Show

ponies in areas where there were no roads or railways, though by that time the majority of pack ponies were Dales.

Although some Fell ponies were still being bred on the open fell as had been the tradition for many centuries, this was not a satisfactory method for the farmers who wanted to use their ponies regularly.

Travelling stallions

Their requirements led to the travelling stallion scheme, which at that time was a system peculiar to the north of England. Each spring, usually on the second Monday in May, the stallion owner would begin a tour of the area, leading his stallion and calling on all the local farms where his services were required. He would follow a planned route, and every farmer would have to provide a field or stable for the stallion, and food and lodging for his owner. They often had to walk long distances over open fens and muddy sheep tracks, in all kinds of weather, and the hospitality at some of the farms was often not very good.

The stallions, however, were kept very fit and the fertility rates were high, which was essential because return visits were difficult. The strain of travelling in this way soon showed up any unsoundness in the stallion and good stallions were always in demand, whereas poor ones were not. This helped to improve the breed in general, and mare owners knew that they were more likely to get a healthy foal. The travelling season usually finished in late July or early August, although August Bank Holiday Monday was later chosen as the last day. From then until the next season the stallions were either turned out to rough it on the fells, or used for general work on the farms.

Fell crosses

In the early 1870s Christopher Wilson of Rigmaden Park, Kirkby Lonsdale, who had kept and bred many different types of pony including turf ponies, began a policy of selecting some of the very best pure-bred Fell mares and crossing them with a pony stallion called Sir George that he had bought in Yorkshire. Sir George, who had been foaled in 1886, was descended from the old Norfolk roadster, and his breeding included famous names like Sportsman,

---

Lingcropper Again

One of the most popular travelling stallions at the turn of the century was Lingcropper Again, who could be traced back to the legendary Lingcropper. He was the stallion who had been found on Stainmore in Westmorland, saddled and cropping the ling heather, but without any rider. No one knows how he got there, but it is likely that he either escaped or was left by retreating mosstroopers after the uprising of 1745. He probably came from Scotland and was a Galloway pony, but was given the name Lingcropper because of the ling heather he was eating when he was found; he became the sire of many good ponies.

Rough quarters

There are stories of travelling stallion owners having to sleep in the same bed as everyone else in the house because there was nowhere else to sleep except in the stable alongside the stallion. Sometimes that was the choice they preferred.

Phenomenon, and Flying Childers. He had won eight firsts at Royal Agricultural Society shows, and his good looks and action, along with the stamina and strength of the Fell mares, produced a new breed of pony which became known as the Hackney.

Christopher Wilson was keen to breed a Hackney pony, rather than a horse, and as the average height of his Fell mares was 13.2 hands and Sir George was only 14 hands, he was able to do so. But to keep down the height of subsequent generations he used to turn the youngstock out onto the moorland and rough ground of Rigmaden, to live as their Fell ancestors had done previously.

His ponies became famous, and won many prizes in the show ring. To everyone's surprise he then sold them all to Lord Daresbury, Sir Humphrey de Trafford, the Marquis of Londonderry, and some other owners, and turned his attention to trout hatching. Nor could he ever be persuaded to take any further interest in ponies, having suddenly lost all interest and enthusiasm for them. At the auction in September 1896, six of his ponies fetched an average of £271 each, and a filly made £900, which were almost unheard-of prices. Until the beginning of the 20th century Hackney ponies, with their extravagant high-stepping action, were particularly popular among tradesmen for delivery purposes.

PONIES ASSOCIATION (UK)

The Ponies Association was launched in October 1988, under the chairmanship of Mrs Joan Lee-Smith. It is not a new society, just a new name, adopted when the Ponies of Britain was dissolved.

Mrs Joan Lee-Smith had been Chairman of Ponies of Britain since 1980, and with her committee had been responsible for the tremendous success which had been achieved during that period. The patron, Mr C R Driver, like Mrs Lee-Smith has a long association with the pony world.

The aims

The Chairman believes in the importance of holding the members' interest, and continually tries to introduce new ideas. She says, 'It would be fatal to just stay as we are, where we are. New ideas, new challenges, and new ground are important for an even more successful and confident organisation.' The aims and ideals upon which Ponies (UK) has been founded have, in fact, never been more urgently needed. Perhaps one of the most important is trying to educate new pony owners in the care and management of their ponies, and the yearly programme is varied to spread knowledge to them and to the younger generation and, above all, to campaign for safety whilst riding either on the road, in the showring or on riding holidays.

The Association enrols new members and registers new ponies daily. They have a variety of equestrian interests and the organisation furthers the interests of members through seminars, clinics and other educational activities, in an endeavour to improve the general management of ponies and horses. Mrs Davina Whiteman, a British Horse Society instructor, holds two-day instructional courses around the country, and these are very successful and always have more applicants than they can cope with.

Mrs Whiteman is also consultant to the Riding Holiday and Trekking Scheme which was started in 1959 by the previous chairman of the Ponies of Britain, the late Mrs Glenda Spooner. It was the first scheme of its kind, and the idea was to improve the management and welfare of horses and ponies in the various trekking centres. Since those days the scheme has progressed, as it was realised that the centres are no longer just concerned with trekking, but cover riding and instructional holidays, as well as activity and adventure holidays.

Davina Whiteman, as a past joint proprietor of the well known Allerton Equitation School, realised it was just as important to have high-class accommodation as high-class horses and ponies and, with this in mind, introduced the 'Star System' to cover accommodation as well as the activity side of

When the Lake District began to be popular with tourists, the Fell ponies again played their part in the life of the area. Hotels and livery stables kept Fell ponies for hire, and families were able to hire a pony and trap for the day, or ponies for a ride over the fells. Some of the livery stables were able to offer a range of driving turnouts, from governess carts to coachman-driven brakes and charabancs. Coaches maintained a regular service over Kirkstone Pass, although the passengers often had to get out and walk when the gradient became too steep; however, they were able to quench their thirst at the Travellers Rest Inn at the top of the pass, the fourth highest inn in England.

Fell ponies were also used for more honest transport duties when they were employed by the Post Office to deliver mail. Even after the mail coaches came into general use in the area in 1785, mounted messenger boys riding Fell ponies were still used to deliver letters to remote places. Old Lingcropper, another Fell stallion descended from the famous pony found on Stainmore, carried the mail between Keswick and Penrith – a distance of eighteen miles (28.8km) – every day for twelve years without a break. Sometimes the Fell ponies pulled a Royal Mail trap, a light two-wheeled vehicle just large enough to carry the postman and a bag of mail. In winter when the

the holiday. There are guide lines on the basic requirements for each star. The minimum standard is white, grading up to green, blue, red and the top grade is purple. This star requires a high standard of hotel accommodation as well as of riding and stable management. There is a strict code of conduct and all centres included in the scheme are required to fulfil their statutory obligations. Centres are inspected every year, and Ponies (UK) is the only scheme to make yearly inspections, which is necessary due to the continual change in conditions in a number of the centres.

Ponies (UK) awards scheme

This scheme, which has similar tests and guide lines to the Pony Club, has been well supported by many trekking centres and a number of them have riders that have achieved green or blue awards and are now working for their red.

The range of the type of tests in the scheme is intended to encourage the progress of the rider from the beginning of his or her riding and general knowledge of horsemanship, through progressive instruction and teaching. Candidates from seven years of age may take the tests, but must have ridden regularly at an approved Ponies (UK) centre for the required time specified for each award, or have competed in a ridden section of one of the Association's shows within the previous two years.

Show section

The organisation has a very successful show section. The shows represent the glamour, the enjoyment and the prestige, but their success is due to the hard work and dedication of those responsible for their organisation.

Both Mrs Lee-Smith and her daughter Davina Whiteman, the show director, have a lifetime's experience in the showing world, and this practical knowledge is of the greatest importance to their supporting teams of officials, stewards and staff. The shows encourage and represent the breeding and use of the best ponies, as well as publicising the native breeds.

Ponies (UK) is the only society organising four shows each year, putting on separate classes for every native breed with supporting classes for riding ponies both in-hand and ridden, show hunter and working hunter ponies, and these classes represent the enjoyment side for members. The three one-day shows are held in various parts of the country and the four-day Championship show is held at the East of England Showground in August and is the final accolade. It stages the finals of the eighteen major Championships for which exhibitors have been qualifying throughout the summer months at the 200 affiliated shows.

The introduction of these championships has done a great deal to encourage the breeding of the right type of ponies, and how best to exhibit them, particularly the native breeds. Mountain and Moorland pony classes have increased tenfold, and are now equal to the riding ponies in their performance in both ridden and working hunter pony classes.

snow became deep a second pony was sometimes used, and the two were driven in tandem.

The National Pony Society was founded on 23 June 1893 to encourage the improvement and breeding of high-class riding and polo ponies. The native breeds played an important part in the breeding of polo ponies at that time, and in 1898 the society opened nine sections in its books for the nine mountain and moorland breeds. It organised committees to supervise the registration of ponies, and the stud books were subsequently opened.

In 1912 a committee was set up in the north of England, separate from the National Pony Society, in order to enforce stricter rules for the registration of Fell ponies, and to see to their welfare. It is not clear when the Fell Pony Committee became the Fell Pony Society,

CITY PONIES

Sue Whitmore describes the number, types and whereabouts of horses in London, and the organisation and activities of the South London Pony Club.

Imagine that you are riding a pony. Where are you in your imagination? In the countryside? In forest or field, on hill or in dale? Few of you will imagine riding along with big red buses as your allies and where the sheep all live in zoos. But did you know that there are approximately 6,000 horses and ponies kept in Greater London, and probably nearly five times that number of regular riders?

Where on earth are all these horses and ponies kept? Hardly any in fields, that's for sure! Those kept in the suburbs of London do usually live in fairly conventional surroundings of stables and fields, but when it comes to the densely populated inner areas of the city, things are very different. Boxes and barracks, gardens and garages, stalls, stables and sheds, underneath the arches, underneath the motorway, look closely anywhere in London and you may well find a horse staring back at you.

A hundred years ago, Tower Bridge was built because the other bridges in the area could not cope with the volume of traffic. Horse-drawn traffic. Tens of thousands of horses were kept in London then, and some of those small stables still exist today.

It was usual for a small tradesman to have just one horse which he would often keep on his premises, just as a trader would today have a van. Indeed in Wandsworth there is a Victorian terrace of very small houses and each still has a single stable in the tiny back yard. The only access now is through the house and I am told that the horses were led in through the hall. It could be true!

Many of the horses kept in London now are working horses. There are carriage horses in Buckingham Palace and cavalry horses in Knightsbridge Barracks. Police horses, dray horses and tradesmen's honest carthorses are to be found all over London – Young's 'Ram' brewery in Wandsworth, situated in the middle of one of the busiest one-way systems in the city, is a magical oasis of Shire horses, dogs, ducks, geese and, of course, a resident ram. Then there are riding ponies and driving ponies kept in small private livery yards, in city farms and children's zoos, and there are the riding school ponies.

In London, the majority of Pony Club members do not have their own ponies and this is reflected in the way events are run. The Pony Club relies to a great extent on the local riding schools to mount its members; the schools are extremely generous with their time, facilities and ponies, often providing ponies free of charge for Pony Club tests, and at very low cost for shows. Many events, and almost all dismounted training, take place on school premises. It is not uncommon for the same pony to have a different rider in each class at a show, yet none of those riders own a pony at all.

Where can all these ponies be ridden? Not in paddocks, fields, or on bridlepaths, for there are none – London does not have any bridleways in the legal sense. All off-road hacking takes place on commons or in parks, where riding is by permission only and not as of right.

This is not, however, as bad as it may seem. The local borough councils are staunch supporters of riding pursuits, and in recent years each of the borough councils in our district has vastly extended and improved the tracks and facilities. There are miles of (virtually) all-weather track within easy hacking distance, and a number of public schooling manèges. As there are no farmers to provide fields in which to stage events, the local boroughs are a veritable

but this probably occurred in 1918 when Lord Lonsdale was President. The war years had been a lean time for the breed, and although Fell ponies were too small to be commandeered by the War Office, many were slaughtered for human consumption. At the first stallion show held at Penrith after the war only five stallions paraded, but the situation steadily improved and by 1927 there were well filled yearling and two-year-old classes.

The society continued to encourage classes for Fells at major shows, and Fell ponies can now be seen at most of the agricultural shows, as well as at the National Pony Society Show, the Ponies of Britain Shows, the Royal Show and other county shows throughout Britain. The Fell Pony Society also runs a stallion show in May and a breed show in August.

> ### The smugglers' accomplice
>
> When the Cumbrian coast was used by smugglers, the spirits, tobacco and salt were transported to the towns of Penrith, Carlisle, Whitehaven and Kendal by Fell ponies, with sacking tied round their hooves to muffle the sound as they carried their heavily laden panniers over the passes along little-known tracks.

mainstay. Permission is always granted to hold all kinds of events on the commons, from pony-driving instructional days to gymkhanas, from full-scale shows to the annual highlight: a one-day event with a tiny, specially constructed 'cross-country' course.

London Pony Club members ride to a high standard. This is partly because it is essential to ride competently when not in the manège. There are, however, some things which are very difficult for the local members to do. Practical experience of grass-kept ponies cannot be obtained unless a member eventually keeps a pony of his own, out of London. As galloping is expressly forbidden on all permitted riding tracks, it is difficult for the more advanced rider to gain experience of riding at speed. And how one occasionally longs to be able to school in an area larger than the standard 20 x 40m manège (even the large ones are a luxury!).

My personal regret is that our district is unable to field a Prince Philip Cup team. This is because the small, fast ponies required for this event are just not an economic proposition for urban riding schools. And even if we could find enough ponies of the right type, we would find it very difficult to find somewhere to practise. It can take hours to get from one end of the district to the other, and this would pose problems since the ponies would still be working animals and required for other duties. One day, perhaps. . .

Even the most foolhardy rider in Central London is aware of the dangers of the road. If you wish to die young, just ride a pony you cannot control, on a track which ends at a main road, as the majority of ours do. We have been involved in the Riding and Road Safety tests since these began, and in 1981, Wandsworth's Road Safety officer held a course to train riding instructors to teach road safety. In my ten years experience of one yard, located on a busy main road, there were only two road accidents. Both were on quiet back streets, and both caused by a reckless driver. Happily neither was serious.

If you ride carefully and courteously, London can be safer than a country road. The horses and ponies are very used to the traffic, and even the headstrong ones tend to behave themselves on the road. Bus and lorry drivers will often stop the traffic to allow a rider to cross a busy road, while local drivers know when you are likely to be on the roads, and are for the most part extremely cautious. Strangers to London are so dumbfounded to see a file of horses that they slow down automatically, to have a good look! Compare this to riding a pony along a narrow, high-hedged or deep-ditched country road, where the locals – who reckon to 'know the road' – drive at speeds approaching mach 1.

Most ponies in Central London are fit and healthy – many are native ponies, who do exceptionally well in this kind of environment. However, the amount of roadwork means that they need to have strong, sound legs, and be well shod at all times; our farriers are local men who understand the conditions and shoe accordingly. Even privately owned ponies are usually kept in communal yards, so it is rare for a pony to be neglected. They are also certain to be regularly exercised, because it is just too risky to allow a pony to get overfresh.

The city dweller who is an obsessive horse-lover will go on keeping horses wherever he can. There are many difficulties, but so many pleasures; the commons are large, beautiful and well managed – neither butchered by herbicides nor poisoned by fertilisers, they are natural nature reserves with an amazingly varied indigenous wildlife population.

While riding quietly along on a pony, many different species of animal, bird, and butterfly can be seen. The unhunted fox is a thing of beauty, glimpsed fleetingly, glimmering palely gold in sodium light. Early in the morning and before the city wakes, we sometimes ride up to the common and watch the sunrise. All the colours of the rainbow, muted in the morning glow, trees and buildings starkly silhouetted against the horizon. It could be anywhere, but it feels like paradise.

Saddlery and Equipment

The saddle, bridle, bit and accessories used on a pony are often referred to collectively as 'tack', and are an expensive but essential investment. The saddle and bridle must be suited to their purpose, and be comfortable for both the pony and rider. Good saddlery is made of the best leather, and though it does not have to be new, the stitching and leather of second-hand tack must be in good condition and the saddle tree particularly must not be damaged or broken.

The saddle and bridle give the rider essential contact and control, and badly fitting tack and hard, dry leather are simply dangerous and uncomfortable. It is best to get advice from an experienced horseman or reliable saddler before purchasing.

Bits and stirrup irons should be of high quality metal. Steel is the ideal material, as it is rustless, retains its shine, and is virtually unbreakable – solid nickel should be avoided as it breaks and bends easily. Stirrup irons must not be too large or too small for the rider's feet. Stirrup leathers can be made of leather, rawhide or buffalo hide: good quality leather looks smartest but can break under pressure; rawhide is virtually unbreakable and is popular for cross-country riding, but does not look as smart for showing or dressage; buffalo hide is recognised by its red colour, and is thicker and 'fleshier' than rawhide. Again, it is virtually unbreakable but can stretch more than the others. As all new leathers will stretch, the stirrups may have to be levelled up with each other after a while.

The bit must be the correct size for the pony's mouth, and must not have worn or sharp joints in it. Bits are measured in inches and the measurement is taken from inside each bit-ring, the smallest being 4½in (113mm) and increasing in steps of ¼ or ½in (6 or 12mm) to 6in (152mm).

BUYING AND FITTING A SADDLE

A good saddle, properly fitted and cared for, can certainly outlive the pony it was purchased for. A badly fitting saddle will be uncomfortable for both pony and rider and will affect the pony's action and performance, and a badly designed saddle will distribute the rider's weight incorrectly and put him in the wrong position. A saddle is rather like a pair of shoes, and will to a certain extent mould itself to the shape of pony and rider. Ideally, one saddle should be confined to one pony and rider, but this is often impractical and is certainly expensive.

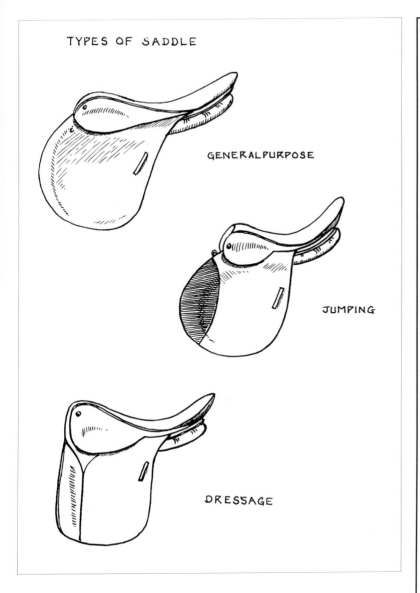

TYPES OF SADDLE

GENERAL PURPOSE

JUMPING

DRESSAGE

The Society of Master Saddlers
This is the official trade organisation embracing the craft of saddlery, and has several levels of membership:

MASTER SADDLER: This category is the pinnacle of the membership and includes highly skilled craftsmen who are capable of manufacturing and maintaining all types of saddlery and harness. Master Saddlers display the Society's wooden plaque showing its emblem in full colour.
APPROVED RETAILER: Retailers of saddlery; the majority can offer a first class repair service but are not qualified to make saddles. This category displays the Society's window sticker.
CRAFTSMAN SADDLER: Formerly known as a 'journeyman saddler'. Usually employed by a Master, or they provide approved retailers with a service on a contract basis.
APPRENTICES: Those who are indentured to a Master for a period of four years. They are taught all aspects of the trade, and when they have served their time and taken the City and Guilds Examination of Excellence, will then be expected to take a position as Craftsman Saddler.
STUDENTS: Those who are undergoing saddlery training at one of the Approved Training Centres, before entering the official apprenticeship scheme with a Master Saddler.

There are various types of saddle and those commonly seen at competitions are the general purpose, the dressage and the jumping saddles. Their design varies in relation to their purpose. The jumping saddle, by reason of the stirrup bar being positioned well forward and with a correspondingly placed flap, enables the rider, using a shortened leather, to carry his weight over the advancing centre of balance of the horse.

In dressage, where the pony's balance is carried more to the rear, the stirrup bar is positioned accordingly and the flap is much straighter to allow for the longer leg position.

The general purpose saddle falls between the above two extremes. A highly recommended general purpose saddle was recently introduced to the market for the non-specialist rider by the Society of Master Saddlers.

Other specialist saddles include the racing saddle and the Western or stock saddle, but in most cases a general purpose saddle is suitable for a pony and any of the tasks its rider may have to perform.

The saddle rests on the muscles each side of the spine and must be

The Haflinger (*opposite, wearing a special decorative headcollar*)

Although usually less than 14 hands, the Haflinger pony is extremely strong and has a great capacity for work. Small but thick-set with plenty of bone, and quite a heavy head which it tends to carry close to the ground when climbing, its great strength and sure-footedness make it an excellent pack and draught pony, and it is now becoming increasingly popular for driving. The village of Hafling, in the Tyrol, is said to be its original home. Haflingers are usually chestnut or palomino in colour with very distinctive flaxen manes and tails; other special characteristics are their long backs, the strength of their loins, and the freedom of shoulder and leg action. In recent years more than a hundred stallions have been registered annually, and modern Haflingers are in great demand and are being exported to many parts of the world. In their native land the ponies are never worked until they are four years old, and there have been instances of them still working at forty.

Variations abroad

Many riders use specially designed saddles when riding Icelandic ponies. The saddles have extended 'fans' at the back so that the weight can be distributed more evenly when the rider sits back. The saddle is also placed further back than usual, and a crupper is generally used. Icelandic horsemen ride with a longer leg, and usually with the lower leg well away from the side of the pony.

cut so as to lie behind the shoulder and its muscle formation. If it lies on the shoulder it will interfere with the movement. This can occur when jumping saddles are cut with too forward a flap or when the shoulder is too upright to allow the use of a jumping flap comfortably. It is built around the tree, which supports and shapes it and is its most vital component. The tree can be made of wood, plastic, or fibreglass and a spring-tree saddle also houses a strip of flexible steel. It forms the foundation of the finished saddle and must fit the pony's back.

Trees are made in three main fittings: narrow, medium and broad, and the actual size of the saddle is measured in inches, from the front of the saddle (the pommel) to the back (the cantle). With the rider in the saddle, too broad a tree will cause the forearch to press on the withers, too narrow a tree will pinch on either side of the withers. An ill-fitting tree cannot be corrected by adjusting the panel stuffing. Standard saddle sizes are 15, 16 and 17in (38, 40.6 and 43cm).

When the saddle is fitted to the pony there must be complete clearance across the withers and along the width and length of the backbone, enough to fit three fingers between the withers and the saddle when the rider is seated.

The channel itself has to be wide enough so as not to press upon the base of the vertebrae, which is wider than the apex.

If the channel becomes closed, the movement of the back is restricted, and any pressure on the spine detracts from the efficiency of the movement – the paces may be shortened and become irregular and the back stiff and hollowed. The lateral suppleness will be affected and jumping ability is reduced as the pony seeks to avoid discomfort when attempting to arch his back.

The panel must bear evenly over the full extent of the bearing surfaces on either side of the spine, so as to distribute the rider's weight accordingly. A panel that is stuffed too high on one side or the other, or a saddle which tips the rider too far to the front or rear, causes the rider to be out of balance with the horse, preventing its free movement and possibly causing galling because of the concentrated pressure over a small area.

While still offering this clearance over the backbone, the saddle should fit as closely as possible to the pony's back. It must not be too long or it will bang up and down on the pony's loins, and will let the rider slip too far back along the pony's back. Saddles of the same type can still vary considerably in shape and design – for example, if the panels are very forward cut, they can hamper the movement of a particular pony's shoulders.

The stirrup bars are attached to the tree and hold the stirrup leathers on the saddle, and they must be positioned so that when the leathers are hanging vertically, the rider's leg is correctly placed 'on the girth'. They must be open ended so that the stirrup leather can slip off should the rider fall with a foot caught in the stirrup.

A good saddler can adjust the saddle to overcome many problems, provided the saddle really is the right size in the first place: stuffing can be reduced or increased, and a narrow tree stretched to allow a better fit. Problems such as the saddle slipping forward on a pony which is very fat or has very flat withers can be corrected by using a crupper. This is an adjustable leather strap with a padded loop which fits under the pony's tail; the other end is fitted to a D-ring on the cantle of the saddle.

BRIDLES

Bridles come in standard sizes – pony, cob and full size – and the throatlash, cheekstraps and noseband are all adjustable by buckles or hooked billets. The reins can be plain or plaited leather, or rubber-covered leather which gives the best grip. If bought second-hand, it is again important to check that all the stitching is secure, particularly on the cheekstraps and reins. A snaffle bridle is suitable for most ponies for everyday riding, but some show classes insist upon a double bridle. In any bridle, the headpiece and throatlash are cut in one from the same piece of leather; the throatlash helps keep the bridle in place but when correctly fitted it will not stop the bridle being pulled off over the pony's head. When it is done up there should be a hand's width between it and the side of the pony's jawbone. The cheekpieces are attached to the headpiece at one end, and the ring of the bit at the other end, and therefore support the bit in the pony's mouth.

BITS AND THEIR USES

The bit and bridle act on different parts of the pony's mouth and head, and as the bit is positioned in something as sensitive as the pony's mouth, it must fit correctly and be suitable for its purpose. There are three main types of bit, the snaffle, the double bridle and the pelham. A pony is usually trained and schooled in a snaffle and may be put in a double bridle for more advanced work or for showing. Unless the pony's mouth has been damaged or spoilt, complicated bits and gadgets should not be necessary.

A correctly fitted snaffle can be checked by holding the bit with a hand on either side so that the joint is straight in the pony's mouth. It should protrude about ½in (0.5cm) either side. If the bit is too narrow, it will pinch the pony's mouth and if too wide, he will be able to get his tongue over it. The height of the bit is adjusted on the cheekpieces – it should not pull upwards on the corners of the lips, causing them to wrinkle excessively, nor should it be so low that the cheekpieces sag outwards when the rider takes up contact on the reins.

Double-bridle bits should be fitted with the bridoon as high as possible in the pony's mouth so that a slight wrinkle shows in the corner of the lips; the curb-bit lies immediately below it. The curb-chain should lie comfortably in the chin-groove, with the lip-strap fitted loosely through the ring in the middle of the chain.

Smooth-jointed loose-ring snaffle This is made of rubber or metal and has a single joint in the middle. It works on the lips, corners and bars of the mouth, and on the tongue.
Egg-butt snaffle This has the same action as a ring snaffle but the barrel-shaped side joints will not pinch the pony's mouth.
Double-jointed snaffles The French snaffle has a rounded central plate which lies across the tongue. It is suitable for a pony with a large tongue or narrow tongue groove as it acts more mildly on the tongue than the other snaffles. The Dr Bristol type has a rectangular central plate which acts severely on the tongue and is not allowed in dressage competitions. It is certainly not suitable for ponies.
Twisted snaffle The metal mouthpiece is twisted and has a very severe action, and is unlikely to be necessary on a pony.
Gag snaffle Another severe bit which works on the lips and corners of the mouth, the tongue and the poll. It is used with two reins and the gag rein should be applied lightly when needed.
Kimblewick This is a single rein pelham, with a port mouthpiece and rounded ends. It can be used on ponies which are too strong when ridden in a snaffle.
Double-bridle bits As explained above, the double bridle has a bridoon bit – either a loose-ring or an egg-butt snaffle – and one of several curb-bits. A tongue-groove curb allows room for the tongue by having a raised arch in the centre of the mouthpiece, and is the most commonly used. A port-curb is very severe and not generally recommended – it has a raised U-shape which presses on the roof of the mouth when the curb-rein is used. A half-moon mouthpiece is curved to allow some tongue room, while a fixed mouthpiece encourages the pony to hold the bit quietly. A milder type is the movable mouthpiece which encourages the pony to mouth the bit. Cheekpieces are used in varying lengths – the longer they are, the greater the

The noseband has its own headpiece strap and is generally a cavesson or a drop, although both the grakle, or 'figure eight' noseband, and the flash noseband are increasingly popular nowadays. Use of a grakle is penalised in any dressage competition (the flash is permitted); only the cavesson-type noseband would be worn with a double bridle. The cavesson noseband must lie below the cheekbones so that it does not rub against them and there must be space for two fingers between it and the front of the pony's face. The browband is a single leather strap which stops the headpiece slipping back; if it is too small, it will pull the sides of the bridle forward, and if it is too big, it will drop down too close to the pony's eyes.

A double bridle is designed to support a bit which carries two reins, a bridoon rein and curb rein. A double bridle bit consists of the 'bridoon' (either an eggbutt or loose-ring snaffle), and a curb-bit with a fixed or moveable mouthpiece and a curb-chain.

Fit for safety

The fitting of saddlery is as important an aspect of safety as its proper maintenance. Saddles and bridles which for any reason cause the horse discomfort and inhibit his movement can create an unnecessary stress situation which inevitably leads to a lowering of the safety threshold. To ride safely it is always best to have a new saddle fitted by a reputable saddler and to consult him about any subsequent adjustments to its fitting.

pressure on the poll and chingroove. When riding in a double bridle the curb-rein should be used gently, and only when required, and should never be used with a drop noseband.

Pelham Combines the curb and bridoon in one mouthpiece and can have two reins attached to the cheekpiece, or one rein attached using a leather

rounding. Some ponies respond well to a pelham, but it will not give the same result as the two separate bits of a double bridle.

Hackamore Is used instead of a bit and acts on the poll, nose and chingroove. There is no mouthpiece but in inexperienced or rough hands a hackamore can cause irreparable damage to these sensitive areas.

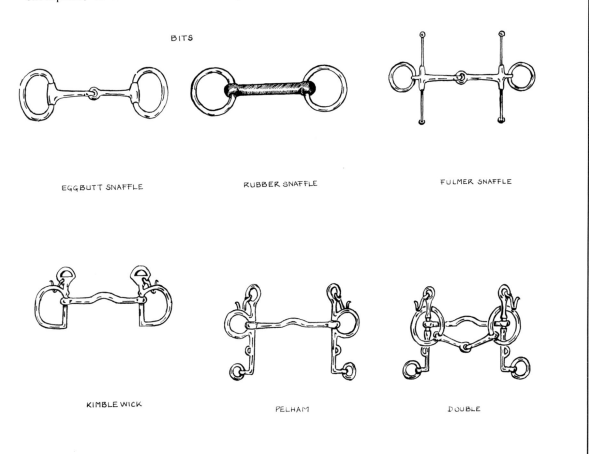

BITS

EGGBUTT SNAFFLE   RUBBER SNAFFLE   FULMER SNAFFLE

KIMBLE WICK   PELHAM   DOUBLE

Buying second-hand
If second-hand saddlery is purchased, the stitching must be safe and the tree must be checked to ensure it is not broken. The cantle should be rigid – if it can be bent backwards or forwards, then the tree has broken. To test a spring-tree saddle, hold it by the cantle in both hands with the pommel pressed against the stomach – the saddle should flex across the waist and seat, and spring back firmly into place. If there is no spring, or if there is more give on one side, then the tree is damaged or broken and is usually irreparable. If a rigid tree saddle is broken, there will be noticeable movement on one or both sides. A rigid tree can usually be repaired by a saddler, who will use metal plates to strengthen it.

SAFETY IN THE SADDLE

One of the most important safety factors in riding concerns good quality saddlery which, if carefully selected, will fit a pony well and should then be maintained to a high standard.

Accidents occur when equipment fails as a result of neglect or misuse, or when the components and the process of manufacture is below an acceptable standard.

An obvious safeguard is to purchase from established saddlers, many of whom are members of the Society of Master Saddlers and are committed to maintaining high standards in respect of materials and workmanship.

The saddle

The saddle and its mountings – the leathers, stirrup irons and girth – are items of equipment which if cared for will last almost a lifetime. But there are points of potential failure which need to be checked regularly.

On the saddle itself the most vulnerable area is concerned with the girth straps and their attachment. The stitching, securing the girth straps to the webs passing round or over the tree, will wear or perish in time and will need to be replaced. Girth straps, however good the quality of the leather, are also subject to wear. When the holes stretch and the leather is in danger of splitting between the holes, new straps

ADDITIONAL EQUIPMENT

Drop noseband Narrower than a cavesson and worn below the bit. It stops the pony opening his mouth too wide, or crossing his jaw. The front should be several inches above the nostrils, and the back should lie in the chingroove. The cheekpieces must not rub on the pony's cheekbones or on the corners of the mouth. The pony must still be able to flex his jaw when it is fitted, but should be unable to cross it.

Grakle, or crossed noseband This is more effective in preventing the pony crossing his jaw as it acts on a wider area. It has two leather straps which cross over on the bridge of the nose – one strap is fitted below the bit as a drop, and the other goes above the bit. It should be fitted for tightness in the same way as the drop noseband.

Flash noseband A cavesson with a drop noseband attached to it. The drop is usually a leather strap which passes through a loop on the front of the cavesson, and can be removed if required. A standing martingale can be used by attaching it to the cavesson.

Kineton noseband This is often effective on a pony that pulls very hard, as pressure from the reins works on the nose as well as the bit – the front of the noseband is adjustable and is fitted to a metal loop on each side;

the loops hook around the mouthpiece of the bit and therefore transfer the pull on the reins to the nose. The front strap should be four fingers' width above the nostrils, and the tighter the strap is, the more pressure is put on the nose rather than on the mouth.

Running martingale The purpose of this martingale is not to stop the pony holding his head too high, but to ensure that the contact with the reins always reaches the bit from the right direction. If the rider waves his hands around or jabs the pony's mouth, the effect will be less if this martingale is used. A strap attaches to the girth and passes through the forelegs; it must then be passed through the bottom of a neckstrap, which supports it and prevents the whole martingale dangling; it then divides into two straps, and the reins pass through the ring which is on the end of each strap. The martingale works indirectly on the bit and can be very severe if badly fitted. Fitted correctly, the rings of the straps should reach to the pony's throat; rubber stops should be used on the reins between the bit and the martingale rings to prevent them catching on the bit or rein buckles.

Standing martingale This is designed to prevent the pony carrying his head too high or tossing his head

should be fitted. The girth straps on cheap saddles, often of foreign manufacture, are frequently of poor quality and their attachment to the tree, sometimes only by tacks, may be so insecure as to be unsafe.

Buckles
'A stitch in time' is a good maxim to observe when it comes to girths, leathers and bridles, but when purchasing any of these items the buckles, and in the case of the bridle the hook-stud fastenings, deserve particular scrutiny.

Avoid the buckle which is obviously poorly finished with the edges left sharp and the tongues loose and perhaps bent. The former cut into the leather and the latter are likely to prove unreliable. Replace bent or loose hook studs immediately.

Stirrup leathers
Stirrup leathers receive the most wear at the point where they turn through the eye of the stirrup iron. It is for this reason that stirrup leathers are made with the tougher 'grain' side (the outside) facing inwards, since the dressing makes it more resistant to friction.

Stirrup irons
Buy stirrup irons made from stainless steel; nickel ones are cheaper but are liable to bend or break. If using a conventional pattern iron,

and hitting his rider in the face. Again, it is fitted to the girth and has a neckstrap, but instead of dividing into two, one strap only passes up and is attached to the cavesson noseband. To fit it properly, hold the strap against the pony's gullet – it should reach as far as the pony's throat.

Irish martingale   This is simply a piece of leather about 4in (100mm) long, with a ring at each end. The reins pass through the rings under the pony's neck. This martingale helps keep the reins in place and prevents them going over the pony's head.

Neckstrap   This is a leather strap which is put around the pony's neck. It gives the rider something to hold onto in an emergency or when learning to jump, and reduces the chance of pulling the pony in the mouth. It is helpful when riding in rough, sloping terrain, especially on a pony with no mane, and should also be used when teaching a young pony or rider to jump. It can be attached to the D-rings on the saddle to prevent it slipping forwards if the pony puts his head down.

Breast-girth   The purpose of both a breast-girth and a breast-plate is to prevent the saddle slipping backwards. This can happen if the pony has very high withers but it is also worn as a safety measure for cross-country riding. A breast-girth has a wide strap which passes around the pony's chest and attaches to the girthstraps under the saddle flap; a narrow leather strap laid over the withers keeps it in place. If it is fitted

too high it will affect the pony's movement and breathing. A breast-plate consists of a leather neckstrap which is attached at the top with two straps to the D-rings on the front of the saddle, or with longer straps to the girth tabs high up, above the buckles. At the bottom it is attached to the girth by a broad strap which passes between the pony's forelegs. There should be a hand's width between the neckstrap and the withers, and the straps from the D-rings should be under no strain when the pony's head is held normally.

Numnah   This is a soft pad cut in the shape of the saddle, and fits underneath it. It protects a sensitive back as it causes less friction than the surface of the saddle and is especially useful when a pony first comes into work. A numnah can also protect the pony's back when used with a spring-tree saddle as this type of saddle concentrates the rider's weight in a small area. If worn when a pony is jumping, it will prevent his rounded back coming into contact with the gullet of the saddle. Numnahs are usually made of sheepskin, nylon sheepskin, sorbo-rubber, sponge or felt. The less absorbent materials such as nylon sheepskin or sorbo-rubber can make the pony's skin sore as sweat will not soak away, so natural fibres are recommended. A numnah and a wither pad can also be used temporarily on a saddle that needs refitting or re-stuffing. However, a numnah should never become an excuse for keeping a badly fitting saddle.

Replace leathers
A wise precaution is to have leathers shortened every so often so as to move the point of contact with the iron. An even better insurance is to replace leathers regularly with best quality new ones; leathers are relatively inexpensive.

choose a heavy one big enough to slip off the foot in an emergency, but not so big as to allow the whole foot to pass through and become trapped. Always wear boots or heavy shoes rather than flat-soled footwear.

Regular cleaning with a glycerine-based soap and reliable 'leather food' preparation is essential if equipment is to be kept soft, supple and serviceable.

When leather is neglected, or is subjected to constant immersion in water (particularly hot water) or dried over heat, it becomes brittle and will snap in use.

CARE AND CLEANING OF SADDLERY

All the pony's tack should be cleaned after it has been used, not just to keep it looking nice, but more importantly to keep it supple, safe and comfortable. Leather has two sides, a 'grain' side which will have been waterproofed and appears smooth, and a 'flesh' side, which has not been sealed so the open pores can receive or lose the nourishment the leather requires. The fat content of leather is what keeps it supple, and must be replenished. Fat is lost every time the leather gets wet or warm. A damp sponge should be used to remove the sweat that clogs the pores and then a nourishing substance such as Kocholine, Flexalan or neatsfoot oil should be applied to the 'flesh' side. Saddle soap, preferably a glycerine one, can be rubbed into the 'grain' side using a damp cloth.

To clean a bridle properly it must be taken to pieces, and similarly, the stirrup leathers and buckle guards should be removed from the saddle. Saddle soap can be used on a daily basis to nourish the tack, but every week or so, a fatty substance should be applied to the 'flesh' side to replenish the fat level. Leather should not be washed with hot water or detergent, nor should it be allowed to dry out in front

of a fire or radiator. Stirrup irons and bits should be rinsed in warm water, and the irons can be brightened up with metal polish. The girth, if it is not leather, should be dried and brushed clean, and washed as necessary (remembering to rinse it well). Numnahs should be cleaned according to the manufacturers' instructions and must be kept dry and well aired.

Saddlery is expensive to replace and repair, and so every care should be taken of it. Never leave a pony loose with his tack on as he may get down and roll with it, or rub it against a wall. When leading a pony, his head should be kept up so that he cannot stand on the reins and snap them. The saddle and bridle should be stored somewhere safe and dry, but not where there is too much heat. If saddlery is to be stored for any length of time it should be taken to pieces and dressed with a preservative such as neatsfoot oil, and then wrapped in newspaper which will allow air to circulate around it. In today's climate of theft and break-in, it is also advisable to have all tack marked with a 'phone number or postcode, so that if it is stolen and later recovered it is possible to identify it, and tack rooms should always be left locked.

THE SADDLEHORSE

Working Ponies

THE PONIES THAT WORKED BELOW GROUND

There are now only about thirty pit ponies working in Britain's coalmines, but in 1914 there were more than 70,000, and even when the coal industry was nationalised in 1947 there were still about 20,000 working below ground. The majority of them have been replaced by conveyors or by diesel locomotives that can pull dozens of mine cars of coal at a time, instead of the one or two pulled by a pony.

Although machines have taken over the work of transporting coal underground, the few remaining ponies still do very useful jobs. When new areas of coal seams are being opened up for mining, ponies are unbeatable for hauling materials and equipment along the new roadways before the permanent conveyors are installed. Very often they have to haul all the component parts of the conveyors before these can be assembled and take over.

The day will soon arrive, however, when the last pony leaves the pits: this will mark the end of a long history of devoted service, which began long before the 19th century boom in coalmining which came as a result of the industrial revolution.

History

Ponies were imported into the pits in large numbers after the 1842 Mines Act, which banned the employment of women, girls and boys below the age of ten who had previously provided much of the underground haulage power. Even before the Mines Act, ponies were being used underground to pull the tubs of coal along and in the 17th century, horses turned the 'horse whims' which worked the underground pumping and winding machinery.

When ponies became needed in large numbers it was the coalfields of Northumberland, Cumberland, Durham, Yorkshire and South Wales which had the most. In the north, Shetland and Welsh ponies were found to be the most suitable for the relatively thin seams, and they varied in height from 10 to 12 hands. In the Midlands where the seams are thicker, there were more Dales and Welsh Cobs in use, and they measured up to 14 hands; the bigger Welsh Cobs were to be found in the South Wales coalfields. Mares were never used underground.

A life undergound

People have often been puzzled as to why pit ponies were not usually brought to the surface during their working lives underground. In some of the more shallow pits they were given summer holidays above ground, but in the deeper mines, where the temperatures were warm and equable all the year round, it was considered that their health might suffer if they suddenly had to face the variable climate above ground.

Famous pit ponies

During the 1930s and the 1940s many pit ponies became well-known as show ponies, and became popular competitors in county shows in many parts of Britain. They also won major awards at the Horse of the Year Show during its early years.

Pit ponies waiting for feed time in their underground stables

Selection and training

Before the ponies were taken underground they were given several weeks' training, and any who were unsuitable were weeded out. At one time they had to work long and hard hours, but ever since the 1911 Coal Mines Act became law, their working hours have been strictly limited and their welfare carefully controlled.

Ponies were not allowed to work underground before the age of four, and they all had to be 'free of glanders', a very contagious disease which ponies used to contract from infected food and water or through a skin infection; it could also sometimes be contracted through the lungs. The disease could prove fatal when it affected the lungs, liver, and other vital organs, and as it was often passed on to the stablemen there was considerable concern at the time. In the early 1900s there were sometimes as many as 3,000 cases a year, but by 1923 only nine cases were recorded, and there have been none since 1926; however, it was one of the very real dangers facing the ponies and their handlers in the days when many thousands of ponies were working down the pits.

Veterinary care

Some of the bigger collieries with a large number of ponies retained the services of a veterinary surgeon, who would examine the ponies several times a year and supervise their care if they became ill. At Tondu in Glamorganshire, where there were more than 160 ponies working in twenty-two collieries, there was even a horse hospital in the stables of a country house which included a dispensary and an operating theatre.

Stabling arrangements

In their underground stables the ponies were situated out of the way of the main roads, but in the intake airway so that they could breathe the same fresh air from the surface as the other mine workers. The stables were lit mainly by electricity, and had concrete floors and brick walls; the natural roof of the mine was usually supported by steel girders. Stalls for the smaller ponies had to be at least 5ft wide and 6ft long (1.5 x1.8m)with a minimum roof height of 7ft (2.1m). The larger animals had stalls 7ft wide and 10 –12ft (2.1 x 3 – 3.6m) long, and the roof had to be 10ft (3m) in height.

The walls were usually whitewashed, but some mines experimented with green walls because it was felt that green would be more restful to the eyes. The ponies had to be groomed each day, and in addition to their other food, grain was provided according to the size of the pony. In more recent years many of the mines had an up-to-date fodder plant of their own where the food was prepared, and the food was specially treated to ensure that it was dust-free.

Care

There had to be at least one experienced horsekeeper in charge of every fifteen ponies – he would make reports about their condition, would ensure that all their harness was cleaned, and kept records of the hours each pony had to work. Their working week was limited to 48 hours and on no account were they allowed to be ridden.

Before they started their working day the ponies had to be

A pit pony hauling a supplies wagon underground at a colliery in the north east of England. Note the eye protection

WORKING PONIES

Shap, the pit pony, is shod underground for the last time at Easington Colliery in Co Durham before being retired when all the ponies were replaced by mechanisation

groomed, fed and watered; the horsekeeper would check that the harness had been put on properly, and the wooden limbers – the portable shafts fitted onto the harness and then attached to the tub pulled by the pony – also had to be checked to see that they were properly suspended and could not cause chafing or injury.

The most important person in every pony's life was his young driver, who collected him from the stables and led him to the coal seam to be hitched up to one of the tubs ready to start work. The lad was also responsible for feeding and watering his pony during the working shift, and for reporting any accident.

Work and fitness

The ponies quickly learned to back up to a tub and then stand still while the limbers were linked, and most ponies knew without looking whether the right number of tubs had been attached. A two-tub pony would remain standing still if three tubs were hitched on, and wouldn't move until one had been removed!

The miners became extremely fond of their ponies and there are many stories told about the deep attachment they had for them – some even lost their lives trying to save their ponies when there had been an accident in the mine. Many of the miners were also very proud of their ponies' intelligence – they knew their work so well that they would often get on with it without being given any directions, and when shotfiring took place and everyone had to take cover, the ponies would know where to go and would take refuge on their own accord.

How many years a pony worked underground depended to a large

A miner and his pony enjoy a breath of fresh air on the surface at a colliery in north east England

extent on the individual pony, and it was usually a matter of fitness, rather than age, which decided when a pony was retired. The average working life of a pit pony, however, was usually between 10 and 15 years, but there were some who were still doing light jobs at 20. For the past seventy years or more pit ponies have been protected by law.

In the past when their working lives came to an end, it was sometimes possible to find them a place in a reputable home of rest for horses or with an animal lover, but the Coal Board always tried to ensure that they never got into the hands of unscrupulous dealers.

Adoption arrangements

The Coal Board still receives letters from people asking for ponies to adopt; however, there are no more available, and the few still working have already had retirement arrangements made for them.

Christmas is for all *the family. Joe and Eva Booth hang up a stocking for their retired pit pony, Trigger*

WORKING PONIES

*These two mares, Broadshade
Searchlight and Broadshade
Bealach, show the typical
mouse dun and yellow dun
colours of the Highland*

PONIES FOR THE DISABLED

One of the greatest joys and freedoms available to disabled people is the opportunity to ride or drive ponies. A pony can give a handicapped person the same feeling of independence that a guide dog can give to someone who is blind. Before the age of mechanisation, disabled people in fact relied upon ponies for transport as there was nothing else available to them; but the idea of ponies being used for therapeutic reasons and simply for the enjoyment they could give originated in Scandinavia. The courage and success of Madame Liz Hartell, the severely paralysed Danish international dressage rider, who won silver medals in the 1956 and 1960 Olympic Games, helped to spread the idea and it was quickly adopted in England.

The Riding for the Disabled Association is based in Stoneleigh, Warwickshire, and is responsible for co-ordinating the work of more than 600 voluntary groups who organise riding and driving for the mentally and physically handicapped, using riding schools and the special centres for the disabled, such as the Diamond Centre near London, to provide this facility. Some of the ponies are donated or purchased, but most are borrowed from people who are also happy to act as helpers on the day. The ponies have to be at least five years old and of a suitable temperament to cope with such vulnerable riders. This does not mean that they are decrepit old plodders – the ponies have to be sound and responsive to the rider's commands. They range in size from small 11-hand ponies to cobbier

types of up to 15.2 hands high for adult riders, and must be reasonably fit and strong as they often have to carry riders who cannot balance themselves, and who are consequently a dead weight on the pony's back. Some hospitals have their own riding facilities so that patients can ride under the observation of their physiotherapists. The Queen allows the Royal Mews to be used for riding for the disabled, and many riding centres offer their facilities free of charge.

Driving ponies tend to be small so that the vehicles they pull can be low to the ground. Vehicles for the disabled date back to the 19th century, and several are on display at the Arlington Court Carriage Museum in Devon. The floor of an early carriage was only about 7½ins (19cm) off the ground, and had a hinged ramp at the back so that a bath chair could be pushed in, and the occupant could then drive the cart himself; some sort of a device would have secured the chair in place. Today, modern carriages are adapted for handicapped drivers either with or without wheelchairs, and competitions are held for them, including the British Driving Society Championships at Smiths Lawn, Windsor.

Sadly, 1988 saw the death of Stella Hancock who has done so much for the riding for the disabled movement, and particularly in increasing the popularity of driving for the disabled. Stella joined the RDA movement in 1981, and was chairman from 1984 to 1987. She introduced regional training days, and an annual two-day conference which is held at

THE HIGHLAND PONIES OF SCOTLAND

The harsh environment of the Scottish Highlands has produced one of the most versatile breeds of pony to be found anywhere in the world, and their history dates back to the 14th century when King Robert the Bruce was known to have preferred Highland ponies to larger war horses. This was probably because of their hardiness and strength, and their ability to cope with rough grazing and harsh conditions. Since then they have been popular with many monarchs, including Queen Victoria who, after 1850, kept many Highland ponies at Balmoral. The royal connection continues today at the Balmoral estate in Scotland, with the Queen's expanding stud; her ponies earn their keep in the traditional manner, carrying deer, being ridden and used for trekking, and as driving ponies.

History

For hundreds of years Highland ponies have been bred to satisfy the needs of sportsmen and travellers, as well as being used for crofting duties. In the 1770s Dr Samuel Johnson made his famous Highland

Highland pony colours

Stallions with white markings, other than a small star, are not eligible for registration with the Highland Pony Society; otherwise the colours are evocative of the pony's homeland – yellow dun, mouse dun, grey dun, cream dun, brown, black and grey. Most ponies carry the dorsal eel stripe, and many have zebra markings on the forelegs. Apart from the small star, any other white marking is also disliked and discouraged on both mares and geldings.

Stoneleigh, and her work abroad led to the formation of disabled riding and driving groups in America, Singapore, Australia, and New Zealand. It was during a tour of Australia and New Zealand that she suffered a fatal heart attack. One of her proudest achievements was the formation of the West Horsley Driving for the Disabled group, and their performance of her Ben Hurs, as she fondly called them, in the 1985 Lord Mayor's show. Her group also performed at the World Driving championships at Ascot. Anxious to encourage better qualified driving instructors, she took the BDS Stage 1 herself, and liaised closely with the British Driving Society to see that as much as possible was done for the disabled. The work of people like Stella has ensured that solid foundations have been laid so that in the future bigger and better opportunities can be fully exploited.

Many disabled riders progress far beyond the weekly lessons in riding schools, and go on to give performances which rival their able-bodied colleagues. In 1987 the first World Dressage Championships for the disabled were held in Sweden, and Britain sent a team who returned victorious with two gold medals. The teams have only four days to familiarise themselves with the horses provided for them. Classes range from simple, walk-only tests to advanced classes which include a rein-back, turn on the forehand, leg yielding, and ten-metre circles at trot and canter.

Some riders simply cannot physically achieve such standards, but the work of the RDA is not about winning medals. The aim is to give every adult and child who is restricted by mental or physical handicap, the freedom of the four good legs and kind mind of a pony.

Despite their disabilities, disabled riders often do well in dressage competitions

Miss Shirley Macgregor with her successful Highland pony Katie winning the Driving Class at the Royal Highland Show

journey on pony-back, and ten years later Robert Burns wrote with affection about his 'Highland filly'. By the end of the century, studs of Highland ponies were being set up by rich landowners such as the Duke of Atholl, and in the 1880s the Department of Agriculture established a stud of the best Highland pony sires at Inverness, for crofters to use. Pedigree records have been kept since 1896, and the Highland Pony Society was founded in 1923. Affiliated societies now flourish in Australia and France, and the export of ponies has become world-wide. Some riding centres in France now use Highland ponies exclusively for riding and driving tuition.

Use for sport. . .

For generations, however, it has been a pony used for carrying sportsmen to the hill, and the day's bag back to the larder. To the Scottish Highland estate deerstalking and grouse shooting have become an economic necessity, and the native Highland pony is used because it is the most economical and practical means of transport by virtue of its sure-footedness and great strength, which enable it to carry up to 20 stones (127 kg) in weight over boggy or rough land.

. . . for trekking

Pony trekking was also started on the broad backs of Highland ponies when in 1952, in order to provide summer work for the animals used for deerstalking, Ewan Ormiston opened the first trekking centre at Newtonmore, in Scotland; since then the activity has spread throughout Britain, with many of the centres also using Highland ponies.

Their kind nature and quick learning ability means that they adapt easily to the daily routine of a trekking centre, and as they vary considerably in size they can carry riders of different weight and riding ability without any problem. They are a natural choice for commercial use as their winter keep is inexpensive since they can live out, and their use in trekking centres has helped to increase their popularity as riding ponies – very often the first contact that many new owners had with the breed was during a trekking holiday.

... for farming
Despite mechanisation, Highland ponies are still being used on some of the smaller farms and smallholdings for light carting and row-crop work, and by hill cattlemen and shepherds for the transport of feed and fencing materials. They are also used extensively in forestry work for dragging thinnings from steep or soft ground, and for transporting bundles of seedlings.

... for pleasure riding
They make, furthermore, excellent riding ponies for every member of the family, and have the build and temperament to carry riders of any age. Many are natural jumpers, and in the show ring they are increasingly successful in side-saddle, mountain and moorland, and working hunter pony classes. In rough or steep country where cleverness and steadiness are essential, they make safe hunters and good long-distance riding ponies.

... for the disabled
In riding for the disabled work their temperament is ideal as they are quiet in traffic and easy to handle in and out of the stable, and have the patience to stand placidly for long periods. Although many disabled riders do not take part in dressage competitions, those who do have found that the Highland's lively paces and easy transitions are a great asset. With riding holidays for the disabled on the increase in Britain, the Highland pony's strength and adaptability are again proving to be invaluable.

... for driving
Because they vary so much in size but are easy to match in colour, Highlands are very popular driving ponies, and they have the qualities which make them an excellent choice for any harness work. They have had notable successes in private driving events and driving trials, whether driven singly or in pairs, as a tandem or a four-in-hand team.

Conformation
There is a saying among Highland enthusiasts that if it is strong and stylish it is unmistakably a Highland: substance with quality, straight action and a typical 'pony' character are the ingredients of a good Highland pony. They vary in height from 13 to 14.2 hands, their backs have a slight natural curve, but their bodies are compact and deep-chested, with well-sprung ribs.

As one would expect with a breed of pony where strength, stamina and sure-footedness are so important, the Highland has strong, powerful quarters and a well-developed thigh and second thigh;

The Eriskay pony
Changing agricultural requirements almost caused the end of the cream-coloured Eriskay ponies from the Outer Hebrides. The last of these charming little working ponies were being fattened for slaughter by a Glasgow horse slaughterer, when they were rescued in the nick of time by Brian Brooks of Hildenborough, Kent. The mare and stallion he saved have helped him to build up a herd at Hollenden Farm Park. About 48in (1.2m) high, they combine elegance with a rugged exterior, and are very friendly with an excellent temperament. Eriskay ponies are fun to drive and easy to keep, but they do not do well on pasture that is too lush.

sloping shoulders with a pronounced wither; legs with flat hard bone, strong forearms and broad knees, short cannons, pasterns which are not too short, and well shaped hard, dark hooves. The forearms are placed well under the weight of the body, and the hocks are clean and flat. Any feather should be silky and not over-heavy, and should end in a prominent tuft at the fetlock.

Highlands carry their heads well. There should be plenty of space between alert and kindly eyes, but a shorter distance between eyes and muzzle; nostrils must be wide. Their necks are characteristically strong but not short, with a good arched top-line and a clean, not too fleshy throat-line.

Keep and care

Although hay should be fed during the winter months, Highlands thrive best on extensive rough grazing. Stallions generally run free with the mares and foaling usually takes place outside. The foals are weaned after six months and fed hay and concentrates, and if this can be done in the stable it will help with early handling. The youngsters should be halter-broken and handled frequently in their formative years, and the process of breaking-in should begin with a little light work at the age of three.

Providing that it has been brought on quietly, a Highland pony should be fully mature at five or six, and will then be in a position to provide its owner with many years of service and enjoyment.

THE VERSATILE ICELANDIC PONIES

Like the inhabitants of Iceland who came from Orkney, Norway, Shetland and the Western Isles in the 9th century, the Icelandic ponies are also immigrants, a mixture of two early varieties of Celtic type. To some extent the ponies are still being used in Iceland as they have been for centuries – as sure-footed mounts for farmers in the autumn sheep round-up, which is looked upon as being very tough work and which usually only the men take part in. The task of rounding up the sheep continues over many days until the early hours of each morning, to get the droves down from the mountain to the safety of the pens. If the snow comes early the job of the farmers, their helpers and their ponies becomes increasingly difficult as they have to plough their way through deep snow.

The sheep round-up, however, is one of those strenuous adventures dreamed of by every young man living in the country, as a way of putting his courage and manhood to the test. Roaming the wilderness for days on end in every kind of weather – including hailstorms, snow and rain – demands stamina, perseverance and resourcefulness. There is dangerous terrain to be tackled, with bogs and swamps, ravines and crevices, steep mountain slopes which have to be climbed, and boulder-strewn river beds to be crossed. At night a few hours' sleep can be snatched in one of the ramshackle drovers' huts, or perhaps a tent, before the search begins again.

When all the sheep have been rounded up it is an impressive sight to see them being driven down the mountain slopes, pouring down in white waves and bleating as they go, amid all the bustle of the riders with their shaggy ponies and dogs. The tired and muddy riders are met by their families, and getting the sheep into the folds usually involves a considerable amount of running about and shouting

Opposite:
The stronger Highland ponies are still used for deer stalking and farm work, and their sure footedness and good balance make them ideally suited for hill work

Horse fights

The horse fight was a popular amusement in public gatherings during the Commonwealth period in Iceland from 930 to 1262, and also in Norway. The stallions fought with fierce cruelty, frequently to the death, and they also often maimed or killed the attendants. Sometimes the spectators' enthusiasm reached such a pitch that fights broke out between the owners and their friends. There are reports of one fight which went on for eleven rounds, and special referees were appointed to decide which stallion was the winner.

There is also a report of a fight to the death between two Icelandic horses which had been sent to Norway as gifts during the reign of Hakon the Old. Although they were only quite small, the Icelandic ponies were, and still are, often referred to as horses. The stallions in those days were bred to fight, and their ability to fight well was at one time the criterion for all really good ponies. Fights were forbidden in 1592, and the last recorded one was in 1623.

Opposite:
The Highland Pony Parade is always a big attraction at the Royal Highland Show

Icelandic salt baths

While the ponies are shedding
their winter coat and before they
are set free in their summer
pastures, it is customary in some
parts of Iceland to give them a
bath in salty seawater. The
ponies, some of them carrying
riders, are made to swim across
a narrow inlet which must be
deep enough for them to become
completely immersed. The best
swimmers are selected to be the
riders. They don't use saddles,
but clasp their feet around the
pony's flanks, and grip the
manes tightly with their hands.

Ancient ancestors

No horses or ponies have been
imported into Iceland for at least
800 years, so not only are the
present-day Icelandic ponies the
same race as those of the Viking
age, they are probably also
descended from the horses used
by the legendary brothers,
Hengist and Horse, when they
invaded England in the 5th
century.

before the job of sorting them out begins.

Much of the farming population turns up to give advice, and the whole sorting process has an air of folk festival. The sorting days in neighbouring districts are timed not to coincide, so that there is an opportunity for everyone to attend more than one of these events. Everyone follows the proceedings with great excitement, and some of the riders call to mind the old-fashioned American cowboys.

Until well into the 20th century the sheep round-up was a hazardous affair for the ponies and their riders, and frequently resulted in the loss of one or more lives – at times, dense fog and terrible hailstorms, as well as deep snowdrifts on the mountains, would lead to the death of all the searchers. Better weather conditions in more recent years and the use of modern technology and equipment, have meant that tragic accidents of this kind are fortunately very rare.

Without their sturdy ponies, many of which are only between 12 and 13 hands high, the Icelander over the years might not have survived in parts of his barren, mountainous and remote island. They were his most faithful and useful servant, carrying him and his belongings from one end of the island to the other and playing an important part in his festivities and celebrations. It has been said that no creature has a greater right to Iceland than the pony, and the truth is that they have created conditions which have had an important effect on Icelandic culture over the years.

Characteristics

Icelandic ponies are usually graded into riding and pack animals, and to a lesser extent, draught animals which can also be ridden. The riding ponies are taught an ambling gait which is comfortable and fast when going long distances. They are hardy and have keen eyesight, and also a very strong homing instinct – the customary way to return a pony after a long ride was to turn it loose and let it find its own way home. They are docile and friendly, although rather independent by nature, but they respond well to the voice.

Ponies of most colours are bred, but they are usually grey or dun. They are short and stocky with a large head and intelligent eye, and have a very short, thick neck, with a heavy mane and forelock. Many thousands have been exported, particularly to countries in Europe. In 1949 the National Association of Riding Clubs was formed in Iceland and at the instigation of Gunnar Bjarnason, the European clubs in Austria, Belgium, Denmark, the Federal Republic of Germany, France, the Netherlands, Norway, Sweden and Switzerland founded the Federation of European Friends of the Icelandic Pony, with a view to organising biennial pan-European shows and races.

The first of these was held in the Federal Republic of Germany in 1970, with each member country entitled to seven entries. The Icelandic owners taking part have always been somewhat at a disadvantage because they are unable to take their ponies back into Iceland once they have left the country, and so they have to be sold abroad along with all their saddles and bridles. This is looked upon by the government of Iceland as being a necessary precaution in order to protect their country's stock, and for the same reason the shows and races can never be held in Iceland.

One Icleandic peculiarity is that each pony has its own set of names which are usually associated with the farm where it was born; and it is not unusual for European owners to travel to Iceland to visit the various farms, particularly as more than ninety per cent of the Icelandic names have been retained by European owners. At one time the Danish club published a catalogue of some 1,200 Icelandic pony names, with explanations of their pronunciation and meanings.

Despite his size, the Icelandic pony has consistently distinguished himself for his fine and variable gaits, his endurance in long distance and cross-country riding, and his agility when properly trained. So much so that courses in treating, training, and riding Icelandic ponies are frequently being arranged in various countries with specialist trainers – often Icelanders – travelling from one country to another.

Attempts to breed a finer type of pony, more suitable as a child's riding pony, by crossing the Icelandic with other breeds, including small Thoroughbreds, have not been successful and the characteristics of both strains have been lost. It does appear, therefore, that the Icelandic pony will not breed true outside its own blood.

Endurance racing

Among the many spectacular events marking the American Revolution Bicentennial celebrations in 1976 were two endurance races for horses and ponies across the American continent, and Icelandic ponies took part in both. One was the Great American Horse Race, which started from Frankfort, New York, on 31 May. Each of the 94 riders had two mounts, and after crossing New York, Pennsylvania, Ohio, Indiana, Illinois, Missouri, Nebraska, Colorado, Wyoming, Utah, Idaho, and Nevada, the race ended on 5 September at the California State Fair in Sacramento, with only 52 riders crossing the finishing line.

The 5,000 kilometre (3,106 miles) trek was the longest horse race ever organised, and there were foreign entries from Australia, France, Germany, Switzerland, Austria and Canada, as well as Iceland One of the Icelandic riders finished thirteenth with both his ponies, and the other came twenty-first, having dropped from seventh place when he had to ride the last 1,000 kilometres (621 miles) on one pony, after the other had died from drinking poisoned water.

Another similar event, the Pony Express Race, was organised from Saint Joseph, Missouri, to Sacramento in California over a distance of some 3,000 kilometres (1,864 miles) starting on 17 July and ending on 15 September. In addition to the ten riders with Arabian and Appaloosa horses, there were four riders with Icelandic ponies, all of whom finished the race, with one taking second place.

In both the races the Icelandic ponies made a considerable impression for their adaptability and qualities of endurance, and in both events they were under the supervision of Gunnar Bjarnason, one of the great authorities on the Icelandic pony. He made sure that the ponies were not stabled along with the other horses at night, but kept out in the open with an electric fence which he erected every night, so that the ponies would feel more at home, as though they were resting in Iceland. Long rests were taken during the hottest part of the day, and whenever the ponies showed any signs of fatigue he insisted that they were rested for one or two days. To begin with, all the ponies were shod in the American fashion with 'Arab plates' but these proved to be disastrous, and Gunnar Bjarnason decided that they should all be re-shod Icelandic fashion, where the frog has constant

The tölt

The one thousand-year isolation of the Icelandic pony has preserved in him some of the peculiarities lost in other European horses and ponies over the past five or more centuries. Among these are the five different gaits. The peculiar gait known as the 'tölt' is of German origin, and there was considerable contact between the Germanic peoples and the Romans during the 2nd and 3rd centuries. Greek artists of the 5th century BC decorated the friezes of the Parthenon on the Acropolis with cavalcades of horses riding to do honour to Pallas Athene, and the men can be seen riding on tölting horses of similar size to the present-day Icelandic pony.

Icelandic horsebreeding law

So far as is known the purity of the Icelandic pony has no equivalent in other breeds. The Icelandic Althing, the oldest parliament in the world, passed a law in 930 during its first year, forbidding the import of horses or ponies; it also passed the first law about horsebreeding in 1891. Ten years later an amendment was added where it was forbidden to let any stallion of more than one-and-a-half years of age roam freely with other ponies, either on the commons or the home pastures.

Above:
Icelandic ponies are docile and friendly, although rather independent by nature

Right:
Icelandic ponies and their riders delighting the crowds at the Calgary Show

Opposite:
Icelandic ponies are becoming a source of pleasure and relaxation to many town dwellers. Note the rider's position

contact with the ground. This was easily done because in Iceland cold shoeing is universal, and many sizes of shoe are available.

The eight Icelandic ponies who took part in the Pony Express Race had already been on the move for six weeks which makes their performance even more remarkable, and they proved to be even hardier than the Arab horses who took part.

There are about fifty riding clubs in Iceland, with some 5,000 members who take part in shows and races, when sometimes as many as 3,000 ponies will gather from all parts of the country – there have been occasions when 700 riders have taken part in one parade.

Distinctive gaits

The five different gaits of the Icelandic pony are unique amongst contemporary European ponies, but they are to be found in many different breeds in Asia, Africa and America; the gaits are employed according to the terrain and the rider's requirements. The walk or step (fetgangur) was used when the ponies were tied together in a train and were carrying loads on their backs and is still used by pack ponies when travelling across country. The trot (brokk) is used when the rider is crossing rough country, and the gallop (stökk) is reserved for occasions when speed is the main requirement, and the ponies will gallop over stony ground and across grassland. The canter (valhopp) is a convenient gait when travelling across mixed terrain, but it is considered to be rather unsightly and so is not very popular with riders. The pace (skeid) is used for short stretches at high speed, and the pony moves in laterals, *ie* both feet on one side move forward simultaneously. In racing the pony starts by galloping, but after 50 metres (47yd) at full speed it must change over into the pace.

Probably the most distinctive gait of the Icelandic pony, is the rack or single foot, or running walk (tölt) when the pony is proudly erect and carries his tail in a typically undulating movement. It is a 4-beat gait in which the feet follow the pattern of near hind, near fore, off hind, off fore, falling at equal intervals. The rider hardly moves in the saddle and it is an ideal pace for travelling over smooth ground.

Few countries give the traveller such a feeling of vast space as Iceland, and travelling on horseback is a magnificent way of seeing the countryside. Many of the riding clubs organise joint one-day tours for their members, usually in the spring, and in Reykjavik and the larger towns provide their members with stables on the outskirts of the populated areas, with easy access to the open country. Often two or more owners will either hire a stable or build one together, and look after their ponies in rotation, with one coming in the morning and the other in the evening.

A great number of riders are seen around Reykjavik and in the countryside during the summer months, at weekends and in the evening, and riding is also becoming more popular in the winter months. The Icelandic ponies are increasingly becoming a source of pleasure and relaxation to the harassed city-dweller: he may enjoy a leisurely ride among the apartment houses, or in frosty weather the frozen lakes make excellent racecourses – a sight not to be forgotten is to see good pacers dashing across an ice-sheeted lake. And there is a special magic surrounding riding over snow-clad hills or along star-spangled beaches in the moonlight, with the Northern Lights dancing across the sky.

The Pony Club

A WORLDWIDE ORGANISATION

The Pony Club is a very special organisation bringing together young people who have a love of horses and ponies. It is the largest association of riders in the world, with almost 37,000 members in Great Britain and a further 100,000 members in twenty-five countries as far apart as Australia and America.

Although the Pony Club is such popular organisation, its members need only two qualifications to belong – they have to be under 21 years old and they must love horses and ponies, although they need not necessarily own one. It began in 1929, when the Institute of the Horse started a junior branch and gave it the name Pony Club. The aim was to interest young people in riding and the welfare of ponies and to offer them a higher standard of instruction than they would probably be able to get on their own.

Districts

The country was split into districts, which tied in with different hunts, and each was organised by a District Commissioner and a local committee. Their policy was to remain closely involved with hunting. The entrance fee charged was 2s (10p) and the annual subscription was 5s (25p). This remained unchanged until 1976 and even in 1989 the annual subscription had only increased to £12 with an entrance fee of £1.

Pony Club camp

By 1930, within just one year of being formed, membership had reached 700 and since then the club has gone from strength to strength. One of the greatest traditions of the Pony Club is the Pony Club camp – it began in 1931 and is still one of the highlights of the year for many Pony Club members. Out of sight of parents for a week, although still under the strict eye of instructors and the camp 'matron', members can really enjoy a week's holiday together with ponies which they either own or have begged or borrowed. The children enjoy instruction in riding and stable management, hacking in the countryside, jumping and other competitions as well as talks, film shows, quizzes and even barbeques.

Everyone considers the annual camp great fun, even if the discipline has to be strict. Tack and turnout are inspected each time the

---

The Pony Club's aim

The Pony Club's aim is to promote sportsmanship, citizenship and loyalty, strengthen members' characters and give them a greater sense of self-discipline. Competition is encouraged, but to make sure that everyone takes part in the right spirit, prize money is not given at Pony Club competitions, and best rider classes are not encouraged.

A shared interest

Although about 90% of Pony Club members own ponies, there is plenty of opportunity for those who do not. They can hire a pony from a riding school or perhaps share one with another club member. Firm friends are quickly made when so many young people, all sharing a common love of ponies, meet together.

A

B

A – D

Anyone taking part in Pony Club mounted games must learn to vault on and off a pony swiftly and correctly

campers ride their ponies, whose comfort comes before their own at all times. Nobody gets tea until the ponies have been fed and watered, and prizes are given for those showing the most improvement during the week.

The wonderful thing about horses and ponies is that they are such character-builders, and they can teach young people a lot more about themselves than many other lessons of life.

Tests

Members are taught how to improve their standard of riding and stable management, and help is given to children to work their way through the various Pony Club proficiency tests. The first is the D test and on passing this members can go on to take the C, C+, B, H and A tests. These tests give great incentive to everyone and are especially useful to those who are planning to take instructors' examinations or go to college to study horsemanship. Members can also take the Riding and Road Safety test which helps them to ride more safely in traffic.

Branches

Pony Club branches exist all over the country and not just in rural areas – there are now several branches in London and in some of the larger towns where, even though the children may have little hope of ever owning a pony, they enjoy riding and looking after ponies; some of these town branches are attached to schools or riding centres. Exchange visits are encouraged between branches and these may take place at home or abroad. Competitions are held between different branches, and again, members may be given the opportunity to compete abroad, or be hosts to visiting foreign branches. All aspects of horsemanship are covered and no one is ever pushed beyond the limit of his ability. Whether their interest is in dressage, jumping, cross-country, mounted games or even polo, there is instruction for everyone.

Rallies

The most regular activity for Pony Club members is the branch rally, when members of the local branch come to a convenient venue for instruction in riding and stable management; this is often followed by some form of competition. Branches may organise other outings and

---

Polo

Pony Club polo is organised by the Polo Committee, who supply training videos and also assist Pony Club branches with the cost of buying polo sticks for their members.

C

D

The Tetrathlon

Another sport growing in popularity is the tetrathlon in which competitors have to run, ride, shoot and swim, and girls are becoming increasingly keen on this event. Pony Club championships are held every year and these are always hotly contested.

Speed, accuracy and perfect understanding between pony and rider are the essentials for success in gymkhana games

often pool their resources to arrange visits to important equestrian events. As well as the ridden rallies there are other meetings where films and slides may be shown or someone well-known will give a talk or demonstration.

THE PRINCE PHILIP CUP

Not many youth organisations can boast national television coverage for any of their activities, but the finals of the Pony Club mounted games at the Horse of the Year Show have, for many years, been seen by television viewers who enjoy the spectacle of Pony Club teams competing against each other in games requiring real riding skill, speed and agility.

The Pony Club mounted games began with the first championship in 1957. They were the idea of His Royal Highness Prince Philip, who suggested to the director of the Horse of the Year Show that they should hold a mounted games event for children, which would be based on the competitions run for cavalry regiments. The gymkhanas which many young riders compete in are also developed from the

Practising on the beach

Practice facilities during the early part of the year are often less than perfect, unless teams have a chance to practise indoors. As soon as the ground is dry enough, however, the fields can be used, and those lucky enough to live near the coast can enjoy early season practices on the beach.

A RECIPE FOR SUCCESS

The phenomenal success of the Eglinton branch in the Prince Philip Cup during the past decade is largely due to the talent and dedication of their enthusiastic trainer, Robert Noble, who has led them to victory six times in the last eleven years. He recalls his early days with the branch.

If someone had told me twenty years ago that one day I would be training Pony Club teams, I would have said they were mad – yet this is the start of my fourteenth season as trainer of the Eglinton Prince Philip Cup team. Firstly, it must be said that Eglinton's success could have been achieved by any enthusiastic trainer for any other club. Eglinton was not a winning team; in fact, it was not even a good one.

My introduction to the Pony Club was in 1974 as a dutiful dad, taking my daughter to rallies and Prince Philip Cup practices – at that time, our branch could scarcely gather together five riders to make a team. Midway through the 1975 season, I was able to take the team to a competition and our partnership seemed good – and shortly after that, I was asked to take over as trainer for the following year.

I accepted, but soon began to wonder what I had let myself in for. Up until then, my real hobby had been breeding and exhibiting Clydesdale horses, but as far as mounted games were concerned, my knowledge of how to run a team was nil – I had never been to the Horse of the Year Show and had never heard of Wylye Valley, Banwen, Croome, or Oakley, and certainly had no idea if those teams could be beaten. However, as long as we had five well-trained riders and ponies, there seemed to be no reason why our branch shouldn't at least be able to equal them.

As trainer, my first priority was to find the children who were keen enough and had some natural ability. With that in mind, I hired a small indoor school for one evening each week, and for the first week, invited some of the local members to come along without ponies and learn to do some of the games on foot. They enjoyed it very much and told all their friends, so that after three weeks I had almost forty children practising Prince Philip Cup games without ponies.

What fun and enjoyment the children have doing bending races, stepping stones, tyres, mugs, sack – almost any race in the rule book can be done without ponies, and it is quite easy to spot the agile and supple children, and teach them the rules of each game without the extra hassle of trying to control ponies at the same time.

We started to practise with ponies in mid-January on the beach at Ayr, and to my delight, all of those children turned up; so in one year the training sessions were transformed from six or seven riders to almost forty of all ages. This was tremendously satisfying and made me realise what potential the children of this branch really had. It was almost certainly this transformation, along with the back-up from the parents, which set Eglinton off on their present run of success.

Training starts each year on the second or third

traditional regimental games originally played in India.

The games are open to riders fifteen years of age or under and resemble a mounted version of 'It's a Knockout', which has proved so popular on British television; they certainly encourage team spirit and co-operation. Some of the events require speed and dexterity while others need a steadier, more accurate approach. Ponies often have to work in pairs, and one of the hardest tasks with a pony with racing on his mind is to train him to stand still while his rider carries out a specific task, such as hitting a target with a ball or posting a letter.

They are great fun, and these games also encourage better horsemanship because the ponies need to be obedient and responsive. There is also great discipline in the training and practice which is needed, particularly for those teams determined to get to the top. Every Pony Club branch can enter two teams for the preliminary round of the competition; these are known as the area finals and are held all over the British Isles, as well as Ireland, during April and May.

> **The Simpson of Piccadilly International Mounted Games**
>
> The Simpson of Piccadilly International Mounted Games create fierce competition for the team places every year. Five riders are picked from England, Scotland, Wales, Northern Ireland and Eire to represent their country and the games are held during the Royal Windsor Horse Show in May, when Windsor Castle always provides an impressive setting. There is also now a competition for the under 12s as well as a recently formed National Junior competition.

Sunday in January, and since we usually finish in mid-October, that means that we train for about forty weeks in the year.

People often wonder why training the mounted games team is preferable to training those for other competitions. In fact I do help with other things where I can, including the Eglinton show jumping team, but the games are special because they are the only competition other than polo where riders compete as a team, and where one rider's mistake can upset the whole team. It is enormously satisfying to see the team improve week by week, and 'peak' just in time for whatever competition they are involved in. The team effort also requires discipline, and this is something which stays with the children for the rest of their lives.

Furthermore, the Cup finals are held at the Horse of the Year Show, and it is the ultimate thrill for all young riders to qualify for one of the largest shows on the equestrian calendar. They can talk to their equestrian heroes, even rub shoulders with them, for a whole week – and I suppose it is also the ambition of many parents actually to take their children there!

Unlike show jumping, where the ponies of Wembley standard can cost thousands of pounds, a perfectly suitable mounted games pony might cost between £600 and £700, and with a little training and patience could become a first-class pony.

The Prince Philip Cup must be the only national title where the champions are on the 'scrap heap' by fifteen years of age. Even the most precocious of those swimming babes would usually still have a year or two, but the Prince Philip Cup is no ordinary test and so it is important to get the riders when they are young.

For many, the games are probably the highlight of their riding life, and the competition caters for the ordinary young member who perhaps lacks the talent or a suitable pony to compete in show jumping or eventing. Moreover, the mounted games provide a schooling ground for the able young rider to be accurate, supple and quick-thinking, and help to develop a rapport between horse and rider.

Over the past decade, Eglinton has a record of which the club may be justifiably proud, but the members are not freaks: the riders do not have three hands, nor do the ponies have some built-in computer to control them. There are five riders and five ponies just like any other branch, but they put up with my honing until they have reached as near perfection as they can get. And without doubt, hard work and dedication are two of the ingredients needed for a successful team.

The successful Prince Philip Cup team from the Eglinton Branch

MEMORIES OF PONY CLUB CAMPS LONG PAST

No one knows who actually invented Pony Club camp, but the suggestion of thirty or more boys and girls, aged between 11 and 17, foregathering for a week with their ponies, could have spelt the biggest recipe for disaster ever. They needed their heads examining! But in the 1930s when camps first started, discipline may have been easier to maintain.

Nevertheless, in spite of the potential for trouble and the unnerving possibilities that the thought of a residential camp engenders, for those who can organise one, it is the highlight of a branch's year – and long may it continue.

For someone who is no longer involved and too ancient to be recalled, this is an easy thing to say. In the 1960s and 1970s it was my responsibility to set up, administer, and run one each year, and I was probably not quite so keen; however, because the camp always gave so many children so much fun it was something which just had to be done.

The night before camp started I used to send up a little prayer – and would heave a sigh of relief when the last camper had eventually departed for home. And in spite of everything, I would do it all again. Everybody had fun, and the children usually learnt more in that week than they did during the rest of the year. There were no indulgent parents around to do all the work. The ponies behaved and worked better as the week wore on, and even if the children were a

Zone finals

After the area competitions, 72 teams go through to the zone finals in August. By that time all the teams will have had more practice and the ponies and their riders will be fitter and much more skilled. As the tension mounts, so does the speed, ingenuity and determination of the competitors and the winners of each of the six zone finals certainly earn their place. The finals are always held at the Horse of the Year Show in London during October.

The Horse of the Year Show

The privilege of competing under the spotlights at the Horse of the Year Show can go to only a few teams, but in the true tradition of the Olympics, it is not only the winning, but the taking part that matters. The mounted games provide opportunities for members in all branches, whether they reach the finals or just enjoy taking part in the early competitions.

Other mounted games

Other mounted games competitions are held to enable more riders to benefit from the fun and the lessons to be learned form the sport. The Zone Final Runners-Up Competition provides a further opportunity for those who came so close to their ultimate goal.This competition is held over a period of two days at Smiths Lawn in Windsor Great Park, and the teams compete for a perpetual challenge trophy (it is held during the National Carriage Driving Championships' week).

The mounted games are always a real team event, catering for riders of varying abilities. Parents often get roped in to help with the organisation and to keep a watchful eye on those taking part. The determination to win must never, however, be the over-riding factor and must not be allowed to spoil the enjoyment of all those taking part. The games are aimed at encouraging true sportsmanship – win or lose – and they seem to be enjoyed as much by the ponies as their young riders.

Lundy ponies

The Lundy ponies are of New Forest origin (see p116) and date back to 1928 when a number of carefully selected mares and fillies were taken to the island, along with two stallions. One of the stallions was of mixed breeding and the other was a small Thoroughbred, and they are responsible for the breed of Lundy ponies as we know them to-day.

good deal scruffier and rather more dirty (baths were anathema!) than usual, the overall turnout of their ponies was better than at any other time.

It is a pity that camps have become so expensive to organise, though this is perhaps inevitable, and rather the way of the world – the fun is still there. The battle with the weather is the same as ever, and the problems of boys and girls (I think we had more boys bent on mischief), missing instructors, lost and wet clothing and tack, and lame and sick ponies, are without doubt still prevalent, and probably always will be.

Stories of camps are innumerable, and many well-known riders still recall the fun they had. My first experience of running a camp was in the 1950s, in the Mediterranean when we handed over our polo ponies for the whole of August to the children who were out there to stay for the summer holidays. Incidentally, the change of activity did the ponies a power of good and they came back to polo refreshed and keen again – there is a lesson to be learnt there!

The camp was in an old castle, which in the past had been the Governor's summer residence – before electricity and air conditioning! It had few amenities, but who minded that for a week? The girls slept in the stables, the ponies were on lines under the trees, and the boys (five of them) were impounded in a turret, with only one door which opened into the hall where the staff lived.

I slept easily under the delusion that all was well, although admittedly I was sometimes suspicious during late evening 'visiting rounds'; however, it was difficult to see how they could possibly get up to mischief.

Some years afterwards I heard the true story, and only the other day did one of the ex-inmates of the turret confirm the truth. Someone had apparently smuggled a rope ladder into the turret, and this was used to get in and out when everyone else was asleep. The target each night was an item of girls' underwear. Who went short is anyone's guess, but with more than twenty girls and only five boys there were probably a few spares around, and such is the honour amongst campers that nobody 'let on' – and for sure the girls somehow got their own back!

I tried many strategies over the following years (a castle and turret were not always available), but not many of them worked completely; and in the end I came to the obvious conclusion: the answer was not to put up any physical barriers, but to allow fraternisation within limits up to a certain time, and then to put everyone on his honour (though a little surreptitious snooping did not do any harm.)

Nearly everyone went to bed quietly – after all, if there was no 'dare', why try? If anyone then set out to break the rules, hopefully my little prayer before camp would work – and as far as I know, it did!

Colonel Pat Langford

Ponies and riders ready for inspection at Pony Club camp

THE NEW FOREST PONY

There have been ponies in the New Forest since the last ice age, and one of the skeletons which has been excavated is of a pony standing about 13 hands and dated around 300 AD. Lying between Southampton and Bournemouth in south-west Hampshire, the New Forest contains within its boundaries one of the largest areas of enclosed land in southern England. Once the hunting ground of kings, it is now a popular place of recreation for the general public, but New Forest ponies still roam its heaths, bogs and woodlands, as they have since time immemorial.

History

King Canute's Forest Law of 1016 records the presence of horses among other wild animals of the Forest, but how and when the ponies passed into private ownership is not clear.

The New Forest pony, like many other native breeds, has always been valued for its hardiness and strength, as well as for its docility and sureness of foot. Arab and Thoroughbred blood was introduced to improve the pony's looks and increase its height, but it was not until the end of the 19th century that systematic efforts were made to improve the breed. In 1891, the Society for the Improvement of New Forest Ponies was founded, and premiums were offered so that suitable stallions would run in the forest. Fifteen years later in 1906, the Burley and District New Forest Pony and Cattle Breeding Society began to register mares and youngstock, and published its first stud book in 1910.

There was a theory at the time that the best way of improving the breed was to introduce stallions from other native breeds, and the earliest stud books show that a curious assortment of stallions were used as acceptable sires. During the early part of the 20th century these included a black Highland with yellow eyes, whose dam was a dun. This was a colour not previously found in the Forest and resulted in some cream foals being born. There were also four Welsh stallions with Deyll Starlight blood whose influence is still apparent, an Exmoor, Dartmoor, Fell, a polo pony which was a Welsh/Thoroughbred cross, and even a Hackney. Two of the foals were by a Basuto pony and one by a zebra, which was a dun with chocolate stripes and, of course, infertile.

Some time earlier in the 19th century Marsque, who was the sire of that great racehorse Eclipse, covered some New Forest mares before Eclipse started to race; and between 1850 and 1854 an Arab stallion, Zorah, belonging to Prince Albert, was offered to improve commoners' mares. They were, however, reluctant to take their mares off the Forest in order to visit Zorah because they suspected, quite rightly, that they would be charged rather highly for his services, and so he was very badly patronised. An Arab stallion turned out into the forest would have found the conditions too hard, and would have had little chance of breeding.

Between 1914 and 1959 registrations of New Forest ponies were recorded in the National Pony Society's stud book, but in 1938 the two local societies amalgamated and no outside blood has been allowed since the mid-1930s; in 1960 the New Forest Pony Breeding and Cattle Society started its own stud book. There are now flourish-

An ideal Pony Club pony

With its free, straight and active action, ideal temperament, and native virtues of strength, intelligence, speed and agility, the New Forest is an ideal riding pony for any member of the family. Most of them jump very well, and they are naturally good at gymkhana events and mounted games – the ideal Pony Club mount.

Ponies and tourists

There are more than ten million visitors to the New Forest every year, and the ponies are one of the main attractions.

Feeding in the Forest

The Forest wetlands and bogs have helped to save many of the ponies because they can eat the bog plants that grow there in the early spring, when there is little else for them to eat.

Private breeding

Two of the most notable features of New Forest pony breeding in recent years have been the large number of ponies which have been bred in private studs, away from the Forest, and the many which have been exported.

ing studs in many parts of Britain, and also studs of registered New Forest ponies throughout Europe and as far away as Canada and Australia.

Versatility and performance

The New Forest is a very versatile breed, and the larger ponies are narrow enough for a child to ride, yet also quite capable of carrying an adult. Sir Berkeley Piggot played a New Forest pony called Hazel at Rheinefield Polo Club for many years, and the ponies have always been used locally for colt catching and cattle herding on the forest. At least one is still being used as a shepherd's pony in Northumberland, and another was recently used for a police coastal patrol in the West Country.

New Forest ponies have been successfully trained for dressage, long-distance riding, cross-country events and polo; they will carry the disabled, and are also surprisingly fast over rough terrain. They have always been raced locally, and the society organises a three-mile point-to-point across the open Forest each year on Boxing Day. It also promotes a 'Performance Pony of the Year' competition, in addition to a summer show and a stallion show.

The 1988 winner of the versatility rosette awarded by the Society was Tildiz Tobacco Leaf. This pony had won points for long-distance riding, hunting and hound exercise, jumping, Pony Club one-day event and Riding Club activities, working hunter pony, dressage, combined training, Western trail riding, side saddle, handy pony, mountain and moorland show classes, hunter trials, gymkhana events, family pony (when ridden by mother and daughter), carriage driving, and also for riding for the disabled, when they reached the finals of the Pony Championships.

Stallions

The stallions are easy to handle, and outside the breeding season most of them are ridden. When New Forest mares are crossed with Thoroughbred or Arab stallions, they produce small riding horses of about 15 hands, which are capable of competing in any sphere.

New Forest ponies are happiest when kept under conditions which are as natural as possible, such as a good grass field with plenty of windbreaks and clean water always available. The ponies are very hardy, and with proper care they can easily live out all year round. They will, however, need hay in the winter, and pony nuts if they are working.

The typical pony

The upper hight limit for a New Forest pony is 14.2 hands, and although there is no lower limit, there are few ponies under 12 hands. They may be any colour except skewbald, piebald or blue-eyed cream. White markings on the head and legs are permitted, and bays and browns predominate. A New Forest pony should always be of riding type with substance. It should have a pony head, well set on, long sloping shoulders, strong quarters, plenty of bone, a good depth of body, straight limbs and good hard, round feet.

A Royal gift

The breed has been famous for its calm and willing temperament since the time when one was given to King James I for his daughter, Elizabeth, when he came south from Scotland.

A family pony

This versatile breed can provide everything from leading-rein ponies to showjumping, dressage and driving ponies, and will continue to give children and adults pleasure in a wide range of activities.

New Forest ponies roam at will over some 60,000 acres of countryside in Hampshire, but unfortunately many of them are killed and injured when they stray onto the roads and are hit by passing motorists

GYMNASTICS ON HORSEBACK

Kate Clancy traces the progress of the award-winning Pony Club display team.

The Pony Club display team, which has become such a popular attraction, again made appearances at a number of shows in the summer of 1988. The team of twenty is selected from members of the Chiddingfold branch of the Pony Club, who have been practising their vaulting hard throughout the winter and spring.

The display team is the brainchild of Mrs Peter Forwood, former assistant District Commissioner of the branch, who organised a musical ride to celebrate the Pony Club's jubilee in 1979. Six years later, she decided to organise a similar but rather more ambitious project with the help of Captain Barry McKie, riding master to the Household Cavalry and who has been in charge of some of their musical rides.

The intention was merely to give a display at the following year's Royal International Horse Show, but the performance was such a tremendous success that the team were awarded the Dorian Williams Memorial Trophy for making the greatest contribution to the show, and they have been in constant demand ever since

In 1986, the team made an appearance at the World Four-in-hand Carriage Driving Championships at Ascot, and in 1987 performed at the European Dressage Championships at Goodwood, and the National Carriage Driving Championships at Smiths Lawn, Windsor.

Nearly a quarter of the current riders are original team members, with the rest being more recent recruits. Their ages range from nine to fifteen years old, and of the twenty, only three are boys. They are all mounted on their own ponies, whose heights range from an 11.2-hand Dartmoor to a 14.2 pony. Anything much bigger would be difficult to vault on to.

Practices for the display begin in early winter, and anyone who is interested can come along and try for the team, regardless of standard.

Every person in the team must be able to perform the basic movement of vaulting on and off, and compulsory practice sessions take place for about three hours every Sunday morning, from November until the first display takes place in May, which is roughly the length of time it takes to train a pony and rider from scratch.

Although the display looks and sounds fairly complicated, there are only a few movements which pose a real headache for Captain McKie. These are the ones that involve combinations of horses and riders, such as when a rider stands on the backs of two ponies coupled at the girth.

The other difficult movement involves one pony being long-reined from the back of another, with a rider vaulting on, standing up, and then doing a shoulder stand. That looks hard, but is in fact the easy bit. It is the long-reining which can present the problem.

As well as straightforward vaulting, other movements are performed at a display, including sequences with the team divided into two rides, criss-crossing the arena one after the other, while jumping through a 'box' of cavalletti. After this, one of the riders usually falls, and tragically 'dies'. Other riders tenderly place the body in a coffin-shaped box, whereupon everybody takes turns in jumping over it. The 'body' then comes to life, and sits up wildly waving its arms between each pony. The finale features two riders galloping flat out down the length of the arena, vaulting continually over the backs of their ponies.

All the ponies are immaculately turned out, with plaited manes and small saddle blankets which are held in place with double-handled rollers. The riders are dressed in jodhpurs, sweatshirts of either blue or yellow, mauve crash hats, and soft shoes. The team goes to as many shows as possible during the summer, but with as many as twenty riders, getting everyone together and in the right place at the right time is something of an achievement in itself.

One of the most prestigious events was the opening of the Gleneagles, Mark Phillips Equestrian Centre, on 2 June 1988. The ponies travelled up by lorry, and the riders flew up, gave the display, and then flew back.

An invitation was received to perform at the Hanoverian horse sales in Germany in October 1988. The team was unable to go, as they have severe financial constraints. For this reason they are keen to attract a sponsor; being limited by large expenses, the team is only able to commit itself to a small number of displays each year. Despite being a great deal of hard work, the vaulting display is tremendous fun, and the riders say that the exercises have definitely improved their balance and riding. Their spectacular performances have already proved tremendously popular at major shows, and they are sure to give audiences further thrills in years to come.

Not to be attempted in your back yard! This specacular display is the result of a great deal of practice and hard work

Competition Ponies

SHOW JUMPING PONIES

Show jumping is still the most popular riding activity among young riders, and show jumping ponies are bought for their speed and jumping ability rather than their looks. Size is also important, because jumping classes are divided according to the size of the pony, and the amount that it has won show jumping at affiliated shows.

BSJA registration

In Britain there are thousands of show jumping competitions held for ponies and their riders every year. The standard varies greatly, but the top ponies show amazing dexterity and jumping ability, and fetch very high prices. They are registered with the British Show Jumping Association (BSJA), and ridden by some of the top young riders in the country, who must also be Junior members or Junior associate members of the BSJA, according to their age.

Junior membership is available until the end of the year that riders become sixteen, and an adult member of their immediate family must be a full member, and able to act on their behalf in all matters concerning show jumping competitions. The ponies also have to be registered in the name of an adult member of the family. Junior associate membership is rather similar regarding the rights and privileges, and is for children who are twelve years of age or over, but under sixteen on 1 January.

Ponies do not need to be registered with the BSJA to be able to jump at the majority of local shows, unless they are shows affiliated to the BSJA. Before competing in a show jumping competition in an affiliated show in which any prize exceeds £7, the rider and the pony must be registered. All subscriptions expire automatically on 31 December, and they must be renewed and the ponies re-registered before members are eligible to compete the following year. Members of the BSJA and their registered ponies are not allowed to take part in any show which is not affiliated to the Association if any prize for show jumping is valued at more than £7.

Grading

All ponies are graded according to their accumulated winnings, which enables competitions to be limited to a particular grade or grades, and this ensures fair competition between ponies of compa-

rable ability. There are more than 3,000 Junior members of the Association, and nearly 5,000 registered ponies.

The first grade of pony is the JD, which enables ponies which have not yet been registered to take part in an official competition, but at an unaffiliated show, until the pony has won a total of £20. It must then be registered as a grade JC, and it will be able to jump at affiliated shows in the very popular JC competitions until it has won a total of £300, when it will have to then go into the top grade and become one of the coveted JA jumping ponies.

Few JA ponies are rides for inexperienced riders. They are fast and keen, and used to jumping against the clock over some remarkably big courses, and their riders have to be well up to the task of handling them. The maximum height for a vertical fence in some of the JA competitions can be as much as 1.40m (4ft 9in), and spreads as much as 1.75m (5ft 9in) for a triple bar. Not the sort of course for a timid or inexperienced rider, but by the time a pony has reached the stage when it is jumping in JA competitions, it has proved that it has the scope and experience to tackle the big courses.

Height

The BSJA now deals in metric units for horse and pony heights, and any animal which is higher than 148cms will not be accepted for registration as a pony. The measurements are always taken without shoes, and a pony which has grades winnings of £50 or more will not be accepted for registration or re-registration until it has been measured under the rules of the Joint Measurement Scheme Limited, and a valid measurement certificate issued to the owner. The measurements are taken in imperial units to the nearest eighth of an inch, and then converted to metric units by using the official BSJA conversion table.

International competition

Ponies competing in international competitions abroad have to have a special passport issued through the BSJA, which includes an official FEI height certificate, along with all the relevant information about the pony. Although ponies may be registered before they are four, they are not allowed to compete in Britain or abroad until the beginning of the year in which the age of four is reached.

The course

It is the responsibility of the judge to walk the course before the start of a competition and to inspect all the obstacles, and if he feels that any alterations are necessary he will ask the course-builder to make the changes. The competitors are allowed to walk the course dismounted before the start of the competition. They are not allowed to walk the course again, unless the track has been substantially altered by the re-siting of the obstacles, before the start of a second or subsequent round, or the jump-off.

At some of the larger competitions the judge may decide to include one different obstacle in the jump-off which was not included in the first round, but it must not be unusual in character, and must conform with the height and spread restrictions applicable to the other fences. A plan of the course, including details of the jump-off, must be displayed in the collecting ring at least 30 minutes before the start of a competition, and the judge will have an identical plan.

The right type of pony

Although show jumping ponies are now frequently bred for the job, there are still many instances of ponies of unknown origin being bought at horse fairs and sales, who have developed into brilliantly successful show jumping ponies. Everything depends on the pony's courage, speed and jumping ability. Looks are of secondary importance – it is the pony which can jump accurately, and in the fastest time, which will win the competition.

WHERE SHOW JUMPING COMPETITIONS CAN BE WON OR LOST

Walk the course

The difference between winning and losing a show jumping competition may not only depend upon a clear round, but also on the seconds gained between fences in a jump-off against the clock. Competitors may even get time faults in the first round of a competition if they don't bother to walk the course properly before the class begins.

There is an old saying: 'If you don't know where you are going, any road will get you there!' It will pay to study the course plan carefully before going into the ring to walk the course. The course-builder will have designed the track to be followed, and the positions of the jumps, to be a fair test of pony and rider. The various different types of jump will be within the height and size limits allowed for that particular competition, and he will usually hope to get enough clear rounds to provide a good jump-off. Most show jumping competitions are sponsored, and so he will hope to provide enjoyment for the competitors and entertainment for those watching.

The judge will have checked that the course is in order before telling the commentator that it is all right to inform the competitors that they can walk the course.

The best place to start is before the start. In other words, having checked where the start is on the course plan, walk through the start and on to the first fence in the same way as you will when you are on the pony. Check you line carefully so that the pony will be able to get a good look at the fence, and have plenty of room to jump.

Opposite:
Up and over the wall

The course plan

According to the rules drawn up by the BSJA, a plan of the course must always be posted somewhere in the collecting ring, near the entrance to the arena. The course plan informs all the riders about the name of the class, whether there are any special rules, if it is also a qualifier for another competition, the speed they will be expected to go to complete the course within the time limit, the fences to be jumped and in which order, and the ones which will be used if there is a jump-off.

Walk the course properly

Although most ponies have a remarkable ability to 'find another leg' and put themselves right at the fence, the rider who has carefully worked out the best approach to each jump when walking the course before the start of the class, will be in a better position to give his pony a chance of meeting each one correctly. The pony will be properly balanced, with rhythm and impulsion, and will have the necessary speed to jump each fence properly, instead of having to 'fiddle' it and lose a lot of time in doing so, quite apart from probably knocking down a pole or two as well.

Be flexible if things go wrong

While walking the course it is as
well to consider the best route to
take if things don't go according
to plan and the pony perhaps has
a fence or two down. The tight
turns which might have been
planned will no longer be
necessary, and it might be wiser
to take a different course so that
he will have a better chance of
regaining his confidence, and
picking up fewer show jumping
penalties, by being allowed to
take a longer and more straightforward approach to the
remaining fences on the course.
By looking at the approaches to
each jump and by walking the
various different lines which
could be taken, a good show
jumping rider will know not
only whether the strides into the
fence may be a bit short or a
little long for his pony, he will
also be working out the
alternative route he will take if a
change of plan does become
necessary.

The approach to the first fence, and to some of the others, may be
partially blocked by another fence, particularly if the competition is
being held in an indoor arena with a limited amount of space
available. If there isn't a clear line to the fence it may be better if your
pony makes his approach leading with one leg rather than the other,
so that he has a better chance of coming into the fence on a good
stride.

Study the jumps *and* the approach
Walking the course is not the time for a good chat with your friends
– because it is the only opportunity you will have of trying to puzzle
out why the course-builder has designed the course in a particular
way, and how you are going to out-think him. He will be trying to
catch out those riders who haven't paid attention, those who, apart
from just checking where each fence is and the order in which they
have to be jumped, have been more interested in turning the event
into a social occasion. He knows that the wise and more experienced
riders will be carefully noting the approach to each fence, the number
of strides between each element of the doubles and trebles, and
whether the poles are particularly light and may be easier to topple
out of their cups. It is only the rider who has a good opportunity to
study each fence beforehand – the first the pony will see of the jumps
is when he comes into the arena , the bell goes, and he is on his way
to the first fence.

Assess the going
If the competition is out in the open there will be a number of other
aspects to consider. The position of the sun can be important – if it
is behind a jump it may be difficult for the pony to see the obstacle
properly, or it may be casting shadows which can also be a problem.
Sometimes courses are built on the side of a hill, which will mean that
the pony will be taking longer strides going down the slope towards
a jump and will probably be going more quickly; however, he will
have to work harder to make the same distance going uphill.

The state of the ground will also have to be taken into consideration. The pony may need studs to get a better grip going into the
fences and on the turns, but what type of stud will be best for the
occasion? If it is very slippery then tight turns may be out of the
question, but again it is a matter of knowing the pony's capabilities.
A sure-footed, experienced, older pony may be able to cope with the
conditions far better than a young animal with less confidence and
experience. It wouldn't be worth upsetting a good young pony with
real potential by making him take unnecessary chances which might
affect his confidence and enjoyment of jumping.

Approaching a fence
A great deal is talked about a rider being able to 'see a stride', which
really means being able to place the horse or pony in exactly the right
take-off spot as it approaches a fence. Many show jumpers think they
can see a stride, but in fact there are far more who cannot, and it is
much better to make sure that when approaching a jump a pony has
balance, rhythm, impulsion, and not too much speed. He will then
have a much better chance of jumping the fence well. The approach
to each jump should begin from the moment the pony lands after the

preceding fence, so it is important to look at the correct line long before the next fence is reached.

Warming up

After taking a final look at the course and checking how much time there is before your pony is due into the arena, it is important to make the best use of the remainder of the warming-up period. Much will depend on the age, experience and temperament of each different pony as to how that time is spent. Young ponies are often excited when they arrive at a show and will need time to settle down. They will need to be walked around and allowed to become accustomed to all the sights and sounds before being asked to concentrate on the jumping.

Old ponies will know what to expect, but they may need to get rid of a little stiffness, particularly if they have been standing in a trailer or horsebox for some time. All ponies need time to limber up so that they are warm and supple before being asked to jump, but they don't want to be worked so hard that they will become tired before being asked to perform. About twenty minutes work on the flat, which means simply walking, trotting and cantering, will usually be sufficient, and the pony will then be ready to have a few 'pops' over the practice fences. The collecting ring can be a busy place, but it should be possible to find a quiet corner where your pony can be ridden round quietly until he is ready to have a practice jump. He should be ridden in a circle, first one way and then the other, so that he will change the lateral bend through his body.

The practice fence

The show should provide two practice fences, one an upright and the other a spread fence. It is not advisable, and in some instances it is also against the rules, to practise over obstacles other than the official ones in the collecting area. The practice fences should be flagged, and must only be jumped in the direction indicated by the flags – the white flag on the left and the red one on the right. Nor is there any point in rushing up to the practice fence and expecting other people to get out of the way. The fence may already be at the correct height for you, but it is always best to have a friend with you who can set the jump at the correct height and put the poles back in place if you knock them off; otherwise you will have to get off every time you want to make an alteration. The usual practice is for your helper to assist in putting up the poles for some of the other riders waiting to jump, and then when they have finished you will be free to choose the height you require.

Always start with the practice fence very low so that the pony can approach it at a trot, or a slow canter; cross poles are popular at this stage, because they will guide the pony naturally to the centre of the jump. The next stage will be to raise the height a little and jump it in a canter, first on the one lead and then on the other, before progressing to a low spread fence, which can then be gradually built up. If the pony makes a poor jump, try to fathom out why, then if you can, correct the problem and jump the fence again. It may be necessary to revert to the previous height for a jump or two, until he is jumping happily again. When he jumps well he should be rewarded with a pat. It is unwise to give him tit-bits just before going into the ring.

Don't show off

Some people use the practice fence as a means of showing off their riding ability to anyone prepared to watch; others use it to see how high their pony can jump; and there are those who rush up at the last minute for one frantic leap before dashing into the ring. None of these riders will get the best from their ponies – they forget that they are riding an athlete, who must be given the best chance of performing well by being allowed to enter the ring in the right frame of mind, as well as being warm and supple.

A word of warning

Don't stop and gossip with friends just before your turn in the ring. You won't do much winning if you don't jump clear, and you won't jump clear without a lot of preparation and sensible thinking. The time for a good chat will be before the prize giving, when all the hard work and thought has been rewarded and you and the pony are waiting to receive that rosette.

Riding over the practice fence will reveal how the pony is feeling and the mood he is in, and it will also enable him to adjust to the going. Jumping in the collecting ring should allow both pony and rider to relax, and gain confidence together by jumping the practice fences when they are placed at the same height and spread as those in the ring. Sometimes it is against the rules to jump practice fences that are any higher. It is important to allow an extra few minutes in case anything goes wrong so that any problems can be sorted out without a panic. Try to finish with a good, confidence-boosting jump, and then walk the pony round quietly to keep him warm and supple until it is your turn to go into the ring.

HUNTER TRIALS AND HORSE TRIALS

Hunter trials are an excellent training ground for potential young event riders, and they and their ponies can be introduced to all sorts of natural fences without having to cope with the dressage and show jumping phases of a horse trial. Hunter trial courses are usually rather more straightforward than those built for horse trials, and they sometimes involve opening and closing a gate during a specially timed section. The fences are usually fixed, without any poles which can be knocked down as in show jumping.

Ponies have to be bold and enjoy their jumping, and there have been many instances of a pony, which has become bored with show jumping, regaining his enthusiasm after being allowed to enjoy himself galloping and jumping across country. The hedges, ditches, post and rails, gates, banks, drop fences and water jumps to be found on a cross-country course provide an exciting challenge to both pony and rider; the ability to complete the course within the time allowed is usually the deciding factor.

Horse trials

Many young event riders gain their first experience of horse trials in the competitions organised by the Pony Club branches. Although the cross-country phase is important, the ponies and their riders also have to take part in dressage and show jumping, which is why eventing is always looked upon as being the test of the complete horseman.

A well-schooled pony is essential – it has to show obedience in the dressage, accuracy in the show jumping, and boldness and agility as well as speed on the cross country. Until quite recently, a pony which could jump well and could show a good turn of foot could overcome a poor dressage score; nowadays, however, a good dressage performance is very important. That is why a good all-round performance is needed to win.

DRESSAGE PONIES

In the same way that riders are finding that dressage is important in horse trials, show jumpers are also realising that dressage training can make their horses and ponies more obedient and adaptable. For some years, dressage has been looked upon by continental riders as being the key to all good horsemanship, and an essential part of every horse and pony's training.

Dressage ponies have to be supple, and be able to perform a set test involving movements at the walk, trot, and canter. Each movement

Tackling a cross-country water obstacle in fine style

is marked out of ten, with extra points being awarded for freedom and regularity of paces, impulsion, obedience, acceptance of the bit, the position of the rider and the correct use of the aids. A smart appearance helps to create a more pleasing picture and is also courteous to the judges. The ponies should be plaited; whips and martingales are not allowed, neither are boots and bandages in the dressage arena, although they may be worn during the warming-up period. Most ponies are capable of doing a reasonable dressage test, and in those competitions where ponies and horses are able to compete in the same class, the ponies have sometimes come out best.

COMPETING WITHOUT TEARS

Anne-Marie Hancock gives some advice on how to make the most of a day at a competition

A day out with your pony can prove to be the greatest fun, but not without considerable forethought and hard work on your part. It is never possible to get 'something for nothing', and a really satisfying day requires a lot of effort and planning. Whether you decide on a competitive or a 'fun' day, it is your choice and do not let anyone bully you otherwise!

With sufficient forward planning, everything will run smoothly and you will be prepared for any and every eventuality. Make sure that you are completely familiar with the rules of the competition, so that you can go into the ring well versed and practised in what you intend to do. If you have never taken part before, go and ask for advice. It is much easier to act on somebody else's personal experience than a wild fantasy dreamed up by you!

Be aware of what you should wear, and if there are any special rulings on the tack you may use. Try not to go over the top with your turnout, as this can be just as much of an eyesore as an untidy horse and rider.

Once you have decided on the type of competition you would like to have a go at, then it is up to you to find a suitable show or event with an appropriate date and venue. Something that clashes with your grandmother's seventieth birthday party may not go down too well, and having to travel miles over land and sea to get there is not altogether practical!

If you are a Pony Club member, your branch should be able to provide you with the relevant information; also, several magazines and the local newspaper publish dates of competitions with the addresses and telephone numbers of their secretaries. It is then up to you to make your entries in good time, and written clearly so that the hardworking secretary knows exactly what you are intending to compete in. Enter classes for which you feel capable, do not overface yourselves or attempt anything totally impractical – it may be fun for experience, but it will be pretty demoralising if you enter a nice family pony in a hack class. Keep in mind that the whole day should be for the mutual enjoyment of you and your pony.

It is much more fun to take a crowd of supporters with you who can share your interest; in which case make sure that facilities for their enjoyment are also laid on. Persuade your mother to produce one of her famous picnics, and encourage your father with remarks about the excellence of the beer tent (don't mention the queues!). A happy crowd of supporters is always a real morale booster, and they can often be a great help just when you need it. Make sure, however, that you ask the sort of people who will enjoy it. Unless they are complete horse addicts, there are not many who can sit all day long watching nothing but horses and ponies, so invite them to a show where there are other attractions which they will find interesting.

Desperately keen support can, however, be rather overwhelming. It is a great pity to see some poor child getting the sharp edge of his trainer's tongue – or worse still, his mother's – because he has failed to come out of the ring with the first rosette. You know your horse's limitations better than anyone. It is often tempting to overdo it, but in the end the greatest enjoyment for both of you will come from being successful at something you can cope with.

Always ensure that everything is prepared by the day before; everything for your pony's and your own maximum comfort, including precautions against our unpredictable weather! Try not to exhaust yourself in your preparations, or get up too horrendously early on The Day – do not forget that you are actually doing it for your enjoyment. There is a lot more to life than winning the blue riband, so bear that in mind; it is a nice goal, but not vital.

Watching some jockeys, one wonders really why they bother at all – the whole performance looks so painfully miserable and dull, and is written all over their faces. It is very important to be dignified, whether you win or lose, and to be a good sport. It is one of the hardest things in the world to be a good loser, but you will be respected for it; it is surprising how often a rider can be seen behaving badly and being angry with his unfortunate mount, totally inappropriately, and mainly because the rider has been over-ambitious or badly prepared.

On The Day, always know exactly how to get to the event – after all the hard work, it would be a shame to arrive late, so allow sufficient travelling or hacking time and enough for a good breather when you get there. Find your way around the showground so that you know exactly where everything is, and then collect your number. There is nothing more flustering than having insufficient time in which to get organised.

If you hack to the competition, find a suitable place to base yourself when you arrive – if it is possible to be near a tree or a hedge for shelter, all the better. If you have been successful in your persuasion of supporters, make sure that there is adequate space for their car or picnic rugs, and that your chosen site will also suit them.

Always be punctual and polite to the stewards, who are usually there on a voluntary basis and specifically to help you. Keep one ear tuned to the loudspeaker system so that you are on the ball and know what is going on. Speak out clearly to the stewards, as with all the hustle and bustle it may be difficult for them to understand (which does not imply that they are often hard of hearing!).

Don't stay on your pony's back longer than you have to; let him rest and enjoy himself as well, as a pony that has been ridden into the ground all day long will be unlikely to give of his best. If there is the chance between classes, why not put him back in the horsebox or let him rest under a tree? It is unwise, however, to let him gorge himself on grass or hay – although *you* know how he will be happiest, so act accordingly. At all times keep in mind that, with the best will in the world and despite all the precautions you might take, accidents can still happen; so, keep switched on!

Try and achieve in your day whatever you set out to do. If you aim to get your young horse into, and around, the show jumping arena for the first time, achieve that and try not to get carried away with the moment. If you do get into the jump-off, it would be very easy to ruin everything by overfacing him and going too fast.

Jumping classes require thought in walking and learning the course. Put your number down at the collecting ring in plenty of time, work out roughly when you will need to be ready; there is nothing more trying for the poor steward than having to call your number for half an hour before you bother to turn up.

If you are showing, do not forget that you are in the ring for the judge to see, so do not disappear to the outside or allow yourself to be 'ridden-off' into the middle distance by other competitors where he will need a telescope to have a look at you. Place yourself well, and not bunched up with a lot of other riders.

You will probably need a 'groom' to come into the ring to help you 'strip' your pony in preparation for the conformation judging, so don't leave this until the eleventh hour to organise. A friend or your mother can usually be persuaded to come into the ring, and it is also nice to have someone to chat to while you are standing in line, as it can often be a long wait.

When you run your horse up, give the judge the chance to have a good look. Run to him and on past so that he can assess the straightness of your horse's movement. If you are asked to perform an individual ridden show, make it clear and concise, showing walk, trot and canter, a gallop if required, and a good halt.

If there is an official prize-giving, either mounted or unmounted and you are involved, make sure that you are present on time, clean and well turned out: it is the least you can do by way of showing your appreciation to the organisers and sponsors.

Hanging around for hours on your pony will only make him bored and tired, and it is easy to forget that once all the excitement is over, you have still got to get yourselves home and to bed! A cheery 'Goodbye' and a 'Thank You' to the secretary for all his hard work and for such an enjoyable day will be well received; and after packing up, you can be on your way home.

The drive or hack will always seem longer when you are tired. Try not to let it overcome you completely, because when you get home you will still have your horse to see to. But it is always enjoyable, when making him comfortable, to reflect on the day's achievements. What you have learned, the new experiences you have encountered, and how much you have enjoyed each other's company – because, let's face it, it could not be done alone.

A (slightly damp) rider shares the apple from the bobbing race with his pony

HOW TO COPE WITH
THE DREADED DRESSAGE

*Former junior international dressage rider, Anne-Marie Hancock, who is now competing at
Grand Prix level, gives some advice on riding a dressage test.*

Was that a loud groan? Are you one of those people who loathe their dressage? Here are some ideas which might help to make it easier to understand and, hopefully, much more enjoyable.

Before you arrive at a competition, make sure that you know the test inside-out and back-to-front! Try and ride it through in your mind, just as you would a cross-country course. Be mentally prepared for anything that might happen so that you are ready and do not react in the wrong way.

It does not make the slightest difference if your mother, your Great Aunt Matilda or your trainer (if you are lucky enough to have one) want you to ride the test: they can give you every morsel of advice they can think of, and more, beforehand but in the end you are the person riding your pony and it is all up to you.

Think of presenting yourself to the judge as the picture you would like her to see: confident, well turned out, and elegant as well if you can manage it. The judges are there to help you; they are not The Enemy, and World War III will not break out the minute you enter at A. Keep it calm and steady, as this enables your judge to have a good look at you; try not to race around the arena – there is no prize for the fastest test of the day!

Riding your test accurately and smoothly is very important. Keeping straight down the centre line can be made easier if you focus on, and keep looking at, either the roof of your judge's car or the crown of her wide-brimmed sunhat. Do not take your eyes off it, and ride all the way up the line, including the halts and transitions, in one forward flowing movement. The moment you look down, the wobbles will begin!

A beaming smile when you salute at the beginning and end of your test will earn you no extra marks, but it will help to build a rapport with your judge. If, through misery or nervousness, you cannot face a smile, try baring your teeth because it has exactly the same effect!

A clear, unhurried and relaxed salute helps to accentuate the halt, and if you are one of those people who takes an enormous gulp at X and then does not breathe again until it is all over, try humming a tune as you ride. This will help you to breathe, is relaxing, and will ensure that you do not pass out half-way through the test!

Simple arithmetic is all that is needed to work out

exactly how to use the arena and where to position the movements correctly. Using the corners does not mean that your poor horse must contort himself through a right angle. He must complete a smooth turn, and you must not allow him to 'escape' or collapse to the inside.

It helps if you do actually turn your head on your shoulders as you progress around the arena and look for the next marker. How do people who appear mesmerised by their horses' necks ever know where they are going?

Diagonals need to be approached by a good turn through the corner: continue this turn out onto the diagonal, then aim and ride for a point on the far track just short of the quarter marker, so that you can join the track smoothly, ready to negotiate the last corner or ride a transition.

Only you know how long it takes for your pony to respond to your aid for a transition. Ideally, it should take place in a single stride, but sadly this is not an ideal world, and you may both need one, four, or even six strides to complete it. The actual transition must take place at the marker, so start to prepare for it as many strides away from the marker as you need. A gradual, smooth and relaxed transition will earn you more marks than pulling helplessly at Bracken and praying that it will be instantaneous.

Imagine circles to be diamond-shaped. Ride to the four points, trying to take only a couple of strides at each one, and miraculously you should find yourself riding a perfect circle.

Twenty-metre circles span the width of the arena: when ridden from C or A, they must reach X; when ridden from B or E, the other two points are on the centre line but unmarked, four metres in from D and G.

A fifteen-metre circle from B or from E must go out to an imaginary point which would be five metres in from the opposite marker; and a ten-metre circle spans the width between the track and the centre line. At F and M the ten-metre circle will go through the points D or G respectively and must fall one metre inside the short side of the arena.

Half-circles involve only three points of the diamond, so a half-circle of twenty metres from E or B includes these two points, and the third invisible point on the centre line.

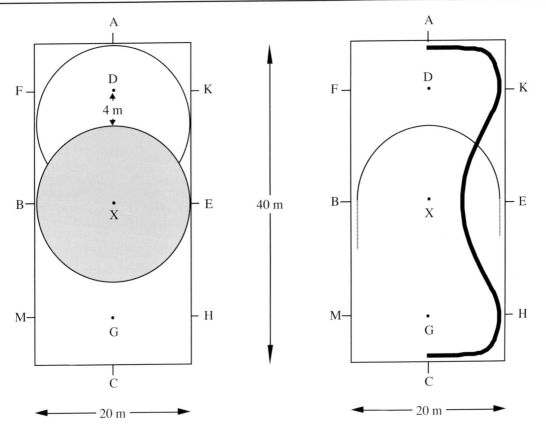

Half ten-metre circles at M and H include a point at G and must fall one metre in from the short side. These half-circles, which are often followed by a return to the track either between E and K, or between B and F, should be ridden as a continuous movement: on completing the half-circle at G, continue for just a bit on the bend of the circle until your pony is lined up with a point on the track – keep your eye on this point and ride straight for it, joining the track in a smooth turn to complete the movement.

Five-metre half circles at B and E, returning to the track before F and K, are ridden in the same way, but the halfway point is an imaginary point five metres between B or E and X.

A loop of five metres in from the track, between H and K or vice versa, is easily ridden as long as you complete a good approach corner. At the quarter marker, aim and ride for the widest point of the loop, halfway between E and X, and then for the point just before the second quarter marker, so that you can finish with a smooth turn back onto the track, and through the final corner.

A serpentine of three loops needs a little care, but is simple when you know exactly where you are going. Imagine the arena divided widthways into three rectangles – the line of your serpentine will follow these shapes. Round off one end of each rectangle so that you complete three smooth loops,

Left: Twenty-metre circles

Right: The fine line show a half-circle of twenty metres from E or B, the thick line a loop of five metres in from the track

and link them with several clear strides on the two straight lines which cross the centre line at right angles.

Although a dressage test is made up of a number of separate movements, try to link them together so that you ride the whole test smoothly and continuously from beginning to end.

Instead of feeling frustrated about your dressage, do ask for some advice. Remember that the judges are not monsters, waiting to attack you every time you pass C. If you ask them nicely they will be only too willing to discuss your problems.

Collecting and reading your sheets at the end of the day will probably provide you with some very good ideas to take away and intelligently chew over. All of us – D-test riders, area horse trials team members, instructors, or dressage enthusiasts – are in the same boat. We are trying to improve and become more knowledgeable about dressage and the training of our horses and ponies. So enjoy yourselves – and good luck!

Show Ponies

THE MODERN SHOW PONY

The clean and streamlined looks of the show pony can be misleading: although it is looked upon by some as being over-cosseted, spindly legged and useless, the modern show pony is actually much tougher than it may seem. Breeding top quality riding ponies has always caused considerable conjecture and argument but English show ponies are now the envy of the world, due in part to the very high standard of the show classes at even the smaller local shows, and also to the quality and choice of the native ponies who still form the basis for breeding the most outstanding ponies.

The characteristics of hardiness, honesty and strength have had to be retained. People want a riding pony to look like one, and those who have tried to breed little horses instead of true ponies have had to think again, especially where lightness of bone has sometimes in the past been mistaken as a sign of quality. The British Show Pony Society was founded in October 1949 to protect and improve the showing of children's riding ponies in Britain, and has been responsible for improving the standard in all showing classes.

A perfect picture – six-year-old Ami Wiggins riding her champion leading rein pony Weston Velvet, led by her mother

The NPS

The National Pony Society works for the preservation and improvement of native ponies, and for the welfare of all ponies, and produces an annual stud book and register of British riding ponies which provides an accurate record of pony breeding. The society stages an annual two-day show for all the native breeds and British riding ponies, and this offers an unrivalled opportunity for people to see British ponies at their best; it also organises auction sales of ponies, many of which are top-class show ponies.

The BSPS

The British Show Pony Society, however, was formed because of the enormous increase in the popularity and number of entries in children's riding pony classes, and is responsible for promoting and standardising classes and competitions for show ponies, show hunter ponies and working hunter ponies, for riders aged between three and twenty-one years. The society also runs two major annual championship shows, and there are also more than 500 affiliated shows.

Breeding the riding pony

Riding ponies for the show ring are usually custom-bred by crossing a native pony with a small Thoroughbred, and then if the result is a filly, putting her back to the native pony. There is often some Arab blood to be found in the best show ponies, but too much will spoil the results.

Stallions which continually produce prize-winning ponies can become almost a cult. One such stallion was Bwlch Valentino, who was by a Thoroughbred polo pony out of a Welsh pony mare. His sons Zephyr and Hill Wind have also been responsible for breeding some outstandingly successful animals.

Some breeders are tempted to use the same bloodlines for the dam and the sire for too long, without any infusion of fresh native blood; this often results in the ponies of frail and weedy quality to be found in some of the show classes and which are the target for show pony critics.

However much care is taken in the selection of the sire and the dam, the result can sometimes be disappointing. To get everything right – grace, beauty, conformation, speed and courage, as well as temperament – is every breeder's hope, and very high prices are frequently paid for top quality animals. Many of these have been exported to ride, to compete with, and to breed from, in all corners of the world. A change of stables and a change of rider, however, doesn't always mean continued success, and producing the right pony and rider partnership at top level is far from easy.

In the show pony classes the judges look for an elegant, free-moving and well-mannered quality pony. The classes start with leading rein and first ridden for ponies not exceeding 12 hands, followed by 12.2, 13.2, 14.2 and 15 hand novice, restricted, and open show ponies. There are also classes for side saddle and pairs. The riders' ages range from three to eighteen years.

The leading rein class

The leading rein class is for child riders of seven years old and under, and the ponies, which must be four years old or over, have two height

---

Pretty Polly

Pretty Polly was one of the best show ponies ever bred. By the Arab Naseel, out of a part-bred 13.2 hands Welsh mare Gypsy Gold, Pretty Polly was bred at St Kells, County Meath by Mrs Stephanie Nicholson, and sold to Mrs Gray, Warrenpoint, County Down as a two-year-old.

She was ridden by Barbara Falloon to win the Dublin Spring Show before being sold to Mr Robert Hanson, coming to England in July 1950. Pretty Polly was then purchased by the late Keith Lee-Smith for Mr Albert Deptford, and joined his string of ponies at the Lee-Smith establishment for nine-year-old Davina Lee-Smith to ride. Polly was shown four times prior to the Horse of the Year Show at Harringay that year, where she won the title of Pony of the Year. She won the same title in 1951, and her great grand-daughter, Holly of Spring, won the Pony of the Year title four years in succession, ridden by Cathryn Cooper and produced by Pretty Polly's rider Davina Whiteman, who was Davina Lee-Smith before her marriage.

The Persian

The Persian is a typical oriental breed, beautiful and full of quality, as well as being high-spirited and speedy, which made it a great favourite with Islam warriors. It was known as a breed for many centuries BC, and is believed to be descended from the Tarpan and possibly the ancestor of the Arab. There are now several different breeds in Persia including the Persian Arab, the Turkoman, the Shirazi, the Yamoote and the Bokara pony.

The 13.2 hands show pony Creden Keepsake, ridden here by nine-year-old Louisa Clarke when winning the Championship at Royal Windsor in 1987. Creden Keepsake went on to become the Riding Pony of the Year at Wembley in 1988

Nicola Madeley and Coney Morning Joy have notched up a long list of successes in showing classes

*Although only eight, Shelly Dixon
is perfectly at home riding
sidesaddle on the ten-year old
pony mare Greenacres Bouquet*

classes, not exceeding 11.2 hands, and 11.2 to 12 hands. They are shown in snaffle bridles with the lead rein attached to the noseband. Perfect manners are essential, and any sign of misbehaviour will be penalised once they are in the show ring.

There are usually two types of leading rein pony: one that looks like a miniature blood pony and is a real eye-catcher, although hardly the right mount for a small child; and the other that is a sturdier type with a 'bombproof' temperament. Much will depend on the judge's personal preference as to which type he chooses on the day.

Every pony should be taught to go on the end of a lead rein while his young rider has just enough contact with the mouth, but the ponies will probably need to be lunged for a while before they go into the ring in case they become too fresh and dislodge their young charges. Those leading the ponies must be smartly dressed in clothes which are suitable for the conditions underfoot. Men should wear a suit and a bowler hat.

The first ridden class

Ponies in the first ridden class must not exceed 12 hands, and should be four years of age or over, with riders nine or under. The judge will be looking for a well-mannered pony which goes quietly and freely forward, with the child obviously well in charge.

As in the leading rein class, the ponies must be shown in a snaffle bridle, but this time they have to be ridden off the lead rein; the riders will be required to walk and trot when going round the ring together, and canter when they do their own individual shows.

The 12.2 hands class

Children of twelve years or under can compete in the 12.2 hand class, provided that their ponies are at least four. As well as being well mannered, the ponies will be expected to have a considerable amount of quality and be suitable for a young rider to show. They need to be well schooled, and their riders will have to show a change of rein at the canter and a few strides of gallop. Many successful 12.2 hand ponies have Welsh blood, but it is important that they are not too thick in the shoulder, and have a long, scopey stride for their size.

The British Show Pony Society

Showing ponies prior to 1950 used to be a very haphazard business, with animals being measured just as they were entering the ring, and riders of various ages. In 1949 the winner of the class for novice ponies at the Royal Richmond Show was found to be a well-known champion of previous years, and ridden by a child well over the age limit; this controversial result led to the founding of the British Show Pony Society. The decision was reached at a meeting called by John Tilling, Peter Knowland and Brigadier Allen, and was attended by Sir Berkeley Piggot and 'Bill' Benson from the National Pony Society. After four hours of furious discussion, a set of rules was drawn up and a panel of judges nominated. Under the chairmanship of John Tilling the society began with 26 members: it now has more than 2,500 adults, 2,000 junior members, and 3,000 registered ponies.

Competing abroad

The British Show Pony Society sends teams to take part in international competitions in many countries, including Eire, Germany, and Scotland.

A good foundation

Many riders who have been successful in other equestrian activities, including show jumping and eventing, started their competitive careers in show pony classes; the same is true of some of Britain's most successful men and women jockeys. As a thirteen-year-old, Guy Landau had considerable success in the show ring with a pony called Cuckoo; in 1987 he rode Lean Ar Aghaidh, trained by Stan Mellor, into third place in the Grand National at Aintree, and then went on to win the Whitbread Gold Cup on the same horse.

BSPS fellowship

The British Show Pony Society awarded its first fellowship to Mrs Joan Gibson, who, as chairman in 1988, led the society through one of its most active and successful years on record. Major developments included the Riding for the Disabled Association championships, the evening performance at the winter show, and the 'growing up' classes for riders up to twenty-five years old, on horses up to 15.2 hands high, which started in 1989.

The society has also been successful in promoting its activities and making itself known to the public. Special awards and scholarships were introduced for outstanding achievements. The BSPS has worked hard to ensure that the ideal of the working hunter pony leads to the improvement of the ordinary pony for the ordinary child, rather than confining it to glamorous looks in the show ring.

The 13.2 hands class

One of the strongest classes to win nowadays is for show ponies which exceed 12.2 hands but are not higher than 13.2 hands, ridden by children of fourteen years or under. For many years breeders have been trying to produce ponies for this class which have a considerable amount of real quality while still retaining all the necessary pony characteristics. Their riders will be expected to perform polished and fluent individual shows, and the ponies will need to have enough scope to cover the ground well. A good overall appearance and a pleasing combination are important.

The 14.2 hands class

It is increasingly difficult to find an outstanding 14.2 show pony with the necessary scope to win the 13.2 to 14.2 hand class, partly because ponies of this size are frequently more like small horses and tend to look too horsey. Some ponies in this class have the necessary pony characteristics but lack the required scope and size.

The successful ponies need to have correct conformation, with a good sloping shoulder and an attractive pony-type head. They must be bold and forward-going, and children up to sixteen years old should be capable of riding them. The riders have to be able to gallop the ponies really well, and give controlled and pleasurable individual shows.

It is important that they really are ponies of quality, rather than small hacks without pony blood, and although being able to gallop, they must be well mannered and obedient and not hot up.

The 15 hands class

Although they cannot really be classed as ponies when they are over 14.2 hands in height, those animals between 14 and 15 hands, ridden by children between fourteen and eighteen years, do serve a very useful purpose. The transition from ponies to larger show horses is not easy for many riders, and this class does offer an opportunity for older children to gain additional experience before going into adult classes. It also offers a chance to children with overgrown 14.2 hand ponies.

The majority of children's pony side-saddle classes are now for ponies four years or over and up to 15 hands, with riders seventeen years and under. As in all the show classes, the ponies and their young riders have to give an individual show to the judges who will be looking for the right type of animal to carry a rider side-saddle, and the overall picture which the rider and pony give will be very important. Keen young side-saddle riders can now compete in junior side-saddle equitation classes, and there are also classes at many shows for pony pairs which are judged on matching looks, turnout and the way in which the ponies go as a pair. The height limit for the ponies is again 15 hands, and the age limit for the riders seventeen.

Novice pony classes

The novice pony classes which some shows are now staging are becoming increasingly popular. There are usually classes for 12.2, 13.2 and 14.2 hands, although sometimes, when there is insufficient time available, there is only one class for ponies up to 14.2 hands. The permitted age for the riders is the same as for the open show pony classes. To be a novice the pony must be four years of age or over and have never won a first prize of £5 or more in any affiliated British Show Pony Society class. Ponies who win a first prize of £5 or more in an open pony class, or an open pony championship, will automatically be classed as an open show pony from then onwards.

Three-year-old ponies can be shown from 1 July of that year, but only in novice classes, and they must be shown in snaffle bridles. Spurs are forbidden in all show pony classes. When judging novice classes the judges will sometimes overlook a certain amount of greenness, providing that they like the general finish of the pony and they feel that it has the right potential.

The hunter type
Since 1984 there have been classes for ponies of hunter type; this has given an opportunity to children who have ponies which may go on to make top quality working hunter ponies or eventers. There are three height and age groups : the first is for ponies not exceeding 13 hands and children fourteen years and under; the second is for ponies not exceeding 14 hands and children of sixteen years and under; and the third is for animals not exceeding 15 hands and riders of eighteen years and under. The judges in these classes are from the working hunter pony panel rather than from the BSPS show pony panel.

The working hunter pony
Not to be confused with the ponies of hunter type, the working hunter pony is a very versatile pony which must have good conformation and manners, but also be able to gallop and jump. Because it is a relatively new class compared with the many riding pony classes, and because more is expected of the working hunter pony, it may still take some time before a level standard is achieved – but its popularity is assured.

For some years now shows have been encouraged to hold classes for working hunter ponies, and for youngstock of that type, and there have been some very impressive champions who are now the foundation stock of the future. A number of studs are catering expressly for the demands of working hunter pony owners, while others are now breeding both types of show pony to cope with the demand.

Working hunter ponies have been increasing steadily in value, and very high prices have been paid for potential champions. The goal of every working hunter pony enthusiast is the Peterborough Championships, held annually in September, and ponies have to qualify for the championships at various shows during the season. It takes a very good pony to win the championships, and so there is every reason why high prices are paid for the few who are successful there.

Judging
The judging in the working hunter pony classes is easier to follow because they are judged in two phases: sixty points are awarded for the way in which each pony jumps a set course of natural obstacles, including its style and manners when jumping, and penalties are given for knock-downs and refusals; and a further forty points are awarded in the second phase for conformation, freedom of action and manners.

Origins of the class
The working hunter pony classes were the brain child of the late Keith Lee-Smith. In 1960, through the generosity of Mr C.R. Driver, a member of the BSPS council, a team of six American children came to England to compete against a team of British children and Keith Lee-Smith, who was also a member of the BSPS council, was invited to train the British team.

When they received details of the suggested Team Championship class, however, the BSPS council realised that the ponies would be required to jump a small course of natural fences, as in the American classes. This caused some concern and twelve children were hastily chosen. They spent two weeks prior to the event at Allerton Equitation School, Alconbury Hill, the Lee-Smith's riding establishment, training their ponies to jump, as British show ponies had never previously jumped.

The team competition was held at the British Timkin Show, Duston, Northampton in August 1960, but although the conformation of the British ponies was far superior to the Americans, they lost marks on jumping and did not win the team event.

After the competition, Keith Lee-Smith suggested to the BSPS council that they should introduce a jumping phase into the pony classes, but the proposition failed to get support and Mr William Benson was the only council member to vote in favour.

It was after this defeat in council that Keith Lee-Smith approached his friend Glenda Spooner and suggested that she should include a ridden pony section at her Summer Show, to be judged on jumping and performance. Glenda immediately agreed – these very popular classes were the first working hunter pony classes, and they continued annually at the Ponies of Britain shows.

continued

continued

In 1969, some nine years later, the BSPS Chairman, Brigadier Allen, agreed to a small Committee being formed to look into the possibility of producing a marks system and a set of rules, including the height of the fences, and to consider a working hunter pony section. Under the Chairmanship of the late Albert Deptford the WHPs held their first Championship at the East of England Showground with about 80 ponies competing.

The ideal working hunter pony

It has been said that the ideal working hunter pony has the looks and substance of a small hunter, the performance of a working hunter, and the size and quality of a pony. Is it any wonder that the search for the perfect working hunter pony is still continuing!

Even so, the standard requirement is more difficult to establish. A show pony type which may be rather plain and lack bone below the knee, will not find success among the working hunter ponies, although some owners of poor quality show ponies have tried. The true working hunter pony must have performance and be clever, willing, bold and agile, as well as being free-moving and fast. Good looks are also important, and a quality pony of hunter type, who looks capable of going well across country and presents a happy picture with his rider, is the one most likely to catch the eye of the judge.

Jumping

The ability to jump fluently and well is important, and a pony which may be rather on the plain side but which is a good, straight, level mover and performs well, will be preferred to the pretty pony with a more flashy movement who does not, however, jump fluently. The main criterion is that he should he suitable for carrying a child well in the hunting field.

Graded classes

There are various classes according to the size of the pony and the age of the rider. The cradle stakes is for ponies not exceeding 12 hands, with riders of nine years and under; the nursery stakes for ponies not exceeding 13 hands and riders of eleven years and under; then a class for ponies not exceeding 13 hands but riders fourteen years and under; then ponies exceeding 13 hands but not exceeding 14 hands with riders sixteen and under; and ponies exceeding 14 hands but not more than 15 hands, with riders eighteen years of age and under. There are also novice classes for ponies who have not won a first prize of £5 or more in a British Show Pony Society affiliated class the previous year before 1 October. Again, spurs are not allowed and the ponies must be four years of age or more.

PONIES THAT ARE PURE GOLD

Palominos have appeared in stories and paintings from earliest history, and in Spain Queen Isabella owned many golden horses and ponies which were known as 'Golden Isabellas', or 'Ysabellas' in her honour. Even so, Palominos are not a breed but a colour, which has been produced in many types of horse and pony from Shetlands to Connemaras and Arabs to Hanoverians, by careful breeding.

The Palomino seems to have originated in Spain, and to have been bred from Arab and Barb and Saracen and Moorish stock. Such animals went with Cortes to Mexico in 1519 and they may have been named after Juan de Palomino, who was presented with one as a gift by Cortes. When the United States of America took possession of California after the Mexican war some 140 years ago, they found many Palominos and continued to breed them for riding, particularly for parades.

It is now a popular colour in many other countries, and the British Palomino Society has been formed to promote the breeding of horses and ponies which are of a high quality and conformation, and which maintain a good colour standard. All Palomino ponies must be of a known and authenticated parentage. Inspections take place between 15 May and 15 September each year, and a panel of inspectors makes sure that only those who conform with all the standards laid down by the society are registered.

The society holds an annual championship show with a large variety of classes, and there is a junior section for those under 16. A points championship scheme is also operated for both in-hand and ridden Palominos which gain awards at shows throughout the country. As well as show classes, Palomino po-

nies can be seen taking part in every sort of activity including show-jumping, eventing, dressage, Western riding, mounted games, long-distance riding and driving.

Most Palominos are bred either by crossing one palomino-coloured pony with another, or by introducing a very light shade of chestnut. Crossing a chestnut mare which has a light mane and tail with a Palomino stallion will almost always produce a Palomino foal. These are usually a light colour at birth, with very blue eyes which can darken with age. The colour of the coat can also change, and manes and tails which start as chestnut also whiten as the pony gets older.

The fine head of Palomino champion Oakley Bubbling Spring

A true Palomino should be a lovely golden colour, rather like a newly minted gold coin, but three shades lighter or darker are acceptable. The eyes should be dark and so should the skin under the coat, and the mane and tail must be white, but white markings on the body are only permissible on the legs and face.

With so many enthusiastic supporters and Palomino ponies taking part successfully in a growing range of activities, the colour is going to remain popular even if the Palomino pony never does become a breed.

139

THE HIGH STEPPERS

Although not often gold in colour, Hackney ponies, with their flashy appearance and movement, have become the golden ponies of the driving world and are much sought-after in many parts of the world.

A smaller version of the Hackney horse, renowned for its stamina and courage, the Hackney pony is sometimes referred to as the ballerina of the show ring. Although the history of the Hackney pony is rather obscure, it is generally believed that the first pony was sired by a 14-hand stallion, foaled in the north of England in 1866 and registered as Sir George. Nothing is known about the breeding of the dam, but from then until the early years of the present century the Hackney pony was widely used by tradesmen for delivering goods.

In Anglo Saxon times riding horses were often referred to as 'nags' from the Saxon word meaning 'to neigh', but with the Norman conquest the word 'Hackney' came into use, and the word was probably derived from the word 'Haquenée', a French derivation from the Latin 'equus' or horse.

The Hackney pony must be of a true pony type, especially its head

The Hackney pony has been replaced by the motor car as a form of transport, but continues to prove its versatility and courage, and is outstanding for private driving purposes and for use in driving trials.

For the purpose of judging in the show ring Hackneys are divided into classes for horses if they are over 14 hands in height, and ponies if they are up to 14 hands. At major shows the pony classes are also divided into those under 12.2 hands, and those between 12.2 and 14 hands.

They are shown in a four-wheel vehicle known as a show waggon, and the harness should be black with a breast collar and brass mountings. After entering the ring, Hackney horses and ponies must trot round in a circle before the judge; they may be asked to 'change the rein' and go round the other way so that he can see the other side of each animal. The judge will make a preliminary selection, then the exhibits are lined up and each pony is inspected for conformation and cleanliness before being sent out one at a time for an individual show so as to assess performance.

The judge will be particularly looking for a fine action, with the leg raised and thrown forward to cover the ground, and not just raised up and back to the elbow. The pony's legs must fall in a true and even

sequence, and be straight and level. To produce this correct picture, presentation is important and a good animal badly presented, perhaps with its head on one side or held too high or too low, will be beaten by a lesser pony that is produced well. The successful pony requires that 'look at me' attitude, combined with elegance.

Cleanliness of the pony, the harness, the show waggon and the smartness of the driver will all be taken into account, and good manners are important. Its conformation and way of going are also assessed: if a judge is still not able to decide between two of the ponies he will ask them to be stood alongside each other and the one with the better conformation will be judged the winner.

To encourage people to own and show their own Hackneys there are now a number of classes at shows for amateur drivers only, and these are becoming extremely popular.

The Hackney Horse Society celebrated its centenary in 1983 and there are now nearly 1,000 members, with an annual breed and harness show being held at Ardingly, by kind permission of the South of England Agricultural Society. Originally, there was a meeting in 1878 at Downham Market in Norfolk of distinguished people who decided to establish a register of the English trotting horse; in 1883 a further meeting was held at Norwich when it was agreed to establish a society for the publication of a stud book for Hackneys, roadsters, cobs and ponies. This decision had the enthusiastic approval of the then Prince of Wales, and the committee unanimously resolved that the society should be constituted as the Hackney Stud Book Society, with the Prince of Wales as the first patron.

During its long history the Hackney Horse Society had many distinguished presidents, including the late King Edward VII, King George VI, and King Edward VIII. The Duke of Edinburgh was also president for two years in 1976 and 1977, and Her Majesty the Queen was the president in 1982 and 1983, during the time of the centenary celebrations.

'No creature in the universe can ever hope to vie with a fine Hackney in "personality", in mien and carriage, and in brilliance of action. The walk is light-hearted, sharp, and true, whilst the movement at the trot (in-hand or harness) holds spectators spellbound. It is literally true to say that it has no serious rivals as a harness horse. Its courage and its placid temper, wearing powers, and soundness are proverbial.'

'Lancastrian' in *The Hackney and Hackney Pony*

THE PONIES OF WALES
Beauty and performance

The first references to Welsh ponies and cobs appeared in the laws of Hywell Dda, or Hywell the Good, in the year 930 when he was the ruler of Deheubarth.

Three different types were mentioned: the palfrey, or riding pony; the rowney or sumpter, which was the pack horse; and the *equus operarius* that pulled the sledges and was the light cob-like working horse.

Several descriptions of ponies and cobs can be found in the Welsh literature of the 15th and 16th centuries, and they have played an important part in the country's economy, despite their comparatively small size.

The Welsh Mountain Pony

The Welsh Mountain pony is one of the most beautiful of the nine breeds now forming the Mountain and Moorland Group and although less than 12 hands in height, it can carry the weight of a Welsh farmer to market as well as being a perfect pony for a small child. Although its origin is remote, the Welsh Mountain pony is believed to have descended from the Celtic pony, and it has certainly existed in the mountains of Wales for a thousand years or more. For hundreds of years these ponies ran wild throughout the country, becoming indigenous to the mountains where their rough existence helped to

Typical characteristics

Welsh Mountain ponies have small neat heads, large eyes set well apart, rather dished faces, fine tapering muzzles which are soft to the touch, deep and well laid shoulders with a good length of neck and short, strong backs, with their tails set high.

A

B

C

A *The Champion Section A Welsh pony Aston Superstar showing off his paces*

B *The Section B Champion Rotherwood Royalist*

C *This Section C foal, Rotherdale Dulais, is in playful mood at the Royal Welsh Show*

D *The Champion Section D stallion Ebbw Victor heading the line at the Royal Welsh Show*

develop the qualities of pluck, intelligence, soundness and endurance for which the breed is now famous.

These very qualities helped to save them from extinction between 1509 and 1547 during the reign of King Henry VIII, when hill shepherds and landowners complained that the ponies were causing too much damage. The king decided that all those which were too small to be used in war should be slaughtered, which meant the destruction of mares less than 13 hands in height and stallions under 15 hands. However, many of them managed to escape because they fled deep into the hills and mountains of Wales where their intelligence and powers of endurance helped them to survive.

These characteristics, particularly in the mares, have also brought success in the breeding of polo ponies, Hackneys and Welsh Cobs.

The Welsh Stud Book and Section B ponies

In 1901, a number of landowners, farmers and other enthusiasts formed the Welsh Pony and Cob Society and the first volume of the Welsh Stud Book was printed. The mountain pony was registered under Section A, and ponies under 13.2 hands were registered under Section B. For many years they were the main means of transport for shepherds and hill farmers, and their quality, good bone, and general substance were typical characteristics.

During the past fifty years the increased popularity of riding among children has resulted in the development of a finer, lighter pony and a few stallions of this type, containing at least fifty per cent of the best Welsh blood, were admitted into the Stud Book.

D

E

F

G

E *Welsh Section C ponies*

F *Welsh Cobs are renowned for their spectacular action, and their handlers certainly know how to show this off to best advantage*

G *A typical Welsh Section C pony*

H *Far from their native Wales, but enjoying the grazing at the Imperial Stud in New South Wales, Australia*

H

143

Influential stallions

The two most influential were Craven Cyrus (foaled in 1927) and Tanybwlch Berwyn (1924). Craven Cyrus was by King Cyrus, who had Arab blood, out of Iron Lady Twilight by Dyoll Starlight. Tanybwlch Berwyn's sire Sahara had Barb blood, and his dam, Brynhir Black Star was by Bleddfa Shooting Star.

A different bloodline in the late 1950s was that of Solway Master Bronze, sired by Coed Coch Glyndwr. He gained his height, however, from his dam Criban Biddy Bronze, who was one of the best saddle ponies of all time. Another influential sire was Criban Victor, foaled in 1944: by Criban Winstan, he also got his height from his dam, Criban Whalebone, who was of cob parentage, and he has certainly been a great influence on Section B ponies in recent years.

Welsh Cobs

Section C in the Welsh Stud Book is for ponies of cob type who are also under 13.2 hands. They share all the characteristics of their larger brothers and are ideally suited for trekking. However, by the 1950s their numbers had dwindled badly, with only three recognised stallions: Welsh Patriot (foaled in 1939) and his sons Welsh Echo (1944) and Teify Brightlight (1949). More recently, the popularity of the breed as a family pony has led to a steady increase in the number of stallions, and there are now large classes of Section C ponies at many of the leading shows in Britain.

It is apparent from early Welsh literature that the Welsh Cob was already well established as a breed by the 15th century, and by the year 1700, farmers were beginning to appreciate that Welsh ponies and cobs could be a great asset when grazed on the hills with sheep and cattle, and a market for them gradually developed. As demand increased, particularly for cobs to do light farm work, hundreds changed hands in the big autumn fairs and more people began to take an interest in their breeding. Stallions were more carefully selected, and four sires who have had a tremendous influence on the Welsh Cob are True Briton (foaled in 1830), Trotting Comet (1836), Cymro Llwyd (1850) and Alonzo The Brave (1966).

True Briton, known affectionately in Wales as 'Ceffyl du Twm Masiwn' – the black horse of Tom the mason – was sired by a Yorkshire coach horse called Ruler, out of a mare called Douse. It is rumoured that Douse was an Arab mare who had been bought from some gipsies. Trotting Comet was a 15.2-hand brown stallion by Flyer, out of a chestnut mare about which very little is known, and Cymro Llwyd was a dun-coloured stallion by an imported mare. He is responsible for the large number of cream- and dun-coloured cobs which have been so successful in the show ring recently. Alonzo The Brave was a 15.2- hand bay of Hackney parentage, but the Hackneys were then much heavier than they are today.

Welsh Cobs have had a great influence on trotting horses, being strong enough to carry an adult but quiet enough to be ridden by a child. They are natural and bold jumpers, with strength and stamina, making them very useful hunters in heavy and difficult country. Their bodies are deep and strong, with short legs and powerful hocks, and the heavier types have some feather at the heels. Registered in the Stud Book under Section D they must exceed 13.2 hands, but many of them are between 14 and 15 hands.

Welsh Cobs in poetry

Guto'r Glyn, a famous poet of the 15th century, describes the pedigree of a Welsh Cob stallion as being the son of Du o Bryndyn – 'He would win a race in any fair field'. In the early 16th century Turdur Aled wrote several poems describing a Welsh Cob stallion called The Abbot of Aberconwy: 'He has the outlook and gait of a stag, eyes like two ripe pears, bulging and dancing in his head, a dished face, a wide forehead, his coat like new silk'.

Driving teams

The increased popularity of driving trials has led to more Welsh Cobs being driven, and they have been particularly successful in driving teams.

Preparing for Competitions

Part of the fun of owning a pony is being able to take part in competitions. Gymkhanas, polo, showing classes, dressage, show jumping, horse trials and hunter trials are all open to ponies which are fit and capable of taking part. Whatever the level or type of competition, pony and rider must be immaculately turned out. This requires careful planning and some preparation in advance, and not just a little extra spit and polish on the day. Well before the first competition, particularly for a showing class, the pony's mane and tail need to be pulled if they are at all untidy. With some of the native breeds of pony, however, the manes and tails are left longer when they are being shown, as it is preferred that they appear in all their natural glory. In those cases, however, the mane and tail should always be thoroughly washed and brushed.

Tail pulling

Pulling a tail means thinning out some of the hairs so that it looks neater and is easier to look after. When the tail has been brushed and all tangles removed, a few hairs at a time should be pulled from underneath the tail dock area. Many people prefer to use their fingers or the hairs can be wound around a mane comb – give them a sharp tug, and that is all that will be needed to remove them. If it is done properly, the pony won't mind at all. The end of the tail can then be cut off square: get someone to hold an arm under the top of the tail and lift it to its natural position – then trim off the end with a large pair of scissors. This is a 'bang' tail. Some ponies have a naturally high tail carriage, and if this is not allowed for before the tail is trimmed it will end up by being far too short. Alternatively, the tail can be left as a 'switch' tail whereby the hairs on either side are simply pulled to about halfway down, and the end is not squared off but left to grow to a natural point. After the tail has been pulled, it can be dampened and put in a tail bandage to keep it in shape. The bandage must not, however, be too tight, or it will cause circulation problems.

Plaiting

Ponies taking part both in show classes and in dressage competitions will also need to be plaited, as a smart appearance creates a good impression. To plait a mane neatly, it must first be thinned out and the hairs shortened to about a hand's width in length. The longer hairs on the underside of the mane can be pulled out in the same way as for

Plaiting a mane

A plaited mane looks neat and also shows off the shape of a pony's neck. The mane is damped down and divided into six or more equal sections. Each section is then plaited, and a piece of thread sewn and plaited into the mane about three-quarters of the way down each, leaving enough thread at the end (about 9in/22cm) for final securing. The plaits must all be about the same length, and if they are not, the ends can be looped over to shorten them. The plait is then doubled over, once or twice, and sewn up securely with a needle and the plaited-in thread. Finally, the forelock is combed and plaited in the same way.

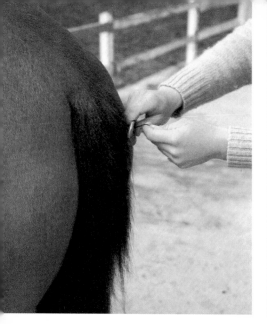

Above:
When pulling a tail, stand opposite the hindquarters and pull the hairs growing underneath a few at a time

Above right:
If the pony is to have a bang tail, the end should be cut off squarely. An assistant should put an arm beneath the root of the tail so that after it has been cut the end will be naturally square

For a mane to be plaited properly, it needs to be thin and silky and about a hand's width in length

the tail. The top hairs, or any hairs which may stand up after plaiting, must not be trimmed or they will form an upright fringe along the crest. The mane need not be pulled all in one go, and working a little at a time often achieves the best results. Some ponies' manes refuse to lie altogether either on one side or the other, and to persuade an unruly mane to stay on the correct side (the 'off' side), it should be dampened down and divided into bunches secured by rubber bands.

Hogging a mane
Cob-type ponies may have their manes hogged, but this leaves them little protection from the flies in summer. The mane is hogged using clippers. Help will be needed to pull the pony's head gently downwards while the clippers are run along each side of the neck, removing the mane from withers to poll. The ridge that is left up the centre can then be neatly smoothed off. The hairs have usually started to grow again after about ten days, and the process must be repeated to keep the hogged mane tidy.

Travelling
Loading Before arranging to take part in a competition some distance from home, it is important to make sure the pony will box easily. The horsebox or trailer should be parked on a level surface so that the ramp does not sway as the pony stands on it. The partitions should be opened wide and the opening made as light as possible – if the trailer has a front unload ramp and top door, open the top door and even let the front ramp down, to maximise light, and to allow the pony to walk right through the trailer if needs be. The person leading the pony should look straight ahead as he walks up the ramp, talking constantly to the pony as he goes. If a pony will not box, it can be because he has been frightened in the past, and his confidence will need to be restored. Feeding the pony on the ramp of the box at home until he has the confidence to enter it for his feed, is often successful. The pony should be rewarded when he does enter the box, and someone should stand with him, reassuring him as the ramp is closed. Some ponies, like humans, are claustrophobic and they can present a special problem.

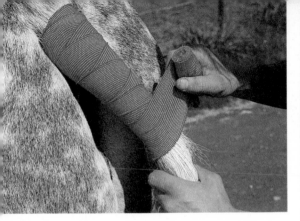

The tail should be damped slightly and put in a tail bandage to keep it in shape. The bandage must not be too tight or it will irritate and cause a nasty sore

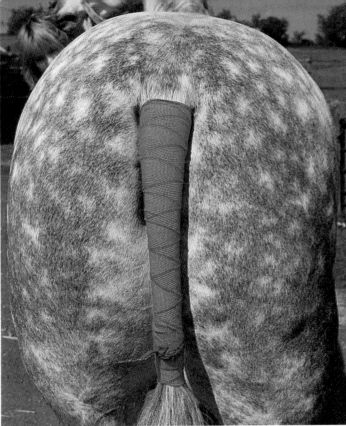

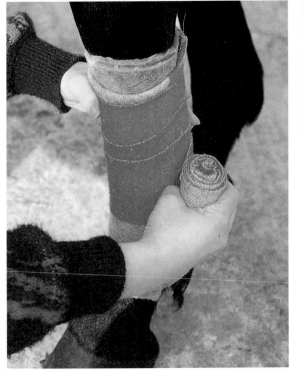

Above:
The bandage should be put on evenly down the tail and then wound back up again, before being fastened neatly with the tapes using a double bow

Left:
Bandages can be used to support the tendons. They must always be put on with a degree of firmness from just below the knee to just above the fetlock joint

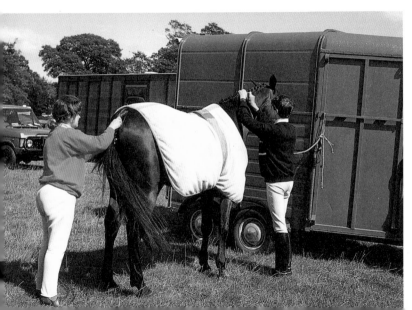

After a competition, the plaits are removed and the pony rugged and bandaged ready to travel home

Ready to go into the horsebox with knee boots and bandages in place

Protective clothing A pony must always travel with protective clothing. He should wear a rug to protect him from draughts, and he will need bandages and boots which will protect knees, hocks and fetlocks, as well as a tail bandage and possibly a tail guard. He must be secured with a headcollar and rope tied with a quick release knot. A head protector can be worn if there is limited headroom or if the pony is likely to try to rear when travelling.

Bandaging Stable bandages are used to protect the legs when travelling, if ready-made travelling boots are not used. The bandages are about 3 – 4in (8cm) wide and 7 – 8ft (2.25m) long and made of woollen fabric or flannel; each bandage is rolled up with the tapes folded in the middle. Starting at just below the knee or hock, it should be wound around the leg as far as the coronet band, and then wound upwards again. The tapes are tied just below the knee, with the knot on the outside of the cannon bone and never on the tendons. Bandages should never be too tight – just firm enough to stop them slipping down the legs. A layer of gamgee or foam rubber can be placed underneath for extra protection.

Knee caps and hock boots These provide important protection for vulnerable joints when travelling; the knee caps can also be used for roadwork as they offer useful protection if the pony is brought down or slips. There are other types of boot which will also protect the pony against injury while he is being ridden: brushing boots for those ponies who are inclined to hit one hind or foreleg with the other as they move; fetlock boots – when a pony gallops, or lands over a jump, the fetlock can hit the ground and be cut by stones or flints, and a boot covering the joint will stop this; and rubber over-reach boots, worn over the front feet, will save injury if the heel of the front leg is struck by the hind leg. Tendon boots support the back of the forelegs and can be shaped to provide added protection to the front of the leg when jumping.

Start early!

Plenty of time must be allowed on the day of the show for the pony to be prepared properly. It is important to arrive at least an hour before the class begins to enable the pony to get used to his new surroundings and let him have a good look round before tacking him up and working him in.

. . . And afterwards

Once the competition is over, particularly if the pony has been across country, he should be sponged down using cold water, and the excess water removed with a sweat scraper. His mouth and lips should be sponged with water, and a sweat rug put on, preferably under a day rug. He should then be walked around until he is cool, and then rugged and bandaged ready for the journey home. If studs are worn they must be removed. The pony can have a drink and a small feed before travelling home, and a haynet will keep him occupied once the journey begins.

When the pony is home, he should be trotted up to see if he is still sound and to get rid of any stiffness. If the weather is mild and he is usually out during the day, he will appreciate a nibble of grass and a roll before being fed and bedded down for the night. The next day, gentle walking exercise will loosen him up.

Plaiting a tail

A tail that is difficult to pull can also be plaited to enhance the pony's appearance. To plait a tail successfully, the hairs on the dock must be allowed to grow long. A small bunch of hairs in the middle of the tail are knotted together with thread to form a bunch which hangs down the centre of the tail. Small bunches of hair from either side of the tail are then taken up and plaited in with the central bunch. More hairs will have to be brought in to form the centre plait as it progresses down the tail. The plait continues to about two thirds of the way down the dock and then only the centre hairs are plaited to form a pigtail. This is looped back under itself and sewn in place with a needle and thread. Tail plaiting is useful on a pony who will not allow his tail to be pulled or if the tail is very bushy.

PREPARING FOR THE SHOW RING

As for any competition, preparation must begin well in advance of the big day. At the start of the season it is necessary to check that the pony is registered with the appropriate society for competing in affiliated shows, that all his vaccinations are up-to-date, and that he has a valid height certificate. When he is first brought in to work he will need slow road work for four to six weeks to let his legs and joints harden and to improve his condition.

Schooling

Basic schooling can then begin as he will have to be fit and supple enough to perform the tasks required of him. A show pony must be taught to walk out well, as jogging in the ring will not gain him any points. As part of this early preparation the blacksmith should check over his feet to ensure that they are developing correctly. The pony will need to be trotted up in hand on a hard surface so that the blacksmith can see if any corrective shoeing will be necessary to improve his action. Something that is often overlooked is the state of the pony's teeth – if there are any teeth problems the pony will not be eating properly and will not accept the bit happily. A veterinary surgeon or horse dentist should look him over thoroughly so that any problems can be avoided.

Feed and exercise

Correct feeding and exercise will enable the pony to put on condition properly, but it is quite an art to feed him so that he is fit and well but

> **Tail bandaging**
>
> Bandaging is only effective if it is done properly. A tail bandage needs to stay in place, but must not be too tight. The tail should be damped down, then with one hand under the tail, about 8in (20cm) of the bandage should be unrolled; the rolled-up bandage is held in the other hand while the loose end is held firmly under the tail. As the bandage is wound firmly and evenly to about halfway down the tail, the loose end can be folded back down and covered by it – it is then wound back up to the top and the tapes at the end are fastened neatly in a double bow, which can be tucked under a fold of the bandage. The bandage is removed by holding it near the dock and sliding it downwards using both hands.

Last minute adjustments before the cross country

Exercise bandages

Exercise bandages may be needed for the competition itself, particularly when a pony is jumping, or the ground is hard. They will stretch and must be worn over gamgee or cotton wool, and for cross-country riding they should be sewn in place, or sticky tape can be wrapped around the bow to secure them. Another useful cross-country tip is to tie the headpiece of the bridle to the first plait with a shoelace, which will prevent the bridle from coming off in the event of a fall.

Beware

A pony should not be allowed to graze at a show as the ground may have been grazed by infected animals.

The extra quality

Whilst hard work and practice can often bring good results in most competitions, when it comes to showing, something a little extra is needed. Even a well-produced pony will still fail in the show ring if he does not have presence – that hard-to-define, aristocratic bearing which is noticeable in many champions. Quality is another essential attribute which should not be mistaken for pretty looks and lack of bone. Quality bone is fine and flat, whereas a more common type of pony will have soft, round bone. A show pony must have good conformation and a good straight action, while the rider also needs a degree of style and showmanship. The most successful ponies are those that love the show atmosphere and play to the audience. Good behaviour is essential, and temperament plays a big part. An easily excitable pony will rarely be a winner in any sphere.

also a sensible ride in front of the judge. Feeding will depend upon the pony's appetite and temperament, and just like people, some ponies are better doers than others. Good quality hay, or haylage, should always be available. Boiled barley and linseed are excellent for putting on condition, and for ponies that do not 'hot up' bran and oats will also be suitable. There are also commercial mixes and cubes on the market and these save time and space in the stable. Quality should never be sacrificed, and it is as well to remember that, as in many things, you only get what you pay for. Carrots and soaked sugar beet can add bulk and roughage to the diet, as do chaff and mollichaff.

Manners

A show pony must remain calm and well-mannered, and he is likely to see quite a few sights when at a modern show ground, including fun-fairs and marching bands. He must face such strange and alarming objects without shying or running away; he must be well balanced and taught to canter and gallop on, without resisting or becoming over-enthusiastic; and as part of his show routine, the pony must be able to walk out and trot back in hand. This is all part of the judging and prizes can be won or lost in this section. If a pony has not been shown before, he should be taken to several small events in the company of other ponies until he learns to be calm and settled on these outings.

Turnout

Pony and rider must be impeccably turned out. The rider should wear clean, well fitting jodhpurs and jacket, a shirt and tie, or stock, and polished jodhpur boots or riding boots. An approved riding hat with a chin strap is of course essential, and gloves should be worn. The pony's tack must be clean and well-fitting. His mane must not be too short or too thin, otherwise after a season of plaiting and unplaiting, he may have very little left.

The tail should be neatly pulled – do not be tempted to cut or dock hairs with scissors, or the pony will end up with a tail looking like an overgrown hedgehog when the hairs start to grow again. The tail should be left long enough so that when the pony carries his tail naturally at the trot, it falls about four inches below the point of the hock. The pony's heels should be trimmed carefully with scissors or clippers.

If a numnah has to be worn on a thin-skinned pony, it must fit as close to the saddle as possible. Show ponies and hacks can wear coloured browbands, but hunters must have a leather one.

STARTING TO PLAY POLO

History

Polo is a game which is now being played in many parts of the world; it has a long history, and flourished in the East long before 600BC – the first international match was played between the Iranians and the Touranians, and very old drawings show that in the reign of Chosroes II, between 591 and 628, the ladies of Persia also played the game. It was first played in England in 1869: officers from the 10th Hussars who were based at Aldershot for the summer used their chargers, some sticks with crooked ends and a billiard ball to play the game of 'hockey on horseback' which they had read was being enjoyed in India. They soon found out that their chargers were not really suitable for the game and sent across to Ireland for some ponies.

Pony Club polo

The popularity of polo in many branches of the Pony Club is growing steadily every year, and young riders can often use their normal gymkhana ponies and turn them into successful polo ponies, although it is important that the pony is introduced to the game very carefully. It is also a relatively inexpensive sport for Pony Club members, because tuition is available and apart from a polo stick, no other special equipment is needed; Pony Club polo is organised and arranged for the one-pony owner. Some polo clubs also have junior members, and tuition can sometimes be arranged there.

Polo is, of course, a team game, played on a polo field with four players on each side, but a keen young rider can easily practise alone in a fairly smooth paddock. Although it is best to use a proper polo ball, initially a reasonably sized plastic ball or even a tennis ball will suffice. Most young riders will want to have a go at hitting the ball as soon as possible; however, it is important to practise holding and swinging the stick, and this can best be done at first by standing on a chair or box. It is also vitally important that a pony is introduced to the stick and ball very carefully before anyone tries to hit the ball from his back. Having a stick waved around him can be very alarming to a pony until he is used to the idea, and can lead to dire consequences.

> **The Argentine pony**
>
> As a result of its extreme handiness as a cow pony, the Argentine has always been much prized as a polo pony. Originally a cross between a Thoroughbred or Arab and a Criollo pony, it soon became the cow pony used by all the cowboys on the estançias, or cattle farms of Argentina.

A certain amount of dash and determination are needed by pony and rider for success on the polo field

Most ponies get used to the riding off process and treat it as a game. They also like to gallop against each other and compete for the line of the ball

Polo facts and figures

A full-sized polo ground must not be more than 300 yards long and 200 yards wide (274 x 182m) if it is unboarded. A boarded ground should not be more than 300 by 160 yards (274 x146m).

The Hurlingham Polo Club issues an official handicap list each year. The highest handicap an individual player can have is 10 goals. Teams are also handicapped, and the maximum for a team is 40 goals.

The maximum duration of play is 60 minutes, divided into eight periods of 7½ minutes each. There should be 3-minute intervals between each period, except for the half-time interval between the third and fourth period which should be of at least 5 minutes' duration. There is no off-side rule in polo, and the ponies can be of any height.

continued

Training the pony

The polo stick Start gently, by showing the pony the polo stick while he is being held by someone else. Rub the head of the stick quietly up and down his nose, and if he doesn't object, continue to rub it slowly over the rest of his face and then down both sides of his neck. It is best to move round to the side to do this, and if the pony begins to get excited or alarmed in any way, the process must be stopped immediately, and not started again until he has settled down. Although very nervous and excitable animals are unlikely to make polo ponies, gentle perseverance will overcome most ponies' objections, particularly when they realise that the stick is not going to be used to punish or hurt them. When the pony is happy about it being rubbed over his face and neck, the process can be continued with the stick being rubbed firmly down the pony's sides, quarters and legs. Hanging a stick in his stable or the field shelter he is turned out in, so that he will have to brush against it to get to his feed, will often help in so accustoming the pony to it that he will ignore it completely.

The ball Once the pony is used to the stick, he will have to get used to the ball. Any white ball will do, providing that it is about the same size as a polo ball; start by tossing it gently against his sides while he is being securely held, until eventually you can do so without him flinching at all. If he continues to seem worried by it, put one in his manger so that he has to nose it to one side in order to get to his feed – this will often do the trick.

Riding off So, once the pony is used to the stick and ball, his training can be continued when the rider is mounted. In polo, ponies are frequently in close contact with one another, particularly in the movement known as 'riding off'; a pony may find this unsettling, but he will have to learn to put up with being bumped by other ponies, sometimes at speed. Riding-off practice can start on a ride with other ponies – even two riders out together can learn to go through the riding-off movements with their ponies. When riding along a track, they should see who can push the other to one side – the rider with his knee in front will usually have the advantage. Put the ponies alongside each other but nose to tail, so that they can be turned first one way, and then the other – each rider will have to learn to press with the outside leg, as this is the important factor in all riding-off.

Most ponies soon get used to the riding-off process, and treat it as a game. They are also competitive by nature, and like to gallop against each other and compete for the line of the ball; the team spirit of the game, being out on the field with other ponies, seems to appeal to them. To be good at polo, a pony needs to be handy, able to stop and turn quickly with the course of play – the player who can do this with his pony will naturally have the advantage, and a good gymkhana pony is normally adept at this already.

Schooling

Polo ponies should be schooled so that they are equally happy leading with either leg when cantering, and to make sure that they do not become 'one-sided'. To improve their balance generally, is is important when exercising at the trot for the rider to rise as much on one diagonal as the other; at the canter, ponies often get into the habit of always setting off on the leg they prefer, so they should be ridden as much on the off-side lead as on the near-side. This is a help when

taking a shot because players usually like their ponies to lead with the off-fore when they are taking a shot on that side. Ponies become very adept at changing the lead again and again as they are swung about by their riders, but when a penalty shot or a hit-in is taken riders usually circle their ponies to get them onto the preferred lead.

For a pony to be able to stop and turn quickly he has to be 'on his hocks'. This can be taught during exercise, first of all at a slow pace, by bringing him to a halt, making him back for two or three paces, and then urging him forward again. When he understands what is required, the same thing can be done at a trot, and then at a canter.

Popularity of polo

Many young riders, girls as well as boys, are taking up polo and with greater opportunities for them to learn, it looks as though polo will continue to increase in popularity. The standard of play at the Pony Club Polo Championships at Cowdray Park has become really impressive, and many of the ponies playing there also give their owners a great deal of fun doing other activities, including Prince Philip Cup games and show jumping.

THE CONNEMARA
Pony of the Emerald Isle

The beautiful Connemara ponies are thought to originate from the horses saved from the wrecks of the Spanish Armada in 1588, but ponies were native to Ireland long before then. They can now be found to the west of Loughs Corrib and Mask, between the Atlantic and Galway Bay, and the area has for centuries been the home of a rather primitive type of pony which for a long time was left to fend for itself in conditions which were wild and hard.

The present-day Connemara is a tough and wiry animal which, like many other typical native ponies, thrives on poor keep, and has become famous as an excellent child's pony. Crossed with a Thoroughbred, the Connemara will also often produce a brilliant competition horse, particularly when courage, agility, and jumping ability are the main essentials.

continued

A polo ball must not be more than 3¼ in (7.8cm) in diameter, and be within 4¼ and 5oz (120 – 141g) in weight. Balls are usually made of willow and bamboo; practice balls are composed of unburstable foam rubber.

During a polo match the rules are administered by two mounted umpires, and by a referee who remains off the field. If the umpires disagree, the referee's decision is final. The match may be played with only one umpire and without a referee, as long as both captains are in favour.

In polo, a goal can be awarded if the ball goes above the goal posts, provided that the umpires agree that it is within the width of the posts. Goals are normally scored when the ball goes between the posts and over the goal line.

The wearing of a helmet, or a polo cap, is compulsory for safety reasons during a polo game.

Since the abolition of the height limit, Argentina has become the leading country for the breeding of polo ponies.

The oldest polo club is the Cachar Polo Club in India, which was founded in 1859 by some British tea planters in Assam.

Versatile Ponies

The popularity of polo in the Pony Club is growing steadily every year, and young riders can often use their gymkhana ponies and turn them into successful ponies for polo.

History

Although its origins are rather obscure, it does have much in common with Highland, Shetland, Norwegian and Icelandic ponies, but there is also undoubtedly a considerable amount of Spanish and Arab blood, which could well have been introduced during the period when Galway merchants were trading regularly with Spain. There are also signs of Andalusian blood. All of this has helped to make the Connemara a pony of high quality and distinction, and much sought-after in many parts of the world.

For hundreds of years Connemara ponies ran in droves in the most inaccessible areas of the mountains, so that the breed remained uncontaminated for some time by other influences. The tough life they had to lead also led to them developing remarkable powers of endurance. Towards the end of the 19th century, however, a number of good quality Welsh stallions were introduced and one of them, Prince Llewellyn, was mated with a native Connemara mare to produce a very attractive little pony stallion called Dynamite. Some years later Dynamite was to become famous as the sire of Cannon Ball, who was the first pony to be registered in the Connemara Stud Book.

In 1923 the Connemara Pony Breeders' Society was formed in Eire to encourage the breeding of good ponies. Connemaras were beginning to be much sought-after by parents who wanted good-looking, docile, intelligent mounts for their children, and they were being recognised extensively as excellent ride-and-drive ponies. The society wanted to encourage the development of the Connemara and also to make sure that it was maintained as a pure native breed.

The Irish are horse-lovers and natural horsemen, and there is no doubt that the performance of their native ponies in the hands of enthusiastic young Irish riders has helped to generate interest in the breed in many other countries. Connemara ponies began to be very successful in Britain, not only as excellent riding ponies and particularly as children's show jumpers, but also as tough and strong harness ponies, being fast and showy and yet capable of covering great distances without tiring.

The Connemara Pony Society was formed in 1946 to encourage the breeding and further utilisation of the ponies in England, and there are now many successful studs with high quality ponies that are becoming increasingly sought-after by overseas buyers. Many have been exported to Europe, particularly to Germany, France, Sweden, Belgium and Holland, as well as to America and Australia, where there is now a flourishing Connemara Breeders' Society.

Conformation

The maximum height for a Connemara is 14.2 hands, but the majority are between 13 and 14 hands, and larger ponies are not encouraged. When the ponies were first being exported from the mountains, bogs and stony outcrops of the western part of Ireland from which they took their name, one of the main difficulties which owners in other countries encountered was the problem of keeping down their size when they were grazed on better land because they tended to become too large, and did not remain true to type. At one time it was reported that a top jumping pony had grown 4in (10cm) when it was six years old after leaving its native Connemara for England!

The Mongolian

The Mongolian pony can be found all over the vast, desolate area of Mongolia, from Manchuria in the east to Turkistan in the west. It is bred and kept in large numbers by the Buriats and other Mongolian tribes, and is extremely hardy. Many of them have been exported to China for racing and polo, and have been crossed to produce what is now known as the China pony.

The breed has a heavy head and shoulders, with small eyes and a thick neck. They are deep chested, and have good quarters and loins, with plenty of bone and feet that are rock hard. The best ponies are to be found in the northern districts of Mongolia, with the smallest, between 12.2 and 13 hands, mainly in the east.

Although the height was limited to 14.2 hands, the Connemara continued to be a first-class utility pony, suitable for carrying a child, or an average-sized adult, and strong enough to do all the work on a small farm or holding in Ireland.

Competitive crosses

Many owners were also quick to realise the potential for breeding competition horses by crossing a Connemara pony with a Thoroughbred. Mrs Bar Hammond's Eagle Rock, although little bigger than a pony, had a remarkable record as an international eventer, and was still winning advanced classes at the age of eighteen when ridden by a fourteen-stone (88kg) man. He was a remarkable character, and when he was eventually retired found it difficult to adapt to a life of idleness, and missed the challenge of the big cross-country fences which he had jumped with such ease.

Colours

Although grey is the predominant colour for a Connemara, there are also many blacks, as well as bays, browns and duns, with occasional roans and chestnuts. The original ponies were dun and had a dorsal stripe and black points, but ponies with these markings are now very scarce.

Connemara ponies are hardy enough to cope well with wintry conditions

Driving Ponies

Don't overtax your pony

Although most driving ponies
are capable of doing most of the
things asked of them, it is
unreasonable to expect too
much, particularly if their
owners are of a keenly
competitive disposition.

Driving is becoming an increasingly popular sport and pastime
among people of all ages. Everyone has his own reason for starting,
but one of the most common is the need to find a use for the outgrown
family pony which no one wants to sell. Frequently it is a pony which
has been ridden by all the children in the family, which has taught
them to ride and then given them their first taste of competition at
local shows and in the Pony Club, so that over the years it has become
more a member of the family and one they would be loath to part with.

The logical answer is to find another use for the pony, and perhaps
at the same time provide a new interest for mother and father who
have probably been looking after the pony for years anyway.
Fortunately the age of the driver does not have to be related to the size
of the pony, although a very small pony should not be expected to be
driven long distances by a very large and heavy man. Ponies are
remarkably strong, however, and a careful choice of vehicle can
sometimes overcome even that problem.

Temperament is vital

A pony which has been with the same family for some time will
probably be safe and sensible anyway, will accept harness-breaking
without any difficulty and will have the necessary temperament to
make a successful driving pony, depending on the choice of driving
activity. Temperament is important with a driving pony. He should
stand quietly to be harnessed and when he is being 'put to' the vehicle
– something which should be carefully noted when purchasing a
driving pony – and he must move off briskly in response to his
driver's command.

Before being persuaded to take the reins of a possible purchase it
is always wise to watch the pony being driven by his owner. This may
seem to be an obvious precaution, but most accidents occur when
ponies are being driven by someone other than their owner, when
there is a strange hand on the reins. Some people don't like mares for
driving because they can be difficult when in season and there is a
feeling that they may also be more inclined to kick than geldings.
There are, however, some very good driving mares, and any problems
regarding temperament can usually be seen when the crupper is
being fitted under their tail – if a mare resents this, or tries to kick the
groom, it may be wise to leave well alone as she will probably prove
to be far more trouble than she is worth.

A suitable pony

People buying a driving pony for the first time would be well advised to purchase one that is not too young, and has had a reasonable amount of experience. An older pony will probably have been well schooled – driving ponies are in their prime when they are between four and ten years old and fetch the most money during that period, but a pony that has been well looked after can give his owner a great deal of enjoyment and success for a further ten years or so. Much will depend on the standard of competition and the type of driving activity he is required for. A pony taking part in private driving activities will usually be able to go on for more years than one which is competing in driving trials or scurry driving.

There is a great deal of enjoyment to be had from taking part in the excellent meets and shows organised by driving societies and clubs throughout Britain, but the choice of driving activity must be carefully considered, and also where the pony is to be kept, before deciding on the type of animal to be purchased.

A suitable vehicle

For private driving classes there are many different types of vehicle available to suit every size of pony, but those taking part in driving trials will also need a specially designed cross-country vehicle. The British Horse Society Horse Driving Trials Group has now set a standard of weights and track widths which governs the size of these vehicles in events. Because of this, the size of the pony can be important, especially as competitors have to have a groom riding with them in the carriage on the cross-country phase to be on hand if help is required, particularly in one of the deep muddy sections. It would be unwise and unfair for a large man to expect a small pony to pull the weight of two people under these circumstances, and a larger, sturdier pony will be required. Furthermore, the overall effect of the complete turnout is important, and it would look ridiculous for a large man to drive too small a pony. Great care must therefore be taken with the choice of pony and vehicle.

Choosing a pony: the native

If the pony is to be kept out in a field for much of the time, a sturdy native breed would probably be the wisest choice. The Welsh is by far the most popular breed for driving, and the Fell is probably the most successful in competitions. They have the strength and stamina necessary for the gruelling cross-country phase and although they are not particularly good at dressage, they are willing and keen to learn, and can be trained to master sufficiently the different movements and paces required in the dressage phase of a driving trials. The larger Dales ponies are more popular with farmers and tradesmen who use them successfully for the light trade vehicles seen at many shows.

Although the New Forest cannot be classed as being very 'showy', it is very suitable for driving, and so is the Exmoor. The Dartmoor, being quite a bit smaller, is better driven as a pair or in a team. The hairy little Shetlands are strong, willing, and remarkably fast and although they do not have the paces necessary for competitions requiring dressage, they have been outstandingly successful in scurry driving events when driven in pairs.

The stylish, high-stepping Hackney ponies with their flashy action

---

Queen Victoria's ponies

On her seventh birthday, Queen Victoria is said to have been given a beautifully matched pair of Shetland ponies with exquisite harness, and a low phaeton, big enough to carry herself and a governess. It was usually driven by a postilion rider wearing 'a neat livery of green and gold, with a black velvet cap'. When she was a little older she was frequently seen out driving in Windsor in her little pony phaeton, with a team of four driven by postilion riders.

The best partnerships

It is important that the pony should have the necessary appeal to the person who is going to drive it, and probably look after it as well – the best driver and pony partnerships have often been a matter of 'love at first sight'.

are in a class of their own, whether driven singly, in pairs or as a team. They are very sharp and quick-thinking and are not really suitable for a novice driver.

Foreign breeds

There are a number of foreign breeds which are beginning to make their mark in driving events and this widens the choice for those just starting; expert advice can be obtained from the British Driving Society, as well as the various breed societies.

Conformation

Having decided on the breed or type of pony, the next step is to choose the right animal. Few are perfect, and it is usually a matter of deciding on the animal which has on average the most good points. A kind, friendly pony is necessary, particularly for a novice driver and if it is going to be looked after at home with help from other members of the family.

It is essential that the pony should stand with his weight evenly distributed over all four legs, and that the quarters should be well rounded and muscled, to give plenty of driving power when he is asked to lean into his collar and give an extra pull. A good deep girth and sloping shoulders are important – if the shoulder is too upright it will be difficult for the pony to move freely when wearing a full collar.

Good legs and feet are probably even more important for a driving pony than they are for one which is being ridden; he is likely to spend far more time trotting along hard roads, and the pounding which his feet and legs will get over the years will usually find out any defects, and weak tendons or bony protrusions on the bones below the knee are a sure sign of trouble. A veterinary surgeon will have to check the true age, because although an older animal will probably be able to perform as well as, or even better than, one that is younger, there may be a considerable difference in the value.

Performance and manners

It is always best when buying a new pony to see him trotted up first without harness so that his action can be studied, as a great deal can be learnt from the way he trots. He should cover the ground in nice easy strides, and should move freely in a straight line with a smooth, not jerky motion. As he trots he should hold his head proudly in front of him, with his ears forward in an attentive manner. His neck should be bent naturally – if it is over-bent behind the ears he has probably had his head-carriage spoilt by the use of harsh mechanical devices.

If the pony seems satisfactory the next test will be the way in which he accepts the harness and stands to be put into the shafts. He should stand still and not fidget, and move off willingly when asked, and when going in a circle he should turn his head naturally in the way in which he is meant to go. It is as well to try him going up and downhill, and to see whether he can cope with both without any bother.

If the pony is being purchased by a novice, someone who is an experienced driver should be asked to make the final judgement, and, of course, every proposed purchase should be vetted.

Opposite:
A good stamp of driving pony – the head says it all

Friend or foe?

It is possible to tell a great deal by looking a pony in the eye – he will usually return your gaze with either a malevolent glare or a friendly gaze, and the secret of his nature will be revealed.

The first collar and shafts

It is believed that the Chinese were the first people to use shafts and to design a form of breeching. They also introduced the driving collar which was later copied by the Romans, who used horse-drawn vehicles extensively when travelling throughout their empire. There is little doubt that as the Romans drove their vehicles across Western Europe, the ideas behind modern harness began to develop.

THE DRIVING HARNESS

Driving harness always looks more complicated than it really is, particularly in the case of single pony harness. Present-day harness still bears some relation to the time when oxen were first yoked up to pull vehicles – in about 2000BC the method of attaching an ox to a vehicle was to use a shaped wooden bar, or yoke, which rested on the animal's neck, and the pole of the vehicle was attached to the yoke. When the ox was replaced by the horse, a breast-strap and traces were added. Eventually the yoke was moved to the horse's back and held in place with a leather strap which was really the first type of girth. Breast-straps had a tendency to slip up and press on the windpipe, and so a further strap was attached to the middle of the breast-strap and passed down between the legs of the horse to be fastened to the girth, rather like the modern breastplate. A pad was placed under the yoke to make it more comfortable and this type of harness was used for some hundreds of years, particularly with the pairs of horses used by the Romans for their chariots.

Materials
Leather has always been the traditional material for driving harness, with patent leather used for collar covering, pad tops and blinkers, but webbing harness is becoming very popular. There are various styles of harness, but the two basic types of single pony harness differ only according to whether a full collar or a breast collar is used. In a full collar harness the collar is fitted round the pony's neck, whereas the breast collar consists of a broad strap across the chest, held up by another strap which goes over the neck.

Collars
The full collar has the advantage of covering a greater area of the pony's shoulder and therefore allows him to exert a greater amount of 'pull'; but the single breast collar is a lot lighter and gives a pony greater freedom of movement, particularly in cross-country driving when tricky hazards have to be negotiated. The full collar should preferably be made for the pony because a good fit is essential. It should lie evenly down his shoulder and have enough room at the bottom for a clenched fist to be inserted by the windpipe, so that no matter how hard he leans into the collar his breathing will not be restricted.

Breathing is also an important consideration when fitting a breast collar: this should go straight across the pony's chest – if it is too high it can obstruct the windpipe, and when too low it can interfere with the pony's action. A neck strap will be needed for ponies being driven in pairs or as the wheelers of a team, especially if there is no breeching, so they are able to hold back on the pole of the vehicle.

Traces
The traces are the two side-straps of strong leather, of two thicknesses and with adjustments at the shoulder end, by which a pony is harnessed to the vehicle. They buckle straight into the end of a breast collar, but with a full collar they attach to a pair of metal hames. The hames used to be made of steel and covered with brass, but nowadays a strong brass and bronze alloy is more frequently used.

The end of each trace has one or two tapered slots for hooking onto the vehicle, although the traces used for light trade and commercial vehicles normally have chains at the end which are more practical for everyday use because they don't wear, and a considerable amount of adjustment can be made.

Shafts

With a single harness, the shafts of the vehicle are supported by a saddle pad held in place with an adjustable girth. There are also fittings for a crupper, and the long leather side panels, or skirts, of the pad are usually shaped to provide a wider area where the shaft tugs will rest. It is important that the pad should not be too small or the tugs will be situated below the wider area and could catch against the girth; this must be fastened tightly enough to prevent the saddle pad from slipping sideways on the pony's back. The back band, which supports the shaft tugs, must be fastened after the pony has been placed in the shafts, and the tugs should have enough room to be able to move up and down slightly to cope with the movement of the vehicle. The tugs can vary in shape, but they are usually oval to allow the shafts to slip through more easily.

Breeching

While the collar and traces are the means by which a pony pulls a vehicle forward, it is the breeching which enables him to hold it back, particularly when going downhill. It consists of a broad strap which goes round the backside of the pony, and is supported by a hip strap which passes over the quarters and through a slot in the crupper back strap. The breeching has large brass rings at each end which are attached to the shafts of the vehicle by breeching straps. Sometimes 'false breeching' is used, when a strong strap is fixed between the vehicle shafts behind the pony; however, this type can only be used satisfactorily when the height of the vehicle shafts at the back of the pony is correct.

Bridles

The bridles used for driving are similar to those used for riding ponies, but they usually have blinkers which need to be adjusted so that the pony's eye is in the centre of the cup. There is a strap or blinker stay, running from the centre of the headpiece which connects the blinkers together, and this needs to be long enough to prevent them from rubbing on the pony's eyebrows. There are various types of noseband used for driving; and the cheek pieces, which usually incorporate the blinkers, have a different fixing for the various driving bits.

Bits

The most popular bit is the Liverpool, which usually has a straight-bar mouthpiece which is smooth on one side, and grooved on the other so that it is rougher; it can therefore be reversed according to whether the pony has a soft or a hard mouth. It is worn with a curb chain and has four different positions where the reins can be attached: these are the cheek, when the rein is simply buckled to the ring of the bit; the rough cheek, when the billet passes round the upright bar while it is still in the ring; the middle bar, which is the upper of the

---

Bits

There is a saying that 'the key to every horse or pony is to be found in the mouth'; in the 19th century there were many different types of bit, and some owners even had bits forged and ornamented to their own particular designs. However, these have all largely been discarded and there are now only about six bits which are generally used for driving.

Bearing reins

Bearing reins can be evil devices if used incorrectly and they are seldom used in single harness, except with Hackneys. Used correctly, however, they can be a major aid to driving, and can help to give a horse or pony a correct and balanced head carriage. They can be particularly useful when driving a pair, or a team when it is necessary to cope with the position of more than one horse or pony's head.

Putting on a bridle

A driving bridle is put on in the same way as a riding bridle. Hold the headpiece in the right hand and the bit in the palm of the left hand with the thumb over the mouthpiece, then put the bit into the pony's mouth using the left hand, while the right hand pulls the bridle onto the pony's head; secure it by doing up the noseband and throat lash.

Take care

A pony should never be left unattended while it is attached to a vehicle, and the bridle must never be removed until the pony has been taken out of the shafts. Once the bridle is removed and the bit has been taken out of the pony's mouth, the driver or groom will have no control – a serious accident can easily occur if a pony takes fright, particularly as the blinkers will also have been removed, and he will perhaps be seeing the vehicle behind him for the first time.

Out of sight, out of mind...

Some governess carts, including one driven by the Queen Mother – then Queen Elizabeth – in the grounds of Sandringham during the war, had a large, circular, high front panel in the dashboard. It was built so that ladies would not have to look at their pony's bottom...

two rein slots; and the bottom bar, which is the lowest, and should only be used in dire necessity.

The bit should be fitted in the pony's mouth so that the bar just wrinkles the corners. If it is too tight the bit will not be in the correct position on the bars of the mouth, and will not be able to work properly. As with a riding bit, the curb chain should be untwisted until it lies flat in the groove, just above the pony's lower lip, and it should be possible to insert two fingers between the curb chain and the jaw when the bit is hanging loose in the pony's mouth. Reins are traditionally made of leather, with long lengths being sewn together to provide the correct length, and they are attached to the bit by means of a buckle and strap.

Harnessing up

Different sets of harness are used when driving ponies in tandem, in pairs, or in teams of four or more, and there are different rules for harnessing up. Because ponies, like horses, are very much creatures of habit, it is important that they should have their harness put on in a set order. The first item should be the collar – in the old days, coachmen were very superstitious about this and considered it to be inviting bad luck if any other piece of harness was put on first. It is, actually, most practical to start with the collar anyway, because the cold leather then has time to warm to the pony's shoulder before he is asked to move off and pull into it. The collar should be put on upside-down so that the widest part is at the top, when it will slip easily over the pony's ears and eyes. If it won't go over easily it may be possible to stretch it by putting a knee into it and pulling it open as far as possible. The hames should be buckled on securely while the collar is still in the upside-down position, and then it can be turned the right way up by bringing it up the pony's neck until it is just behind the ears, and rotating it gently in the same direction as the way the mane lies.

The saddle and breeching can then be placed together onto the back of the pony, with the saddle slightly behind its correct position so that the crupper can be put in place. This is done by standing alongside the pony, taking the crupper in the right hand and lifting it up so that the left hand can be put through it. The left hand can then be run over the pony's quarters and down the tail until the end of the bony part is reached. The tail can then be lifted gently, but firmly, and with the right hand the crupper can be slid over the doubled-up tail and allowed to rest in the correct position around the base of the tail. With the tail lowered, run a forefinger around the inside of the crupper to free any small hairs which may still be trapped and which could cause discomfort. The saddle can then be lifted forward until it is in the right position, and any necessary adjustment to the back strap can then be made to ensure that the crupper is held firmly in place.

The girth should be done up tightly, but the back band will need to be left loose so that it can be adjusted when the pony is between the shafts. The reins may be put on before the bridle, but if the pony is not being taken out of the stable immediately they will need to be looped up safely out of harm's way. Next, the pony should be bridled up, and he will then be ready to be taken to the driving vehicle to be 'put to'.

PUTTING THE PONY INTO THE VEHICLE

The term 'putting to' is used for attaching a horse, or pony, to a vehicle. Safety must always be a prime consideration, and both harness and vehicle should be checked to ensure that everything is ready before the process of putting the pony between the shafts takes place. It is never wise to go driving without the help of a competent groom who should also be available when 'putting to'. The pony should be held a short distance in front of the vehicle, with the groom standing in front to prevent him from moving as the vehicle is rolled gently forwards; the points of the shaft should be well above his back. The shafts can be lowered when they are in the right position to slide into the tugs, and the groom can help by reaching forward to slip the tug over the shaft on the opposite side to the driver. The tug stops on the shafts will prevent the tugs from being too far back.

The traces should be connected while the groom is still standing in front of the pony, and it is important to make sure that they just pull the collar onto the shoulders of the pony while the tugs remain correctly positioned in the centre of the saddle skirt. The breeching strap should be fastened around the shaft by passing it through the breeching dee on the outside of the shaft. The breeching strap can also be placed around the trace, provided that in doing so the trace can

---

Princes Anne

Her Royal Highness the Princess Anne became the 1,000th member of the British Driving Society, and to mark the occasion she drove a pair of Haflinger ponies belonging to the Queen, to a French cane-bodied chaise, and took them to both the Royal Windsor Horse Show and the BDS annual show.

THE BRITISH DRIVING SOCIETY

As Europe emerged from the trauma of two world wars there was a resurgence of interest in horse-drawn vehicles, and in 1957 the British Driving Society (BDS) was formed to bring together the growing band of driving enthusiasts, and to encourage and assist those who were interested in driving horses and ponies. Area commissioners were appointed for the various counties of England, Scotland, Ireland and Wales, and they were asked to organise instructional meetings, picnic drives, social gatherings, film shows and various other events where driving enthusiasts could get together and compare notes.

Members were given instruction on driving and the correct methods of harnessing-up by those with the necessary driving experience; and being able to discuss problems and learn from each other's mistakes helped the driving movement to grow. Many of the smaller shows began to introduce driving classes and became affiliated to the society, and the black and yellow rosettes presented to members attending the shows, in addition to the red, blue, yellow and green rosettes awarded to the prizewinners in the competitions, soon became a familiar sight on the walls of harness rooms all over Britain.

The Royal Windsor Horse Show became a popular venue for drivers, and on the Sunday afternoon an official meet was held each year. After gathering on the showground, the BDS members would drive through the beautiful Home Park and past the turreted walls of Windsor Castle, and along the banks of the River Thames.

As more people took an interest in carriage driving, vehicles hidden away in barns and outhouses and often long forgotten were rediscovered and lovingly restored; and all the while, the demand for suitable carriages, driving harness, horses and ponies grew.

Finding suitable carriages and driving equipment became a considerable problem until John Mauger, a partner in the firm of Thimbleby and Shorland (the well-known auctioneers), appreciated the growing need for driving vehicles of all kinds and started the Reading Carriage Sales. Held at regular intervals throughout the year the Reading sales have become a Mecca for driving enthusiasts from all over the world. Buyers come from Europe and from countries as far apart as America, New Zealand and Australia, and collections which have lain undiscovered in those countries have been sent to Reading to be sold. Some of the vehicles which for years had been looked upon as scrap now fetch many thousands of pounds. Driving bric-à-brac also now finds a ready market, and membership of the BDS, and the hundreds of driving clubs throughout Britain which are affiliated to the society, is growing steadily each year.

The Carriage Association of America was formed in the mid-1960s, and was followed by the American Driving Society in 1974 whose aims are similar to those of the BDS. There are also similar organisations in other countries, including thriving societies in New Zealand and Australia.

INTERNATIONAL COMPETITION

Driving trials in Britain come under the aegis of the BHS Horse Driving Trials Group, and during the past sixteen years a growing number of driving clubs have become affiliated to the group. They also organise social and competitive events, and their novice driving trials have become ideal venues for those wanting to compete for the first time.

The growth in the popularity of driving trials as a sport is largely due to His Royal Highness, Prince Philip; in 1969 he was president of the Fédération Équestre Internationale, and saw four-in-hands from Germany and Hungary competing. At a previous meeting of the Fédération he had discussed the possibility of creating an international competition for carriage drivers with the Polish delegate, Eric Brabec, and after watching the competition for the four-in-hand teams he now realised that a formula for an international event would be feasible.

On his return to England he discussed his plans with Colonel Sir Mike Ansell, who was a senior member of the FEI Bureau and a well-known organiser of equestrian events, and persuaded him to devise a driving competition based, in principle, on the ridden three-day event: on the first day the drivers would first of all have their carriages inspected, and then do a dressage test. There would be a cross-country on the second day, with various sections which would include a number of different obstacles, or hazards, which the drivers would have to negotiate. On the final day, instead of the show jumping phase which the riders have to tackle, the drivers would have to test their driving skill and the speed and suppleness of their animals by negotiating a course marked by cones laid out in pairs in the show ring. Discipline and accuracy in the cones competition is essential, and it is from this phase in driving trials that scurry driving has developed.

As any sport progresses, the rules are continually being updated, and carriage driving is no exception. The FEI rules, however, were drawn up only to cover competitions for teams of four horses, so the national rules drawn up by the BHS Horse Driving Trials Group cater for events where singles, pairs and tandems can take part, as well as teams, and there are classes for ponies in each of the different divisions. Since 1975 there have been national championships in Britain for all classes, from singles to teams, and they are always hotly contested.

still make a straight line from the trace hook on the vehicle to the point where it is attached to the collar.

Harness care

Harness needs to be cleaned every time it is used, and washable leather is used for breast collar lining, breeching lining and pad tops, which are all parts which press onto the pony and get particularly dirty. Webbing harness is often used for driving trials because not only is it light and durable, it is also simple to clean.

THE CHOICE OF VEHICLE

Various factors have to be considered when choosing a driving vehicle, and it is sometimes difficult to decide which should come first, the pony or the carriage. Sometimes it is a matter of finding a vehicle to suit a particular pony, and it will be important to ensure that they both complement each other and form an attractive turnout. The size of the driver also has to be taken into consideration, particularly if it is planned to enter competitions. Sometimes it is the other way round, and it is a question of finding a suitable pony to go with a carriage that may have been picked up as a bargain at a sale. In either case, the vehicle and the pony must go together.

A wide variety

There is a wide variety of vehicles available at greatly differing prices, from simple and relatively inexpensive exercise carts to beautifully built and maintained show carriages; there is also a

Royal drivers

As children, Princess Elizabeth and Princess Margaret frequently enjoyed driving their little grey pony 'Snowball' to a spindle-sided governess cart in the grounds of Windsor Castle. Although when she grew older Her Majesty the Queen became more interested in riding, she still continued to drive and encouraged her children to do so. During a state visit to India in 1961 she was seen driving a pony to a phaeton, and later at Windsor, when Prince Andrew was still a toddler, she took him for a drive in Queen Alexandra's little cane bodied phaeton, drawn by a pair of New Forest ponies. In 1976 Prince Charles thrilled members of the British Driving Society when he drove a smart pair of greys to a demi-mail phaeton in the concours d'elegance class during the society's annual show on Smiths Lawn at Windsor.

relatively new breed of custom-built competition vehicles, some of which have independent suspension, disc brakes, and seats which can be adjusted according to the weight of the driver. People taking part in driving trials will need a more traditional carriage for the dressage and the cones phase, and a specially built vehicle for the cross-country. Most drivers, however, get their fun from more leisurely pursuits – ambling round the country lanes, perhaps going to some of the fun events organised by the many driving clubs, or taking part in the relatively new sport of long-distance driving.

Showing
Most of the larger shows have driving classes, in addition to the shows run by the British Driving Society, and showing has become a very popular driving activity at all levels. The most popular section is the single pony class, mainly because of cost, but also because there are so many excellent ponies available for both the novice and the more experienced driver, and there is a range of driving vehicles to suit the ponies which will not cause too much of a strain on their owners' financial resources.

Most of the ponies used for showing, except for some of the heavier native breeds, seem to have an air of daintiness and style about them which is ideally suited to some of the beautiful traditional driving carriages of the past. Although the older, original vehicles are much sought-after, it is possible to buy modern replicas which have been built along traditional lines.

Types of vehicle
A suitably sized, **stick-back gig** is a very popular vehicle for a pony and is excellent for the show ring; the **ralli car** can also be obtained in a range of sizes, some of which are suitable for ponies. This type of vehicle is based on the style of the **dogcart** and was built in large numbers during the early part of this century. It was designed to suit the requirements of a family, and can carry two adults and two

Driving trials can be hazardous, as Ian Gilbert found when he tipped up with Whitefield Sundance in the last hazard at Drumlanrig

Nine-year old Heidi Eagle and Jester make a very attractive turnout in the Light Trade class at Windsor Horse Show

children with enough space under the seat for a picnic hamper – essential for family outings on a warm summer's day. The ralli car is a particularly safe vehicle for carrying young children, because it has panel sides which curve upwards to finish in a mudguard over the wheels, which means that they are well out of reach of inquisitive young hands.

The very popular **governess cart** was also considered as being particularly safe for carrying children. Many of them have survived and can be seen in showing classes each year, and often with children on board, enjoying every minute and bringing back memories of more elegant times. The governess carts were originally built in large numbers (which is probably why so many of them still exist), and they were bought by the more wealthy families for their governesses to take the children out for a drive. They were considered to be particularly safe to drive because their familiar tub-shaped body was usually hung on elliptical springs within a cranked axle, which gave the vehicle a very low centre of gravity so that it was much more difficult to turn over. There is only one door at the rear which has the handle on the outside, within the reach of the driver but out of the reach of children. One of the main drawbacks is the driving position, because the governess had to sit at an angle in the right rear corner which could become uncomfortable on longer journeys. It is also difficult to get out of a governess cart quickly to get to the pony's head in an emergency. Even so, it is still a very popular and attractive carriage for a small pony.

The majority of driving vehicles for ponies have just the two wheels, but there is a four-wheeled pony phaeton; however, although there are still some elegant examples to be seen in carriage museums in various parts of the world, there are not many still in regular use.

THE FJORD
The little yellow horse

Known in Scandinavia as 'the yellow horse', the Fjord is invariably a golden dun colour. Most of them have a clearly defined stripe along their back, and many also have zebra markings on their legs. They often have cream tips to their ears, but there should not be any white – only a small star or snip on the head is permitted. They get their name from the fjords of Norway, where they had to learn to adapt and thrive in the inhospitable climate to be found there, but these remarkably tough little ponies no doubt migrated to Norway some thousands of years ago, when most of Europe became joined together.

The Fjord bears quite a resemblance to the original wild horse which was named after its discoverer, Colonel N. Przevalski, in the 19th century. It has similar markings and colouring to its wild ancestor, although it is a good deal taller. The Fjord of today stands between 13 and 14.2 hands, but is usually referred to as a horse – it is certainly a sturdy animal capable of hard work. The Fjord, however, has no official height limit, unlike most of the other breeds. Apart from their very distinct colour and dorsal stripe, they can also be easily distinguished by their straight and usually erect manes, which have a dark centre with cream or blonde hair on either side and which are traditionally trimmed into a distinctive crescent shape. Their tails have a mixture of cream and dark hairs.

In its native Norway the Fjord has been used extensively for pulling loads of all kinds and really doing the work of a small horse, which is probably another reason why it is usually referred to as a horse instead of a pony, despite its size. It was so successful as a work-horse, and so extremely economical to keep, that its popularity quickly spread to other Scandinavian countries, and also to Germany. During the early part of this century there was a need for taller animals, and although the Fjords had previously stood about 13 hands high, some of them went up to 14.2 hands as a result of selective breeding.

As with so many breeds, they became involved with the needs of war; during World War II most working horses were commandeered by the German army for draught work, and breeders were ordered to produce smaller pack horses – as a result the Fjord returned to being a 13-hand pony. After the war, when everything started returning to normal, breeders began to produce larger animals. When controlled breeding is set back, however, it takes a long time to re-establish a height, and it is interesting to note that only now, more than forty years later, are the larger Fjords beginning to become more common.

Performance testing
The Fjord has been a very popular breed in Denmark where they are very strict about breeding lines, and only the very best, well proven animals are used at stud. Stallions have to undergo a strict examination

---

Varied uses

Fjords are very versatile and can be used for many purposes: they are used for driving as well as for dressage in Denmark; for rounding up cattle in the United States of America; and for long-distance riding in Germany.

Archaeological evidence

The Fjord is known to have inhabited Norway since prehistoric times and can be seen depicted in rock carvings and engravings in Norwegian caves.

The Viking influence

The Vikings are known to have bred and kept ponies which were very similar in type to the Fjord. They may well have taken some of them to Britain which may account for the noticeable similarities between the Highland pony and the Fjord.

---

as two-and three-year-olds, and they are checked for temperament as well as for conformation, wind and action.

Those that pass the examination are given permission to breed but only for one year, and they must then return to be examined by a panel of judges for their final selection. As well as again checking each stallion's temperament and action, the panel will also carry out ridden, driven and endurance tests. Finally, each stallion's pedigree is given a thorough examination to make sure that there are no proven genetic faults in his ancestry, and if he fails on any of these tests he will not be accepted for breeding purposes. The failure rate is high, and stallions do not get a second chance to qualify – they are usually gelded straightaway and used for riding; this policy ensures that only top-class stallions are used for breeding. The mares must undergo a similar set of tests. Because of these stringent qualifications the breed has remained virtually unchanged for hundreds of years, without any infusions of outside blood, and all the Fjord breed societies are keen to ensure that the situation does not change.

The Fjord is acknowledged to be an ideal ride-and-drive animal, being well up to weight and in many cases able to carry a rider weighing 14 stone (88.8kg) or more, as well as having a strong constitution. The body should be muscular, well coupled, with a deep chest and girth, and the limbs must be clean, with good dense bone and short cannons. There is a small amount of feather on the heels, and their hooves are strong and hard.

The neck of a Fjord is short, strong, and frequently crested, and they have a thick mane and tail. Sometimes their heads are slightly dished, but they must have large, wide-apart eyes, and small, neat ears. It is probably their temperament which is most remarkable: they are usually kind, friendly, willing and adaptable, and seem to enjoy human company. Even the stallions are easy to handle.

Fjords in Britain

Fjord horses were introduced into Britain from Norway by the Hon. Jean Bruce during the 1930s, but it was not until after World War II that they began to gain in popularity, when the late Mrs Janet Kidd imported a number in the 1960s. She first saw these unique animals in Copenhagen when she went there to watch her son, Johnny, competing as a member of the British show jumping team. She watched a party of students taking part in a carnival procession in the centre of Copenhagen, blowing trumpets, and riding on gaily decorated floats pulled by Fjords.

She was so taken by the Fjord's looks and temperament that she decided that she wanted some for her Maple Stud in Surrey. Shortly afterwards she bought two pairs from Denmark and Norway, and since then the Maple Stud has been breeding and exporting youngstock all over the world, including to the Arab State of Oman.

Most of the Fjords in Britain originate from Denmark, but it was particularly the Hon. Mrs Kidd who was responsible for the breed's considerable increase in popularity in the 1970s, when she drove her Fjord ponies so successfully in driving events that for some time they were almost unbeatable.

In 1983 the Ausdan Stud, run by Lyn Moran, the secretary of the Fjord Horse Society of Great Britain, and John Goddard-Fenwick, imported two top-class Fjord stallions from Denmark in order to

Fjord and valley-horses

Two different types of Norwegian Fjord are recognised. There is the fjord-hest of western Norway, and the doele-hest or valley horse of the interior. Their characteristics are the same, but the fjord-hest is probably the more ancient and the original type.

At work and play

Fjords are still used for a variety of agricultural work on some of the smaller, remote farmsteads. They are also used as pack ponies, as well as for riding and driving, and their hardiness and sure-footedness makes them ideally suitable for mountainous areas.

The Hucul

Like the Konik, the Hucul is probably a direct descendant of the original Tarpan, which dates back to the Stone Age. Its ancestors have flourished in the Carpathian mountains for thousands of years, and the modern Hucul is a powerful and elegant pony used mainly in harness, although the larger ponies are sometimes ridden. The breed is noted for being extremely docile and sensible. They are usually bay or dun colour, but piebald Huculs are not uncommon.

ensure that the animals being bred in Britain would continue to be of the high standard required by Denmark, and without any notable inbreeding. Before the stallions were chosen they discussed the various breeding lines with Mrs Kidd, so that they would complement those already in the country. The Danish breeders were particularly helpful, and were anxious to ensure that the British breeders should be able to keep up the standard of Fjord horses.

Lyn Moran and John Goddard-Fenwick went to Herning to see the stallions being put through their paces, and were particularly impressed by the strict discipline demanded by the judges. As a result of their visit two stallions, Ausdan Svejk and Ausdan Otto, began the long journey to England in November 1983. They now stand alongside Maple Klaus, a very successful stallion previously owned by Mrs Kidd. The Ausdan Stud has a number of 'Maple' Fjords.

The British Fjord Horse Society has introduced a performance testing scheme, initially for stallions only, similar to that used in Scandinavia. There are now some 160 pure-bred Fjords in Britain,

THE SPOTTED PONIES OF BRITAIN

There have been spotted ponies in the British Isles for many centuries. They appear in many illustrated manuscripts, oil paintings and drawings, and they were obviously widely used both in peace and in war. The most common size seems to have been a sturdy cob of about 14 hands.

Two illustrations of spotted ponies can be seen in the Worksop Bestiary, which a canon of Lincoln Cathedral gave to Worksop Priory in 1187AD. A parchment dated 1298 also survives among the accounts of Edward I's campaign at Falkirk, in which the clerks have listed cavalry expenses and estimated the values for replacing some 800 animals. One of the clerks wrote: 'Robinettus filius Pagani habet unum equum Powis vairon precii xxv mar', which being translated explained that Robin Fitzpayne had a spotted Welsh Cob valued at £16 13s 4d.

Another pony which fits the same description appears in an illustration in the 15th century manuscript of the Chronicles of Sir John Froissart, which shows 'The Duke of Gloucester arrested by the Marshall and sent to Calais'. On the right of the picture King Richard is seen riding away with his entourage, and the only one looking back at the Duke is a little cob, which is chestnut with darker spots. He has a beautiful little head and strong quarters.

The British Museum has a 'Military Roll of Arms showing Jousting Knights from an English Heraldic Manuscript and containing 160 pairs of combatant horsemen before 1448'. One of the knights looks rather underhorsed on a leopard-spotted cob.

The harsh laws which came into force against ponies in Tudor times seem to coincide with the disappearance of the smaller spotted ponies from fashionable equestrian paintings of the time. The larger Spanish horse was becoming popular, however, and it was from that animal, taken to the Americas by European armies, that the spotted Appaloosa horses descended. It is consequently quite wrong to refer to the British spotted ponies as Appaloosas. Despite the emphasis on heavy horses, many people in Britain continued to breed native ponies and the spotted ponies became preserved in certain bloodlines, especially in Wales and the South-West.

By the mid-19th century spotted ponies were back in fashion, and there is a print of a woman, thought to be Queen Victoria, driving a blanket-spotted pony to a pony phaeton, although it is not certain that it is the queen.

In 1946 the British Spotted Horse and Pony Society was formed to keep a register of all animals, and to make sure that the colour was preserved. In 1976 the horses formed their own register, but the British Spotted Pony Society has continued to care for the ponies, ie, up to 14.2 hands.

The society maintains a register for stallions, mares and geldings of known breeding, but stallions are only accepted with a veterinary certificate. There is also, for the time being, a temporary scheme for ponies of unknown or unregistered breeding who are of good quality, and conform to the required breed characteristics. They can be for riding or driving but they must be sound and have good conformation.

Three different types of marking are eligible. The

Maple Brantly, Fjord pony champion at Royal Windsor 1981

leopard variety can have spots of any colour on a white or light-coloured background; the blanket type refers to ponies having a white rump or back on which are spots of any colour; and the snowflake type has white spots on a foundation of any colour. Piebald or skewbald markings with any of these three different types are not permissible.

The typical characteristics of any spotted pony are white sclera round the eyes; hooves which are yellowish white and black in vertical stripes; and mottled flesh marks on the bare skin.

To demonstrate the ponies' versatility, the society runs a performance award scheme every year which gives owners a chance to show what they and their ponies can do, whether it is in showing classes, eventing, driving, long-distance riding, jumping, or Pony Club activities like mounted games.

Many of them do well in international events, like Karen Bassett's team of registered leopard-spotted ponies, who won the Carriage Driving Points League Championship for the second successive year with maximum points in 1988, as well as the Famous Grouse National Driving Trials Championships.

Because there are so many different types it will take many more years to establish the spotted pony as a breed, but they are becoming increasingly popular and many of them have now been exported to America, Canada, Germany, Holland and Australia.

Karen Bassett with her champion team of spotted ponies on their way to another victory in a driving trials competition

and five stallions which have been approved for stud duties. Three of these are in Wales and the other two are in Scotland and Cornwall.

Since the British society was formed in 1982 steady progress has been made towards popularising the breed for riding and driving, and the performance testing for stallions now includes testing under saddle and in harness, including a mini-marathon.

Breeding mares must conform to standard so far as bloodlines are concerned, even though they are not performance-tested, and blood typing is another safeguard. Voluntary branding has been started, and all foals in Britain must be branded with the society logo and their stud book number on the saddle area.

The society organises tours to see Fjord horses at work in Scandinavia, and encourages Fjord owners to take an active interest in the future of the breed in Britain.

THE REDUNDANT PONY

What can be done with a pony that has been outgrown by the riding member of the family?
Jo Kemp was faced with this dilemma, but discovered a happy solution

This knotty problem exercises the minds of most pony-owners at one time or other. Sometimes it is possible to make the decision to sell, and so allow another child the benefit of a bombproof pony – a knowledgeable home is carefully chosen and all is settled.

Unfortunately, many find this action impossible. Small ponies, be they good, bad or indifferent, tend to wriggle their way into their owners' affections and to contemplate a sale seems criminal, and rather like selling a member of the family!

Unless they are old or infirm, however, ponies need to work. They enjoy a change of scene; being cooped up in the same field day after day bores an active pony, as much as being housebound irritates a human. Another solution would be to lend the pony to a suitable child, although an agreement should be drawn up so that both owner and lessee know exactly what they are respectively responsible for.

The solution which our family finally arrived at may appeal to many others who are in the same situation. My riding days had been over for some time, but I had always wanted to try my hand at driving. Nothing fancy, you understand, just British Driving Society rallies and pottering around our county lanes.

A farming friend who had driven horses and ponies all his life once told me: 'The forward-going child's pony is no good as a driver. Choose the reluctant, lazy mount to put between shafts.' Honeybunch certainly qualified on that count. Over the previous two years, my daughter had worked hard to persuade Honey to respond properly. She eventually became quite good at Pony Club rallies, but she was seldom in the right frame of mind at shows. Ability and inclination must go hand in hand for success and with our combination they did but rarely. Certainly a lazy ride, what would she be like as a drive?

I decided to work with the pony myself, so that we learnt together. Advice from driving friends was invaluable but I am convinced that knowledge of the animal's character and her respect of, and trust in, me, made the training trouble-free.

The first phase of the training was achieved with the help of my twelve-year-old daughter. We fitted the harness on Honeybunch; long-reined her round the village; attached a tyre to the traces for her to pull up and down hill, and finally put her between the shafts of a flat cart, bumping and swaying it as Honey stood near her stable. The pony took all this in her stride, and was therefore considered ready to be 'put to' properly. For the next phase I was helped by the owner of the nearby riding school, who also knew the pony well.

Our 'hilly home' is not suitable as a training ground, and so we long-reined her to the village car-park, put her to an exercise cart and taught her to turn around there. Honey was extremely skittish and had misbehaved on the long-reining session, but once 'put to', she seemed to put her mind to learning the task with a will.

The training programme was as follows:
Day 1 Fitted harness on pony.
Day 2 Long-reined a short distance, groom at H's head.
Day 3 Long-reined a longer distance of about a mile.
Day 4 Long-reined for about 2 miles.
Day 5 Long-reined a short distance with tyre.

Day 6 Stood between shafts, cart rocked by groom.
Day 7 Put to and taught to turn to left and right.
Day 8 Pulled cart and whip round village, 1½ miles.
Day 9 Put to at home, pulled up hill for first time.
Day 10 Driven from riding school, many distractions!
Day 11 Driven round lanes, had to stand still for 20 minutes.
Day 12 Longer drive of approximately five miles.
Day 13 Followed another turnout on a seven or eight mile drive.
Day 14 Driven on her own again, a bit 'spooky'!
Day 15 First BDS Rally, 13-15 miles!

The whole process took six weeks from the first time she was harnessed up until the first British Driving Society rally, although Honey had only worn the harness fifteen times in all! It was not as difficult a task as I had imagined.

The BDS rally began at 2.30pm on a hot summer's day and Honey was marvellous in every way. Our turnout was the last in the line as I did not want to upset anyone (in every sense of the word!) if Honey misbehaved.

Unfortunately, the pony ahead of us could not cope with the hilly terrain, and my poor pony had to pass her leader and trot on for miles without sight or sound of the others. We found a gymkhana, but again she had to trot on past. We were both delighted when we saw the other turnouts at halfway house; my groom and I had begun to wonder if we were driving along the wrong road!

Things were very different during the second half of the drive. Honey had realised that she needed to trot when the leaders increased their pace. This made life a little difficult, and I spent a great deal of time and effort keeping her head at least an inch or two away from the exercise cart in front of her!

At 5.30pm we returned to base, tired but very happy. All had gone much better than expected. Well, nearly all.

Honeybunch came through with flying colours, but not so her whip (that's me!). I had been so concerned about the pony that I had forgotten about myself. I have to confess to have taken part wearing only tee-shirt and jeans. Everyone else, needless to say, was wearing full gear, including hat, gloves, jacket and driving apron.

Sorry Honeybunch, I've let the side down . . . again!

Do's and don'ts for beginners

Do choose a steady, sensible, bombproof pony! An animal that bolts away from a bus is no use for driving.

Do have at least one knowledgable adult helping at all times.

Do have a good groom who can quickly go to the head of the pony whenever necessary.

Do proceed cautiously. Ponies have very limited powers of concentration so short frequent lessons are most effective.

Do keep calm. If you are worried, hide your fear from the pony at all costs.

Do remember your control is limited to reins, whip and most important of all, your voice. When driving round the local lanes I like to change pace using my voice alone, as this encourages Honey to keep listening.

Don't learn with an Arab or a Hackney! Leave these to the experts.

Don't ruin things! If a new job is learnt quickly, don't be tempted to continue for longer. If boredom sets in, a clever pony may try all sorts of manoeuvres and you may not be able to control him.

Don't force a frightened pony. If the animal is genuinely worried by a new task, reassure him and stop the lesson as soon as you can, before he misbehaves. The next time you try the same lesson he will probably accept it perfectly.

Happy driving to you all!

Honeybunch and her new exercise cart. This was only the second time that she had been between the shafts

The Pony's Health

THE HOOF AND SHOEING

We take it for granted that ponies were created to be ridden, and putting metal shoes on their feet seems a natural progression so that they can be ridden on the roads – but ponies were never designed to carry a rider's weight, nor were their feet designed for shoes. A greater understanding of the pony's hoof will underline the importance of good foot care and shoeing.

The hoof's structure

The outside of the foot is made up of the wall, the sole and the frog. These are non-sensitive horny structures which have no nerve or blood supply, and this is why nails can be driven into them without causing pain. The wall has a glossy outside surface which reduces the amount of evaporation from the horn and helps prevent it becoming dry and brittle. It grows downwards continually from the coronet like a finger-nail, though on an unshod pony it wears down with use and rarely becomes overgrown. However, if a pony is not let out or exercised, or is left to stand continually on soft ground and his feet are not attended to, it will become too long unless the blacksmith trims it back.

The sole The sole is meant to protect the sensitive interior of the hoof from injury, although it is not particularly thick and can quite easily be bruised or punctured. It has a slightly concave shape which gives a better foothold.

The frog The frog has a rubbery feel to it and acts both as a shock absorber, and to help prevent the foot from slipping. It is wedge-shaped with a rough surface, and is the first part of the foot to make contact with the ground.

The hoof inside Inside, the foot is a different story to the hard, horny appearance of the outside. The hoof houses a number of small bones, including the vulnerable navicular and pedal bones, and these are surrounded by layers of sensitive flesh called laminae. Unlike the horn, the laminae have both blood and nerve supplies, and this is where pain and damage occur.

Injury Problems arise when the hoof is damaged inside because the rigid wall will not allow it to swell up, as would happen when other parts of the body are injured or strained. The bones inside the hoof can become displaced or deformed as pressure from infection or inflammation builds up, leading to permanent unsoundness. Injuries

---

Limited movement in the foot

The wall and sole of the foot are relatively rigid but the laminae and frog have limited movement – as the frog comes in contact with the ground, it is pressed inwards and expands. This forces the ends of the wall slightly outwards and allows some movement inside the foot.

The shoe must fit the foot

A good farrier will look for signs of uneven wear on the shoe before he removes it, and may alter the shape of the new shoe to correct any faults in the pony's action. The sides of the shoe may be built up or lowered to distribute the pony's weight more evenly across the foot.

The farrier at work:
Removing an old shoe by cutting
through the clenches with a buffer
and driving hammer

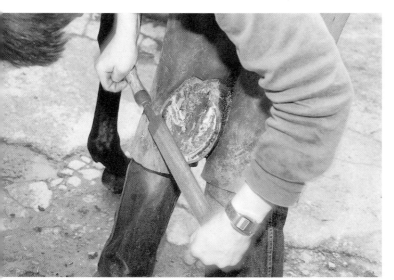

Rasping the hoof to give it a level
surface

Fitting the shoe to the size and
shape of the hoof

175

to the foot such as punctures or bruising will usually require poulticing to reduce swelling and pain, and to draw off any pus.

Shoe ponies regularly

Ponies are shod because riding on roads and hard surfaces wears the hoof down faster than it can grow, and metal shoes will prevent soreness and stop the pony's feet from breaking up. The shoe protects the wall from wear, but of course it continues to grow (about ½in/1cm a month) and so the shoes have to be removed even if they have not worn down, and the wall cut back regularly. A pony usually needs shoeing every four to six weeks; if the front of the hoof, the toe, grows too long, the pony is liable to trip, and a pony in heavy work on the roads may need reshoeing more frequently. The farrier must be called if the shoe is loose or has come off, if the shoe has worn thin in places, if the clenches are sticking up through the wall, or if the foot is too long or the wrong shape.

Removing the shoes

The old shoe is taken off by raising the clenches with a buffer and driving hammer, nipping them off, and levering off the shoe with pincers – the clenches should pull out cleanly without tearing the wall. The hoof is prepared for the new shoe by cutting back any overgrown horn with a drawing or toeing knife; if there is a lot to cut away, a horn cutter is used. Any raggedness on the frog or sole is trimmed and the hoof is rasped to give it a level surface, ensuring that the frog will still come into contact with the ground when the new shoe is in place.

Hot shoeing

The shoe should be made to fit the hoof, and the hoof should not be trimmed or rasped to fit the shoe. Because of this, hot shoeing – where the shoe is tried on first and then adjusted so as to be an exact fit for the foot – is more satisfactory than cold shoeing, where a ready-made shoe is used.

Poulticing

Commercial poultices such as Kaolin or Animalintex can be purchased in a made-up form. Kaolin can be used cold or heated in an oven; to heat Animalintex, boiled water is cooled to the required temperature (usually blood-heat) and poured over it. Before applying the poultice, it should be tested against the skin of the elbow to make sure it is not too hot for the pony. The heated poultice is placed against the injured area, covered with a waterproof material such as a plastic bag, and held in place with gamgee and a crêpe bandage.

Alternatively, a poultice can be made with bran and Epsom salts. The pony's shoe should be removed, his leg bandaged, and vaseline smeared on his heels. A handful of Epsom salts is added to a hot bran mash which is put in a strong plastic bag. The pony's foot is put in the bag and the bran packed underneath the hoof. It can be held in place with a poultice boot, or a piece of sacking. If the pony is liable to eat the dressing, Stockholm tar can be smeared around it to discourage him.

TYPES OF SHOE

Plain stamped This is simply a piece of iron shaped into a horseshoe with holes stamped in it and a toe-clip drawn from it. It would only be suitable for a pony in slow work as there is no protection against slipping, brushing or knocking.

Hunter shoe This is made of concave iron which reduces suction on soft going as well as increasing the grip. The heel of the front shoe is narrowed and shortened to reduce the risk of the hind shoe catching it, and the toe of the hind shoe is rolled (set back and rounded off) to reduce injury from over-reaching. There is sometimes a calkin on the outside heel, where the last ½in (1.2cm) of the shoe is turned downwards and forms a built-in stud which helps the pony if he has to stop quickly. For the same reason the inner heel has a wedge, which is less likely to cause brushing than a calkin. Originally designed for hunters, these shoes are suitable for any pony needing extra grip, such as fast work on grass.

Anti-brushing shoe Brushing is when a pony injures a leg by hitting it with the opposite one. To minimise the risk of damage, the inside of the shoe is feathered and fitted close in under the wall. Being slightly higher on the inside, it makes the pony carry his foot outwards.

Grass-tip This is often used when a pony is turned out to grass but not ridden. It is a thin, half-length shoe put on the toe to stop it splitting.

Surgical shoes Some injuries, malformations or disease, can be helped by fitting these.

Horseshoes are forged from different types and weights of iron depending on the work the pony will be doing. Once the shoe has been shaped, nail holes are stamped into it and the clips formed – a front shoe usually has one toe-clip, and a back shoe two quarter-clips to secure them in position. In hot shoeing, the shoe is heated until it is red-hot and is then held briefly and carefully against the hoof – the hot shoe sears a mark around the bottom of the wall and when it is taken away, the blacksmith can see what adjustments need to be made. When the shoe is the exact shape, it is cooled in water and nailed on. The first nail is usually put in near the toe.

The nails are hammered in carefully to make sure they do not puncture the sensitive tissue inside the wall, and the nail ends, or clenches, which then protrude from the wall, are then turned over and hammered down, and any roughness removed with a rasp. The toe-clips are tapped gently into place and the area where the shoe and wall meet is rasped to reduce the chances of cracking.

If a pony does a lot of jumping or work on slippery roads, the farrier can be asked to tap out **stud holes** in the shoes. Road studs can be fitted or screwed into the outside of the hind shoes to give grip on slippery surfaces. Made of hardened metal, they wear down more slowly than the shoe and provide a rough surface for a better grip. For jumping, studs can be used on both front and hind shoes if necessary.

A pony can be worked **unshod,** as long as hard, gritty roads and flinty tracks are avoided. This will save on shoeing charges, allow the pony a better grip, and reduce any injury if he kicks. His feet must be given time to adjust to the changeover from wearing shoes to being unshod, and until nature has responded to the situation by giving him harder, stronger hooves, care must be taken not to make him sore. His feet will still need regular attention from a farrier to keep the surface even and to stop the wall cracking or splitting.

One of the latest developments in shoeing has been the introduction of **glue-on shoes.** These originated in America where they were designed for horses whose feet had been damaged so badly that shoes could not be nailed to them. Dr Ric Redden, an equine foot specialist from America, and Helmuth Dallmer of West Germany, have both designed different types of plastic shoe for problems such as limb deformities, and weak tendons in foals. Dr Redden believes that the continual breeding and racing of Thoroughbreds has led to them developing lighter feet and thinner soles and walls which cannot always withstand conventional shoeing.

The flexible nature of a plastic shoe allows the hoof to expand and flex as it would in its unshod state. They are made up of a lightweight alloy racing plate, covered in polyurethane, with plastic tabs which hold the shoe to the wall of the hoof.

The tabs are fixed in place using a special glue which sets in ten seconds. A knife blade or modified pincers are used to pry the tab away from the surface of the wall when they need to be removed. Manufacturers are confident that the shoe can withstand the stresses of hunting, racing and three-day eventing. A horse called Rambulara enjoyed a twelve-to-one win in his first race wearing glue-on shoes. They were fitted six weeks before the race, and showed little sign of wear. Glue-on shoes are more expensive than conventional shoes at this early stage in their development, but as their use increases, the cost should come down.

'Prefabricated' shoes

Once the farrier is familiar with the shape of a pony's feet, he can make up the shoes beforehand specially, and there should be no problem.

The right size nail

If the correct size of nail is used, the head of it will fill the nail hole. If the head is too big it will stick out and wear away too quickly; too small a head will lead to a loose shoe as the nail hole will not be filled.

A metal stud has been screwed into the shoe to give the pony more grip when jumping across country

Travel him home

If a pony goes severely lame and is in obvious pain, he should be taken home in a horsebox or trailer.

CAUSES AND TREATMENT OF LAMENESS

Unfortunately, lameness can be an all too common occurrence, and every rider should have some idea of how to identify the problem and what to do about it. If any unevenness is felt when riding, a check should be made that no stones have got lodged in the foot. If there is no obvious cause for the lameness, the pony should be led home, keeping on the grass wherever possible.

Which leg?

In less obvious situations, to find out which leg the problem concerns, the pony should be walked on hard flat ground. Severe lameness will be obvious at the walk, but if this is not the case, then the pony should be trotted up. If he is lame in a front leg, as the sound leg touches the ground, the pony will lower his head, but as the lame leg touches down, he will raise his head to try to take the weight off it. If he is lame in both forelegs he will keep his head raised, and will not stride out. If he is lame behind, he will lean more on the sound leg – this is best seen by standing behind him and watching for uneven movement of the hindquarters; he may also drag the toe of the lame leg.

The cause of lameness can often be found in the foot and this should be checked for anything sharp or any sign of heat. If there is nothing obvious there, the rest of the leg should be felt for heat, swelling and pain. It is not always possible to find any definite cause or damage and diagnosis is best left to the veterinary surgeon or, in some cases, the farrier.

Bruised sole This affects the horn of the sole and the sensitive tissues underneath. It is usually caused by picking up a stone or by riding on rough, hard ground and the sole may be pink and tender. Some ponies have very flat feet and thin soles which are prone to bruising. They should be shod with a leather pad covering the sole.
Treatment: The shoe should be removed and the foot poulticed for three days.

Corn These usually occur on the inside of the fore feet and are bruises under the heel of the shoe. They can be very severe and fester, and are indicated by heat in the heel region. Badly fitting shoes or excessive paring of the heels can be the cause.
Treatment: A veterinary surgeon or farrier will remove the shoe and pare out the corn. A surgical shoe will probably be fitted and a bran poultice applied.

Laminitis This is a swelling of the sensitive laminae inside the hoof, and is a serious and painful disease as the wall of the hoof cannot expand to take the swelling. Ponies are susceptible to it and it is usually caused by too much food and not enough work, particularly too much lush grass in the spring, or too much heating food when stabled.
Treatment: The veterinary surgeon must be called and the pony put on a strict diet.

Pricked foot If a nail is driven too close to the sensitive tissues inside the foot it will cause pressure in this area and subsequent lameness.
Treatment: When the nail is removed, the pony will usually go sound straightway. If not, the foot will need to be poulticed to draw out any pus.

Navicular This is a condition which causes the navicular bone to become rough, and makes contact with the tendon very sore. It is often caused by concussion but can be hereditary.
Treatment: Navicular was always considered incurable but some modern techniques are bringing success.

Pedal ostitis This is damage to the pedal bone and is similar to navicular.

Sandcrack Brittle feet can lead to this condition, which

A pony being trotted up for the veterinary surgeon to check for lameness

basically is a crack running down the wall from the coronet.

Treatment: If the pony is lame, the veterinary surgeon should be called. If not, the farrier can prevent the crack spreading by making a groove across it with a hot iron. Cornucrescine, or some other substance, can be rubbed into the coronet to encourage healthy growth and Biotin given in the feed.

Seedy toe This is an infection of the hoof, usually caused by a blow to the hoof or by bad shoeing. A farrier will know how to treat it.

Under-run sole This is caused by a sharp object penetrating the foot and damaging the sensitive inner structure.

Treatment: The foot will require poulticing.

These are some of the causes of lameness which stem from injury to the foot. Many of the injuries require poulticing, which means applying a hot substance to the injured area to draw out pus, reduce swelling and pain, and to clean out wounds.

OTHER AILMENTS AND REMEDIES

If an injection is given properly, the pony will not feel any discomfort

Injury and illness is obviously distressing for a pony, is expensive in both time and money, and can often be guarded against. A pony should be checked over at least once a day and the owner must be able to recognise signs of ill-health and discomfort.

His coat should be glossy and flat, and the skin loose and supple. The eyes should be bright and the membranes salmon-pink. The body should be free from heat and swelling and well filled out, not tucked up or blown out. The pony's urine should be thick, and colourless or pale yellow, and the dung should be soft but not sloppy.

When at rest, the normal respiration rate is 8 to 12 inhalations per minute. This is best measured by standing behind the pony and watching the rise and fall of his flanks. His temperature should be 38°C and his pulse rate, 36 – 42 beats per minute.

The pony should be fed regularly, with no abrupt changes in diet and according to the work he is doing. Worms must be controlled by regular dosing with an approved medication and he should be vaccinated against

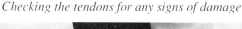

Checking the tendons for any signs of damage

A New Zealand rug can cause rubbing if it does not fit correctly and must be checked regularly

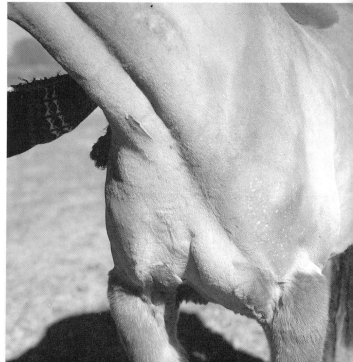

tetanus and influenza. Some competition entries will not be accepted without an up-to-date vaccination certificate.

His teeth should be checked every year by a veterinary surgeon and rasped if necessary, and his feet should be picked out and checked daily. If the pony is not thriving, even if his pulse, temperature and respiration rate are normal, and he is being fed and worked properly, do not ignore the problem. Seek expert advice as this may be an early sign of a problem yet to surface.

Every pony owner should have a first-aid kit at home, and a smaller one for travelling. The kit should contain the following:

Animalintex dressing and Kaolin paste for poulticing
Antibiotic powder and antiseptic cream
Vaseline or zinc ointment
Witch-hazel for galls
A jar of vapour rub
Stockholm tar
Epsom salts
Crepe and cling-type bandages
Cotton wool and gamgee
Gauze
Surgical tape
Safety pins
Scissors
Veterinary thermometer

The telephone number of the pony's usual veterinary surgeon and farrier should also be at hand.

A pony's temperature is taken by inserting the thermometer in his rectum; it must be shaken down to read zero and the end should be greased with a little vaseline to make insertion easier. Hold the pony's tail out of the way and insert the bulb end to about two-thirds of its length – the thermometer must be held firmly to prevent it being drawn into the rectum. After half a minute, remove it and read the temperature – the normal temperature of different ponies may vary but an average is 38°C (100.4°F).

A pony's pulse rate can be tested in three places – under the lower jaw, by pressing this facial artery against the bone; on the inside of the foreleg, at knee height, where the artery crosses over the bone; or on the pony's cheek, just behind the eye. The pulse should be felt with the fingers, not the thumb, and an average is 36–42 beats per minute. Ponies and youngstock may have a faster rate of up to 45 beats per minute.

If a stable, or equipment, has been used by a pony with a contagious disease, these should always be disinfected. Any bedding and leftover feed should be burned, and the buckets, manger and stable scrubbed with a disinfectant; tack and rugs should also be washed with disinfectant and then cleaned normally. If possible the stable walls should be limewashed, and any unvarnished woodwork coated with creosote.

If there is any doubt about a pony's health, the veterinary surgeon should be called out. In cases of

lameness, it is worth remembering that the farrier is a foot specialist, and can be called out before the veterinary surgeon. Have the pony ready for inspection, and make sure there are washing facilities and hot water available. The veterinary surgeon may give complicated and lengthy instructions which must be understood, remembered, and carried out strictly: write them down if necessary.

Medicine may have to be given to the pony and the vet will normally give instructions as to how this should be done. If it is to be given in the feed, it should be mixed with something which will encourage the pony to eat, such as molasses or sugar beet. Some medicines can be dissolved in water but a check must be made that the pony drinks the water and does not leave it or knock it over.

If medicine is mixed to a paste with treacle it can be smeared on the back of the tongue – the pony's tongue must be held out to one side, and the paste applied with a smooth wooden stick or spoon. This can be harder to do than it sounds and assistance will probably be needed. Some other treatments which may have to be carried out at home by the owner include bathing, cold hosing, hot tubbing, hot fomentation or poulticing.

Bathing wounds Cotton wool and warm water with antiseptic or a mild salt solution can be used to gently clean out the wound.
Cold hosing is a simple treatment for the legs to reduce pain and swelling from strains. The pony's heels should be greased with vaseline to stop them getting sore, and a steady trickle of water should be hosed over the hoof, gradually working up the leg until the injured part is reached. Hosing should continue for 20 minutes and should be done at least twice a day for best results.
Hot fomentation is helpful if a poultice cannot be applied, and can be done after hosing. Two large pieces of thick material are soaked in hand-hot water and Epsom salts. One piece is squeezed out and the hot cloth held over the swollen area. When the cloth is cool, it is re-immersed in the hot water, and the second cloth is applied. The process is repeated, and the water kept hot by adding to it from a boiled kettle.
Hot tubbing is a similar process to fomentation but is used for injuries to the lower leg or foot. The foot is scrubbed clean and lowered into a bucket of hand-hot water and salt. The leg can be tubbed for 20 minutes, several times a day.
Poulticing A ready-prepared poultice can be used, or a bran poultice can be made (*see* The Hoof and Shoeing p.176). The prepared, hand-hot poultice is applied to the wound, covered in a waterproof material and then held in place for at least 12 hours, and can be effective for two to three days; if there is poison in the wound it should be changed more frequently.

There are numerous diseases and injuries that can afflict a pony, but the following are some of the ones which a pony owner is most likely to come across:

Azoturia Cramp in the muscles of the loins and quarters: the pony will move only with difficulty; he will sweat, have a temperature and breathe faster than usual, and his urine may be brown. Sometimes known as 'Monday sickness' because it was prevalent amongst working horses who were rested on Sunday but still given full rations, and then faced with work on Monday. Work/exercise should be stopped immediately, even if halfway through a hack, or irreparable damage may be done to the affected muscles. The pony must be kept warm and given a laxative such as a warm bran mash; in more severe cases the veterinary surgeon may give an injection to relax the muscles. Azoturia can recur, and so particular care must be taken over the exercise and diet of an affected pony.

Bog spavin Fluid builds up in the joint capsule and shows as a soft swelling on the inside of the hock. Heat is not present and lameness only occurs if the swelling interferes with the pony's action. Shoes with high heels and rolled toes will reduce the strain. Cold treatment and pressure bandaging will be needed if the pony is lame.

Bone spavin An enlargement of the bone on the lower and inner side of the hock often caused by a young pony being given too much work. In the early stages any lameness wears off with exercise, but the condition is usually permanent.

Bots are parasites that live in the stomach. The pupae pass out of the stomach in the pony's droppings, and mature into flies which lay their eggs on the pony's coat, usually on his legs. The pony licks them off and they pass into the stomach where the cycle is repeated. To try and break the cycle, the eggs can be removed from the pony's coat using a safety razor.

Breaking out Having cooled off, the pony starts to sweat again; the sweating is patchy and the pony sometimes cold, and it must be rubbed/wisped dry or it may catch a chill. Always make sure the ears are dry.

Broken wind is a chronic lung condition. It can be caused by an allergy, or if a pony is strenuously exercised while it has a cough. The pony will have a deep, persistent cough and his flanks can be seen to heave twice as he breathes out. Dusty feeds and bedding should be avoided.

Canker A serious condition where parts of the hoof become spongy and give off a grey or white discharge. Veterinary attention is needed immediately.

Capped knees and hocks Caused by a blow to the knees or hocks. They can be treated by hosing, resting and poulticing.

Colds and coughs Treatment will vary depending on the cause, but if the pony is coughing, has a temperature and a runny nose, the veterinary surgeon should be called. The pony must not be ridden until he has been checked.

Colic is a name given to any type of abdominal pain – ponies cannot vomit so any stomach upset is particularly distressing for them. The pony will keep looking at his flank and may kick at his stomach. He will swish his tail and as the pain increases he will try to roll or lie down; in severe cases, he can become violent and throw himself about. The pulse rate may rise to 80 or 90 beats per minute.

The veterinary surgeon must be called as colic can be fatal; the pony should be kept warm with a blanket and walked around, so that he cannot kick himself or lie down. Colic can be caused by worms, poor diet, irregular feeding, insufficient exercise, or by gulping down cold water when he is overheated and sweating.

Cracked heels The skin in the hollow at the back of the pastern becomes sore and scabby and cracks appear. The heels must be washed and dried with a clean cloth and a soothing lotion such as Dermobion applied. Before exercise, petroleum jelly or lanolin can be smeared on the heels.

Dental problems A pony's teeth need to be in good condition for him to graze properly and regular rasping should keep them smooth and level – have them checked every year. As a pony gets old his teeth may become loose or sharp, and a tooth may even have to be removed to stop it cutting his cheeks or lips.

Girth gall Areas of skin near the girth become thickened and sore; this usually happens to fat ponies whose skin is soft because they are unfit. The pony should not be ridden until the sore patch has improved and then the girth should be padded – a clean motor-cycle inner tube often does the trick.

Humour or hives A skin condition seen as numerous weals under the skin. It can be caused by a digestive disorder, or by external influences such as nettlerash. Bran mash and Epsom salts usually put things right, otherwise antihistamines may be required.

Lice Small insects, less than ⅛in long (about 2mm) and brown, which get into the mane and tail of ponies when they are in poor condition. They cause a great deal of itching which results in bald, sore patches where the pony rubs himself. Animal insecticides can be used to get rid of the lice.

Mange Now fortunately a rare condition, it is caused by a parasite that affects the skin near the mane, tail and legs. There may be slight swelling in the pony's legs and a rash. The veterinary surgeon should be called, and the pony's grooming kit, rugs, and other items of clothing should all be disinfected.

Mud fever An inflammation of the skin on the lower leg more common in ponies with white hair on their legs. The legs must be kept dry and clean and a soothing lotion such as Dermobion applied.

Ringworm Caused by a fungus which forms circular bald patches on the pony's skin. People can also become infected and the pony's tack and grooming kit must be disinfected. The pony should be isolated and the veterinary surgeon called.

Strangles is a contagious, serious disease, particularly in ponies in poor condition. Swellings appear on either side of the throat and the pony has difficulty breathing. There will be a nasty, thick, white discharge from the nose. A veterinary surgeon must be called and the pony isolated and kept warm.

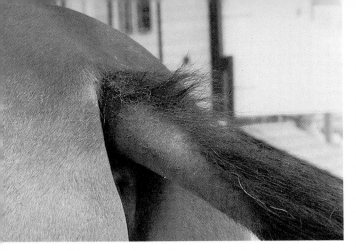

This pony, suffering from sweet itch, has rubbed its tail raw

Sweet itch Small midges cause irritation around the mane and tail, and the pony will often rub himself raw. He should be kept indoors during the day and a soothing lotion applied.

Thrush A disease of the frog of the foot which results in a smelly discharge. If the feet are not picked out properly and the pony is stood in dirty, damp conditions, he may get thrush. The frog area must be cleaned with soap and water. When it is dry, Stockholm tar can be applied.

Worms Parasites which live inside the pony and are usually picked up from the pasture. Ponies always carry a small number of worms, but if the level of infection builds up, the pony will become *ill*. Worms prevent the pony getting the full goodness from the food he eats and can cause permanent damage to the lungs and intestines. Regular worming, at least four times a year, is needed.

Wounds All wounds should be cleaned with a mild solution of salt water – strong disinfectants should not be used as they can damage the healing cells. The wound should be dressed with wound powder or cream, and remember that it must not be hosed clean initially as this can drive dirt deeper into a fresh wound. If the cut is deep or bleeding excessively, the vet must be called. Swelling can be reduced by hot and cold dressings, and a pressure pad can be applied above a wound to reduce the bleeding, or a tourniquet used. This must not be too tight, however, and should be released every fifteen minutes, to let the blood circulate.

It is important that a pony is protected against **tetanus** with a vaccination, as it can be fatal.

Remember. . . Never be afraid to call the veterinary surgeon – it can save money and the pony's life.

THE SAD DECISION

Owning a pony carries with it many responsibilities, but apart from making sure that he is kept happy and well fed, there may be a time when an owner is faced with the very distressing situation of a pony with an incurable illness, or one that has been badly injured, or perhaps is suffering too much because of old age and is no longer able to enjoy life.

When faced with any of these situations, an owner must do what is best and kindest for the pony and accept that it must be put out of its misery as quickly as possible.

Fortunately, many ponies live quite happily until they are more than twenty years of age, and some even live beyond thirty, but for the owner who has to have a pony put down the British Horse Society, the Royal Society for the Prevention of Cruelty to Animals, and the National Pony Society have provided some very important Do's and Don'ts.

DON'T

* Allow anyone to take your pony away alive without supervision.
* Panic or allow natural emotion to affect your pony.
* Allow anyone inexperienced to attempt its destruction, even if this avoids delay.
* Create problems and distress for your pony by demanding injections or dope, except on veterinary advice.

* Move an injured animal unnecessarily or take a suffering pony away from his normal surroundings.
* Allow a pony with a broken limb to be transported live to a slaughter house.
* Try to influence the person in charge, or override his decision.

DO

* Face facts calmly and with determination to do the best possible thing for the animal.
* Consult a veterinary surgeon, licenced horse slaughterer, RSPCA inspector or huntsman. For their telephone numbers, consult the telephone directory, Yellow Pages, or telephone the police.
* If you encounter difficulties, the local BHS welfare officer will be able to offer advice on the facilities available.
* Accept that the correct use of the humane killer is the kindest method for the pony.
* Either stand by your pony yourself, or get a reliable friend to keep him calm and confident. Distract him with food or titbits if possible.
* Follow exactly the instructions of the expert. He will also advise you on disposal.
* In the case of an old pony who is not in pain, accompany him or send a trusted friend if he has to travel to the slaughter house, and wait until he is destroyed. In most abattoirs appointments can be made.

GLOSSARY

Aids A rider uses his legs, hands, seat and voice to communicate with a pony – these are natural aids. Spurs, martingales and whips are artificial aids.

Anti-cast roller A surcingle with a metal arch on top which prevents the pony from rolling over in his box.

Arch-mouth pelham A bit with an upward curve in the mouthpiece.

Artzel A white mark on a pony's forehead.

Azoturia (or Monday morning sickness) affects the muscular system.

BHS British Horse Society.

BSJA British Show Jumping Association.

BSPS British Show Pony Society.

Back at the knee From a side-view, the knee slopes backwards and appears concave; the cannon bone appears to slope somewhat forwards and there is little room for tendons and ligaments.

Balance The distribution of weight between the pony and rider.

Bandages Protective pieces of material wrapped around the legs and tail.

Barrel A horseshoe used to relieve corns or sidebones in which a piece of metal is welded across the heel to give support and place extra pressure on the frog.

Bearing Altering the surface of the teeth to disguise a pony's age.

Behind the bit When a pony refuses to accept and hold the bit.

Bib martingale A running martingale with a triangular piece of leather between the straps.

Bit The mouthpiece of the bridle.

Bitless bridle or hackamore: a bridle with no bit which acts on the pony's nose, chingroove and poll and is more severe than many people realise.

Blanket clip Removing the pony's hair from the neck, belly and tops of the legs.

Blaze A white mark down the full length of the pony's face.

Blemish A scar left from a previous injury which does not affect the pony's performance.

Blistering An artificial way of inducing severe inflammation of the skin to try to promote healing.

Blood horse An English Thoroughbred.

Bog spavin A painless, soft swelling on the inside of the hock.

Bone spavin A hard, bony swelling on the inside of the hock.

Bore When a pony leans on the bit.

Bone Used in describing a pony's conformation, and refers to the circumference of the bone below the knee.

Bounce fence Two fences with no stride between them.

Bowed hocks A sign of poor conformation, the toes turn inwards and the hocks point outwards.

Breaking-in The earliest stages of a pony's training, when he is introduced to a saddle and bridle and eventually a rider.

Broken knees The knees are permanently scarred after an injury.

Bridoon One of the two bits used with a double bridle.

Bringing up The process of bringing a pony in to be largely stable-kept, and getting it fit, after he has been kept at grass.

Brushing When the pony strikes his fore- or hind-leg with the foot of the opposite leg.

Brushing boots Leather, felt or synthetic fabric (plastic) boots with padding which protect the inside of the leg against brushing from the opposite leg.

Cade foal A hand-reared foal.

Cadence When a pony's paces have rhythm and impulsion.

Calkin A raised piece of metal on the heel of the shoe which gives extra grip.

Camp When a pony stands with his fore and hind legs as far apart as possible.

Canker An infection of the sole of the foot.

Cannon bone The bone between the knee and the fetlock. It should be relatively short and flat.

Cast (pony) When a pony has lain down and cannot get up, usually because he is stuck in the corner of his box or against the manger.

Cast (shoe) When a pony loses a shoe.

Cavalletti Small wooden jumps, each consisting of a pole bolted at each end onto a cross-piece; it can therefore form 3 different heights as it is turned over. Used for schooling a pony before jumping.

Cavesson A padded headcollar which has the lunge rein attached to the front of the noseband.

Cavesson noseband A standard leather noseband on a bridle.

Centre line In a dressage arena this is the line down the middle of the length of the school, between markers A and C.

Change leads, or leg When a pony changes the leading leg when cantering or galloping; also when the rider asks the pony to lead with a different leg when cantering.

Clench The point of the nail which sticks out through the wall of the hoof when the pony is shod. It is twisted off and hammered over to secure the shoe to the hoof.

Close-coupled A pony with a short back and strong loins.

Cold-backed A pony with a sensitive back; he may buck or play up when the rider first gets on, and will dip his back down when the saddle is put on. A numnah can reduce the problem.

Cold-blooded Describes the heavy horse breeds and heavy types of pony.

Cold hosing Using a stream of cold water to reduce swelling or pain.

Colic A disorder of the pony's digestive organs.

Colt A male foal.

Concussion Jarring of the pony's legs when jumping or working on hard ground. Also describes some injuries or blows to the brain.

Condition General fitness and well-being and the state of the muscles and skin.

Conformation The shape of the pony and the way he is made up.

Contact The 'feel' taken up by the rider's hands from the pony's mouth, through the reins.

Coronet The sensitive band around the top of the wall of the hoof, from which the horn grows.

Cow hocks Hocks which turn inwards (the feet consequently turn outwards).

Cow kick When a pony strikes out forwards with his hind-leg.

Cracked heels Inflamed skin in the hollow of the pony's heel.

Crest The upper part of a pony's neck.

Crib-biting A stable vice, when a pony continually grabs hold of something with his front incisor teeth and sucks air into his stomach.

Dish face When a pony's face is hollowed inwards *ie* is concave; usually seen on Arabs.

Dishing Incorrect action when the pony throws his front feet outwards, instead of straight forwards.

Disunited canter When the leading fore and hind leg appear to be on opposite sides.

Dock The bone in the tail.

Double bridle A bridle with a bridoon and a curb bit and reins for each bit, *ie* a snaffle rein and a curb rein.

Dressage Training the pony to be obedient to the rider's commands.

Drop noseband A narrow noseband which is done up below the bit to stop the pony crossing his jaw.

Dumped toe When the toe has been rasped and rounded off to fit the shoe.

Electuary Medicine which has been made up into a paste for administering to the pony.

Ergot A small horny growth found at the back of the fetlock joints.

Extension When the pony lengthens his stride at the trot or canter.

FEI Fédération Équestre Internationale.

Falling in/out When a pony loses balance on a circle and the shoulders or quarters move off the true circle.

False ribs The pony's last pair of ribs are held together with cartilage and are not attached to the sternum.

Farrier A person qualified to fit and make horseshoes

Filly Female pony under four years of age.

Foal A pony under one year old.

Frog The V-shaped wedge on the sole of the foot which acts as a shock absorber.

Full mouth At six years old, a pony is described as having a full mouth.

Galls Sores from chafing of the girth or saddle etc, or swellings on the legs.

Galvayne's groove Once a pony is ten years old, a brown mark appears on the corner incisor teeth, and grows down the teeth as he gets older.

Gamgee Cotton wool covered in gauze which is used under bandages for warmth and protection.

Gelding A castrated male pony.

Good doer A pony which keeps in good condition even on very moderate feeding.

Going The state of the ground; **way of going** describes the movement or outline of the pony.

Groundline The baseline at the bottom of a fence from which pony and rider judge the point of take-off.

Hackamore *see* bitless bridle.

Hand The standard used to measure a pony's height - one hand equals 4in (10cm).

Hard mouth When a pony's mouth becomes insensitive to the bit because the nerves have been damaged.

Hollow back A very dipped back.

Hot up When a pony becomes over-excited while being ridden.

Independent seat When the rider can move and control his legs, hands, seat and body independently while riding.

In-hand A pony being led.

Keepers Leather loops which keep the ends of the leather straps on the bridle in place.

Knee spavin A bony growth on the back of the knee.

Lameness Uneven stride due to injury or pain.

Leading leg When cantering on a circle, the inside fore leg should appear to be leading each stride.

Left rein To be 'on the left rein' means that the pony is moving to the left.

Loose box Individual indoor accommodation for ponies.

Lungworm A parasite which occurs in the bronchi; the pony picks them up from the pasture, and is more likely to be affected if grazing with donkeys, which are the natural hosts. Lungworm can cause damage to the lungs.

Mare Female pony.

Martingale Item of saddlery used to control the pony's head, or the direction of pull on the reins.

Nappy When a pony refuses to go in the direction its rider asks.

Native pony A pony breed native to the British Isles, *eg* Exmoor, New Forest, Welsh or Connemara.

Near- and off-sides When seated on a pony, the near-side is to the left and the off-side is to the right.

New Zealand rug A waterproof rug for outdoor wear in a field.

Numnah A protective pad worn under the saddle.

Oestrus The ovulating cycle of a mare, *ie* when she is fertile and will accept the stallion.

Over-face Asking a pony to jump beyond his ability or training.

Over-reach A wound received from the hind hoof striking the heel of the foreleg.

Pelham A type of bit which incorporates a bridoon and curb on one mouthpiece.

Points The term used to describe the different parts of the pony's anatomy.

Pony An equine animal measuring less than 14.2 hands high.

Pulling Thinning out the hairs of the mane or tail.

Quartering Grooming only one part of the pony at a time by folding back the rug.

Rasping Filing back the teeth or feet.

Roller Broad leather or canvas surcingle which goes right round the pony's body and keeps the rugs in place; it is padded to avoid putting pressure on the withers.

Run up the stirrups Slide the stirrup irons to the top of the leathers.

Saddle horse A wooden stand on which a saddle can be cleaned or stored.

Saddle soap A special glycerine soap used to clean saddlery.

Saddle tree The frame around which the saddle is built.

Salt lick A hard block of salt for the pony to lick in the stable or field.

Splint A small bony growth between the splint bone and the cannon bone.

Spring-tree Describes a saddle with a strip of metal in the tree which makes it more flexible.

Stable vice Bad habits which the pony developes in the stable, usually from boredom.

Stale To urinate

Stallion An uncastrated male pony.

Staring coat A sign of ill-health when the coats looks dull and appears to stand on end, instead of being flat and glossy.

Strapping A thorough grooming, given after exercising the pony.

Strike off The first canter step when the leading leg is established.

Surcingle A girth which goes right round the pony's body to hold a rug or saddle securely in place.

Sweet-itch A condition which irritates the mane and tail.

Tack All the items of saddlery and equipment used for riding and training ponies.

To turn out To put a pony out to graze.

The turn-out General appearance of pony and rider.

Twitch A stick with a soft piece of rope on the end which is twisted around the upper lip and used to restrain a pony during operations such as clipping, veterinary examinations etc.

'Underneath' a fence When a pony takes off too close to a jump.

United canter When the leading fore leg and hind leg both appear to be on the same side of the pony.

Vetting When a pony is examined by a vet for general soundness: this is done prior to a pony being purchased; in the course of competitive events such as long distance-riding or 3-day horse trials; for insurance purposes; etc.

Warm-blooded A pony with Arabian or Thoroughbred blood in its ancestry.

Weaving A stable vice where the pony rocks to and fro by shifting his weight from side to side.

Wind Describes a pony's breathing or respiration process.

Wings High extensions either side of a fence, which support the pole and discourage the pony from running out.

Withers The point of the pony's back where the neck meets the backbone. A pony's height is measured from the ground to his withers.

USEFUL ADDRESSES

The British Horse Society
British Equestrian Centre, Stoneleigh, Kenilworth,
Warwickshire CV8 2LR

British Driving Society
27 Dugard Place, Barford, Warwick CV35 8DX

Association of British Riding Schools
Old Brewery Yd, Penzance, Cornwall, TR18 2SL

British Equestrian Federation
British Equestrian Centre, Stoneleigh, Kenilworth,
Warwickshire CV8 2LR

British Equestrian Trade Association
Wothersome Grange, Bramham, Nr Wetherby,
Yorkshire LS23 6LY

British Equine Veterinary Association
Hartham Park, Corsham, Wiltshire SN13 OQB

British Field Sports Society
59 Kennington Road, London SE1 7PZ

British Harness Racing Club
Bryn Goleu, Bryniau, Dyserth, Rhyl, Clwyd LL18
6ER

British Show Jumping Association
The British Equestrian Centre, Stoneleigh,
Kenilworth, Warwickshire CV8 2LR

Horse Driving Trials Group
The British Horse Society, British Equestrian Centre,
Stoneleigh,Kenilworth, Warwickshire CV8 2LR

Hurlingham Polo Association
Ambersham Farm, Midhurst, West Sussex GU29 OBX

National Association of Farriers & Blacksmiths
Avenue R, 7th St, National Agricultural Centre
Stoneleigh, Kenilworth, Warwickshire CV8 2LG

The Pony Club
The British Equestrian Centre, Stoneleigh, Kenilworth,
Warwickshire CV8 2LR

Pony Trekking & Riding Society of Wales
32 North Parade, Aberystwyth, Dyfed SY23 2NF

Riding for The Disabled Association
Avenue R, National Agricultural Centre, Stoneleigh,
Kenilworth, Warwickshire CV8 2LR

Royal College of Veterinary Surgeons
32 Belgrave Square, London SW1X 8QP

The Scottish Trekking & Riding Association
Tomnagairn Farm, Trochry,
By Dunkeld, Perthshire

The Side-Saddle Association
Highbury House, Welford, Northampton NN6 7HT

Society of Master Saddlers
The Cottage, 4 Chapel Place, Mary St., Bovey Tracey,
Devon TQ13 9JA

Ponies Association(UK)
Chesham House, 56 Green End Road, Sawtry,
Huntingdon, Cambs PE17 5UY

The Riding Clubs
British Equestrian Centre, Stoneleigh, Kenilworth,
Warwickshire CV8 2LR

Pony Club Magazine
EPG Publications Limited, Finlay House, 6 Southfields
Road, Kineton Road Industrial Estate, Southam,
Warwickshire CV33 OJH

The Ada Cole Memorial Stables Ltd
Mr E B Collier, Director, Broadlands, Broadley Common,
Nr Nazeing, Waltham Abbey, Essex EN9 2DH

The Ancient Order of Pack Riders
Mrs C R Stone, Fridays Acre, Bromyard Road,
Stoke Bliss, Tenbury Wells,
Worcestershire WR15 8RU

British Appaloosa Society
Mr Michael Howkins, c/o 2 Frederick Street,
Rugby, Warwickshire

Connemara Pony Breeders Society
Mrs P MacDermott, 73 Dalysford Road,
Salthill, Galway, Ireland

Dales Pony Society
Mrs J C Ashby, Assistant Secretary,
196 Springvale Road, Walkley, Sheffield S6 3NU

Dartmoor Pony Society
Mrs M Dansford, Fordons, 17 Clare Court,
New Biggin Street, Thaxted, Essex

The English Connemara Pony Society
Mrs M V Newman, 2 The Leys, Salford,
Chipping Norton, Oxon OX7 5FD

Eriskay Pony Society
14 Braid Road, Edinburgh

Exmoor Pony Society
Mrs D Mansell, Glen Fern, Waddicombe,
Dulverton, Somerset TA22 9RY

Fallabella Society
Lady Rosumund Fisher, Kilverstone Wildlife Park,
Thetford, Norfolk

Fell Pony Society
Mr Clive Richardson, 19 Dragley Beck, Ulverston,
Cumbria LA12 OHD

Fjord Horse Society of G.B.
Miss Lyn Moran, Glynarthen, Llandysul,
Dyfed SA44 6PB

Hackney Horse Society
Miss S Oliver, 34 Stockton, Warminster, Wilts

The Haflinger Society of G.B.
Mrs Robins, 13 Park Field, Pucklechurch,
Bristol BS17 3NS

Highland Pony Society
Mr Ian Brown, Beechwood, Elie,
Fife KY1 9DH

Horses and Ponies in Need
Glenda Spooner Trust, Emmetts Hill,
Whichford, Warwickshire CV36 5PG

The Icelandic Horse Society
Mrs E G Thorburn, 12 Clare Court,
North Berwick, East Lothian, Scotland

International League for the Protection of Horses
67a Camden High Street, London NW 1 7JL

Medical Equestrian Association
The Medical Commission on Accident Prevention (At
the Royal College of Surgeons),
35 – 43 Lincolns Inn Fields,
London WC2A 3PA

National Pony Society
Col A R Whent, Brook House,
25 High Street,
Alton, Hants GU34 1AW

New Forest Pony & Cattle Breeding Society
Miss D MacNair, Beacon Corner,
Burley, Ringwood, Hants BH24 4EW

Peoples Dispensary for Sick Animals
21 - 37 South Street, Dorking,
Surrey RH4 2LB

Shetland Pony Stud Book Society
Mrs Barbara M McDonald, Pedigree House,
6 Kings Place,
Perth PH2 8AD

Side Saddle Association
The Acting Secretary, Mrs Maureen James,
Highbury House, Welford, Northampton, NN6 7HT

Welsh Pony & Cob Society
Mr John Pritchard, 6 Chalybeate Street,
Aberystwyth, Dyfed, SY23 1HS

Worshipful Company of Farriers
Mr F W Birch, 3 Hamilton Road, Cockfosters, Barnet,
Herts EN4 9EH

Worshipful Company of Saddlers
The Clerk, Saddler's Hall, Gutter Lane,
Cheapside, London EC2V 6BR

ACKNOWLEDGEMENTS

'A Passion for Ponies'
The authors are grateful for the help they have received from Deborah Sly in the preparation of the book, and to the following who provided information or photographs:

The Lady Fisher
Mr J F T Pritchard, The Welsh Pony & Cob Society
Mrs M Mansfield, Secretary of the British Show Pony Society
Colonel A R Whent, Secretary of the National Pony Society
Mrs M Danford, Secretary of the Dartmoor Pony Society
David Mansell, Secretary of the Exmoor Pony Society
Clive Richardson, Secretary of the Fell Pony Society
Mrs E Seymour, Wantsley Farm
Penelope Shephard, Secretary, The Coloured Horse & Pony Society
Mrs P Howell, Secretary of the British Palomino Society
Jackie Elias, Secretary of the Icelandic Horse Society of Great Britain
Mrs M V Newman, Secretary of the English Connemara Pony Society
Keith Beeston, British Coal
Nicola Campbell, Secretary, British Caspian Society
Lyn Moran, The Fjord Horse Society of Great Britain
Miss D Macnair, Secretary of The New Forest Pony Breeding and Cattle Society
D M Paterson, The Shetland Stud Book Society
The Pony Club
The British Horse Society
The British Show Jumping Association
The British Driving Society
The Riding for the Disabled Association

The authors and publisher would also like to thank the following for supplying illustrations for this book. We apologise if acknowledgement to any photographer has been omitted.

Bob Langrish
D Mansell
Trevor Meeks
National Coal Board
Gilsons
K Ettridge
Iaian Burns
Kate Willings
Bob Elford
Sue Feast
Dayne Jenkins
Equestrian Services
Expo Life
Highland Pony Gazette
Valerie Russell
Dales Pony Society
Mrs E Seymour
Oliver Joyce
Lady R Fisher
Mrs Jo Kemp
Mrs P Carvosso
Mrs G Sant
Ian Wilton
Thomas Fall
Chris Moller
Photographers International
Raymond E Chaplin
Brian Stidwell
Kit Houghton

Index

Page numbers in *italic* denote illustrations

Ackram Rose, *61*
Acland family, 18
Acorns, fatality from, 54
Action, how to judge, 33
Adults, ponies for, 15
Advertising for pony, 30
Age:
    consideration when buying,
      28, 29
    how to tell, 26
    minimum for selling, 33
Allerton Equitation School, 80, 137
American Revolution Bicentennial
    races, 105
Ancestors of pony, 12-13
Andalusians, 56
Ansell, Colonel Mike, 165
Anti-brushing shoe, 176
Arab horse, 6, 12, 151
Argentine miniature horses
    (Falabellas), 6, 45-8, *45, 47*
Argentine pony, 151
Arnwood Stud, Sussex, 40
Aston Superstar, *142*
Ausdan Stud, 169-70
Azoturia, 181

Balmoral Bramble, *79*
Bandages:
    exercise, 150
    tail, 145, 149
'Bang' tail, 145, *146*
Barley, as food, 66, 150
Bassett, Karen, 171, *171*
Bearing reins, 161
Bedding, 64
Beginner's pony, 13-14, 26ff; *see also*
    Child, suitable pony for
Bits, 84, 88-9, 161-2, *89*
Blaze, meaning of, 16, *16*
Body brush, 66, *65*
Bog spavin, 181

Bone spavin, 181
Booth, Joe and Eva, *97*
Borrowing, instead of buying, 20
Bots, 56, 181
Box, loading into, 146
Bradford cart, *75*
Bran, as food, 66, 150
Branding marks, 19-20
Breaking out (renewed sweating), 181
Breeching, 161, 162
'Breed', meaning of, 13
Bridles, 84, 88-9, 161; care of, 92
British Caspian Society and Trust, 49;
British Driving Society, 99, 164, 166
British Fjord Horse Society, 169-70,
    172
British Horse Society, 8, 20, 182;
    Code of Practice for saleyards,
    32-3
British Horse Society Horse Driving
    Trials Group, 157, 165
British Palomino Society, 138
British Show Jumping Association,
    120-1, 123
British Show Pony Society, 132-3,
    135-7
British Spotted Horse and Pony
    Society, 170
British Timkin Show, 137
Broadbent, Mark, *163*
Broadshade Bealach, *98*
Broadshade Searchlight, *98*
Broken wind, 181
Brooks, Brian, Eriskay pony herd, 101
Brooks, Joe, *121*
Browbands, for show ponies, 150
Bruised sole, 178
Brushes, for grooming, 66, *65*
Brymor Mimi, *60*
Buckles, 91
Buying:
    avoiding cost of, 20

choosing right pony, 26-34,
    156- 7, 159

Calmady-Hamlyn, Miss, 36
Canker, 181
Capped knees and hocks, 181
Caspian horses/ponies, 6, 48-9, 50
Catching, in field, 55
Chaff, as food, 68
Chiddingfold Pony Club, 118
Child, pony suitable for, 13-15, 26-31,
    49, 117, 154, *27, 29*
Choosing a pony, 13-15, 17, 21, 26-34,
    156-7, 159
Clancy, Kate, 118
Clarke, Louisa, *134*
Clipping, 55, 71, 146, *70*
Clothes, for competitions, 128, 150
Clydesdales, 58, 62
Coal Mines Act (1911), 94
Coat:
    healthy, 179
    special Exmoor, 21
    see also individual breeds
'Cold-backed', 30
Cold hosing, leg treatment, 180
Colds, 181
Colic, 181
Collars, driving pony, 160, 162
Colour *see* individual breeds
Combing, 67, 71
Companionship, need for, 52, 71
Competitions:
    advice on, 128-9
    preparing for, 145-50
Concentrates, as feed, 54
Coney Morning Joy, *134*
Conformation, 30
    driving pony, 159
    show pony, 150
    see also individual breeds
Connemara pony, 153-5, *155*

Connemara Pony Breeders' Society, 154
Corns, 178
Cost:
    buying, 14, 20, 28
    keeping, 15
Coughs, 181
Course plan (show jumping), 123
Cracked heels, 181
Cramp (azoturia), 181
Creden Keepsake, *134*
Crib-biting, 71, *71*
Criollo pony, 56, 57
Cross-country event, *127, 149*
Crosses, successful, 120
Cruelty, protection against, 8-10, 68
Crupper, 156, 162
    Icelandic pony, 86
Cubes, as food, 66, 150
Curry comb, 66, *65*
Cuts, treatment of, 56

Dales Galloways, 62
Dales pony, 57-63, 73, 77, 79, 157, *14, 57, 58-61, 75*
Dales Pony Improvement Society/ Dales Pony Society, 62
Dandy brush, 67, 71, *65*
Dargue family, Bow Hall, Westmorland, 78
Darkhorse Avval, *50*
Dark Horse Caspian Stud, 50
Dartmoor Breed Society, 36, 37
Dartmoor cross-breds, 37
Dartmoor pony, 34-7, 157, *35, 37*
Dartmoor Prison, ponies used at, 34
Deadly nightshade, 54
Diamond Centre for Disabled, 98
Disabled, riding for, 98-9, 101, *99*
Dixon, Shelly, *135*
Dogcart, 166
Dorian Williams Memorial Trophy, 118
Dressage, 85, 89, 126, 126-7, 130-1, *131;*
    for disabled, 98, 99, *99*
Driving ponies, 101, 140-1, 156ff, *100, 158, 163*
Droppings/dung:
    normal, 179
    removal from fields, 53, 56

Eagle, Heidi, *167*
Easington Colliery, County Durham, *96*
Ebbw Victor, *142*
Eglinton Prince Philip Cup team, 112-13, *113*
Eohippus, pony ancestor, 12

Eriskay pony, 101
Exercise bandage, 150
Exmoor pony, 18-23, *19, 23*
Exmoor Pony Society, 19-22

Falabellas, 6, 45-8, *45, 47*
Falabella Miniature Horse Society, 48
Farriery, 174-7, 178, 179, 180, *175*
Fédération Équestre Internationale (FEI), 165
Federation of European Friends of the Icelandic pony, 104
Feed:
    Exmoor pony, 23
    for show condition, 149-50
    stabled pony, 69, 71
    types of, 66
    winter, 52, 54
    see also Grass
Feet/shoes, 23, 55, 174-9
Fell ponies, 57, 62, 73, 75-9, 81-3, 157, *77, 79;*
    crosses, 79-80
Fell Galloways, 76
Fell Pony Committee/Society, 82-3
Fences, show jumping, 125-6, *11*
Fencing, 24-5, 52, *9, 52*
Field, size needed, 24, 52
First-aid kit, 180
Fisher, Lord and Lady, Kilverstone Wildlife Park, 48, *45, 47*
Fitzmaurice, Sebastian, 48
5,000km trek (USA, 1976), 105
Fjords, 6, 168-70, 172, *171*
Flaked maize, as food, 66
Foal:
    cost of breeding, 51
    minimum age for selling, 33
Fortescue, Earl, 19
Forwood, Mrs Peter, 118
Foxglove, *37*
Freeze-marking, 20, 54
Friesian horses, in Roman Britain, 12-13

Galloway pony, 76, 79
Gates, right type, 52
Gibson, Mrs Joan, first fellowship of BSPS, 136
Gilbert, Ian, *166*
Girth gall, 181
Glenda Spooner Memorial Fund, 69
Glenda Spooner Trust, 9, 69
Gleneagles, Mark Phillips Equestrian Centre, 118
Glue-on shoes, 177
Goats, driving, 166
Goddard-Fenwick, John, 169-70
Gorsbridge, *121*

Governess carts, 157, 162, 165, 167-8
Grass:
    area needed, 52
    cuttings, illness from, 54
    danger of showground, 150
    maintenance of, 24, 25, 52-3, 56
    worms in, 56
'Grass laminitis', 53
Grass-tip shoe, 176
Great American Horse Race (1976), 105
Green, Frank, of Dulverton, 18
Greenacres Bouquet, *135*
Gresham Assurance Group sponsorship, 40-1, 42
Grooming, 65, 66-7, 71, *65*
Gymnastics, on horseback, 118, *119*

Hackamore, 89
Hackney ponies, 80, 140-1, 157, 159, 161, 173, *140*
Hackney Horse Society, 141
Haflinger pony, 86, 164, *87*
Hames, to put on, 162
Hancock, Anne-Marie, 128-9, 130-1
Hancock, Stella, 98-9
'Hand', definition of, 6
Harness:
    care of, 165
    driving, 160-2
Harnessing up, 162
Hay, 55:
    types of, 68
    winter feeding, 54
Haylage, 68, 150
Height, 6, 121;
    for show ponies, 34, 133, 135-8
    see also individual breeds
Hemlock family, poisonous, 54
Hickstead, *11*
Highland ponies, 99-103, *98, 100, 102*
Highland Pony Society, 99, 100
History, of ponies, 12-13, 61;
    see also individual breeds
Hives, 181
Hogging a mane, 146
Holiday riding, 72-5, 80-1
Hollenden Farm Park, Kent, 101
Honeybunch, 172-3, *173*
Hoof:
    injuries to, 174, 176
    structure of, 174
Hoof-oil, 67
Hoof-pick, 67, *65*
Horsage/haylage, 68, 150
Horse, definition of, 6
Horse fights, as amusement, 103
Horseshoes, how made, 177
'Horse-sick' pasture, 53

Horse trials, 126
'Horse whim', seventeenth century, 93
Horse of the Year Show, 112, *121*
Hot fomentation, 180
Hot shoeing, 176
Hot tubbing, 180
Hucul pony, 170
Humour or hives, 181
Hunt, Rachel, event rider, 22
Hunter classes, 137
Hunter shoe, 176
Hunter trials, 126, *44*

Icelandic ponies/horses, 6, 86, 103-8, *106*
Illness and injury, 56
Influenza, vaccination against, 179-80
Injection, how to give, *179*
International Caspian Stud Book, 49
International competitions, 121, 135, 165
International Falabella Miniature Horse Society, 48
Iron ore mines, ponies used in, 77

Jester, *167*
Joint Measurement Scheme Limited, 121
Joyce, Oliver, Quimper Stud, 40-3, *41, 43*
Joyce, Victoria and James, 42, *41, 43*

Katie, 100
Kemp, Jo, 172-3
Kidd, Mrs Janet and Hon Mrs, 169-70
Kilverstone Wildlife Park, Thetford, 47, 48, *45, 47*
Knight, John, of Exmoor, 18
Konik pony, 63

Lameness, 178-9, *178*
Laminitis, 23, 31, 53, 178
Landau, Guy, 136
Langford, Colonel Pat, 115
Leading rein class, 133, 135, *132*
Leasing, alternative to buying, 20
Leather, care of, 92
Lee-Smith family, 80-1, 133, 137
Leng, Virginia, 37
Lice, 56, 181
Linseed, as food, 67, 150
Loading, into travelling box, 146
London, ponies in, 82-3
London Pony Club, 83
Londonderry Stud, Bressay, Shetland, 39, 41
Lord Arthur Cecil Cup, 36
Lundy ponies, 114

Macdonald, Vicki, 25
Macgregor, Shirley, *100*
McKie, Captain Barry, 118
Madeley, Nicola, *134*
Mail: delivered by pony, 81-2
Mane:
    hogging, 146
    plaiting, 145-6, *146*
Mange, 181
Manual of Horsemanship, 10
Maple Brantly, *171*
Markings, Exmoor for registration, 19-20
Markings, face and legs, 15, 17
Martin, Richard, MP, 8-9
Martingales, 90-1
May Queen IX, *61*
Medicine, giving of, 180
Menelek, prize spotted stallion, *46*
Merychippus, 12
Mesohippus, 12
Middle Ages, ponies in, 57
Millstone Hotspur, *60*
Mines Act (1842), 93
Molasses, as food, 67
Mongolian pony, 154
Moran, Lyn, 169-70
Mouldy hay or silage, 53
Mucking out, 64, *64*
Mud, problems of in field, 25
Mud fever, 181
Munkton, Colonel, 19

National Association of Riding Clubs, 104
National Pony Society, 8, 21, 82, 133, 182; Exmoor Division (1899), 19
Native breeds, 13
Navicular, 178
Neckstrap, 91
New Forest pony, 116-17, 157, *117*
New Forest Pony Breeding and Cattle Society, 116-17
New Zealand rug, 56, *54, 179*
Noble, Robert, 112
Norfolk breeds, 58, 61, 62
Norwegian Fjord horses, 6, 168-70, 172
Nosebands, 89, 90
Novice pony classes, 136-7
Numnahs, 91, 150

Oakley Bubbling Spring, *139*
Oatmeal gruel, 67
Oats, as food, 66, 150
O'Brien, Mrs, Anwood Stud, 40
Ogle, Debbie, *37*

Pack-horse bridges, 77
Pack ponies, 57, 60, 77-8, 79, 169; tin carrying, 36
Palominos, 138-9, *139*
Pandora, a Falabella, *47*
Part-Bred Dartmoor Register, 37
Pedal ostitis, 178
Persian pony, 133
Peruvians, 56
Phaetons, 157, 168
Pit ponies, 93-7, *94, 96*
Plaiting:
    mane, 145-6, *146*
    tail, 148
Plastic shoes, 177
Poisoning, symptoms of, 53
Poisonous plants, 53-4, *53*
Polo, 6, 36, 150-1, *151-3;* Pony Club, 110, 151-3
Polo Pony Society, 34
Polo and Riding Pony Society, 36
Ponies, meaning of term, 6
Ponies Association, 80-1
'Ponies Bill' (1970), 8-9, 68
Ponies of Britain, 8, 68, 69
Pony club, 10, 28, 34, 109-19, 128; camp, 109-10, 114-15, *115* competitions, 111-14, 126, 128, *110, 111, 121* display team, 118, *119* in London, 82-3 polo, 151-3, 110 Prince Philip Cup, 112-13 proficiency tests, 110 rallies, 110, 112
Pony Express Race (USA, 1976), 105
Poulticing, 176, 180
Practice fences, 125-6
Price of buying, 14, 20, 28-9
Pricked foot, 178
Prince Philip, 112, 165, *77*
Prince Philip Cup, 112-13, *113*
Przevalski, Colonel N., 168
Pulse rate:
    how to tell, 180
    normal, 179
    with colic, 181
Putting down, 182
'Putting to', 164-5

Quartering (grooming), 67
Quimper Stud, 40-3, *41, 43*

Races, endurance (USA, 1976), 105
Ragwort, 53-4
Reading Carriage Sales, 164
Registered ponies, 34; *see also* individual breeds
Reins, when harnessing, 162

Respiration rate, normal, 179
Ridden classes, 135-7
Riding for the disabled, 98-9, *99*
Riding for the Disabled Association, 98-9
Riding holidays, 72-5
Riding Holiday and Trekking Scheme, 80
Riding and Road Safety tests, 83
Ringworm, 181
Romans, time of, 12, 160
Rotherdale Dulais, *142*
Rotherwood Royalist, *142*
Royal Highland Show, *100, 102*
Royal Society for the Prevention of Cruelty to Animals (RSPCA), 8, 182
Royal Welsh Show, *142*
Royal Windsor Horse Show, 164, 165, *79, 134, 167, 171*
Rugs:
    in field, 71
    when travelling, 148

Saddle horse, *92*
Saddles, 84-6, 89, 90-1, 92, 162, *85;*
    Icelandic ponies, 86
Safety, 89, 90, 91, 162
Sales of ponies, cruelty at, 69;
    Code of Practice for saleyards, 32-3
Salt in diet, 63, 67
Sandcrack, 178-9
Schooling:
    for competition, 149
    polo ponies, 152-3
Scottish Galloway pony, 57-8, 62
Second-hand saddlery, 90
Seedy toe, 179
Shafts, 160, 161
Shap, pit pony, *96*
Shelter, field, 25, 52;
    see also Stabling
Shetland/Dartmoor cross, 37
Shetland pony, 38-44, 157, *38, 39, 41, 43*
Shetland Pony Stud Book Society, 38, 40, 41
Shoes/shoeing, 23, 55, 174-7, *96, 175, 177*
Show jumping, 120-6, 129, *11, 122*
Show ponies, 14-15, 132-44, 166, *13*
Show waggon, 140
Siberian ponies, 12
Sidesaddle, riding, *135*
Simpson of Piccadilly International Mounted Games, 113
Skerraton Peanuts, *37*
Sly, Debbie, 40-3

Smuggling, ponies used in, 83
Snaffles, 88
Snip, face mark, 16, *16*
Snowhope Purple Heather, *57*
Society of Master Saddlers, 84, 85
Sock, leg marking, 17, *17*
South American breeds, 56
Sponge, for grooming, 67, *65*
Spooner, Glenda, 8-9, 68-9, 137
Spotted ponies, 170-1, *46, 171*
Stable rubber, 67
Stable sponge, 67, *65*
Stabled pony, feeding of, 69, 71
Stabling/shelter, 23, 25, 63-4, 66, *64;*
    disinfecting, 180
Star, face mark, 16, *16*
'Star System' for holiday riding, 80-1
Stick-back gig, 166
Stirrups, 84-6, 90, 90-1
Stocking, leg mark, 17, *17*
Strangles, 181
Stream, best depth for watering, 25
Stripe, face mark, 16, *16*
Stuart, Colonel Alec, 21
Stud books *see* individual breeds
Stud holes in shoes, 177, *177*
Sugar beet pulp, as food, 67
Sunglow Karalina, *58-9*
Surgical shoes, 176
Sweet itch, 56, 182
'Switch' tail, 145

Tack, care of, 92
Tail:
    bandage, 145, 149, *147*
    plaiting, 145-6, 148
    pulling, 145, 148, 150, *146*
Teeth:
    care of, 180, 181
    telling age by, 26
Temperament, good, 31, 156
Temperature:
    normal, 179
    to take, 180
Tetanus, vaccination against, 179-80
Tetrathlon, Pony Club, 111
Thefts, guarding against, 54, 92
Thrush, 182
Tin, Dartmoor pony carrying, 36
Trace-clip, 56
Traces, 160-1
Trail riding, 73
Training for harness pony, 172-3
Transit of Animals (Road and Rail) Orders, 33
Transy Stud, 41
Travelling a pony, 146, 148, *147, 148*
Travelling stallion scheme, north of England, 79

Trekking, 73-4, 100-1
Trials:
    hunter and horse, 126-7
    driving, 157, *163, 166*
Trigger, *97*
Trotting race ponies, 78
Tschiffely, Aimé Felix, 57
Turf ponies, 78

Urine, normal, 179

Vaccination, 179-80, *179*
Vanners for town work, 62
Vehicles:
    for disabled, 98
    for driving, 157, 164, 165-8, *75*
Veterinary surgeon:
    examination when buying, 32
    'grass laminitis', 53
    if poisoning suspected, 53
    wounds, 56
Vices, 71

Wallace, Mrs Ronnie, 18
Watering, 25, 52, 54, 71
Water tank, field, 25
Weaving, 71
Weed killer, poisons from, 53
Welsh cobs, 141-4, *143*
Welsh pony, 141-4, 157, *55, 142, 143*
Welsh Pony and Cob Society, 142
Welsh Stud Book, 142, 144
West Horsley Driving for the Disabled group, 99
Weston Velvet, *132*
Wheat, as food, 66
White face, meaning of, 16, *16*
White fetlock, 17, *17*
Whitefield Sundance, *166*
Whiteman, Mrs Davina, 80-1, 133
White Willows Darwin, champion Dartmoor stallion, *35*
Whitmore, Sue, 82
Wiggins, Ami, *132*
Wilson, Christopher, Kirkby Lonsdale, 79-80
Windsucking, 71
Winstay Shah, *50*
Winter feeding, 52, 54
Wisp, for grooming, 67
Working hunter classes, 137, 138, *58*
World Dressage Championships for disabled, 99
Worms, 53, 56, 179, 181, 182
Wounds, 56, 180, 182

Yorkshire roadster, trotting pony, 61